Nagabe

-a's Memories-

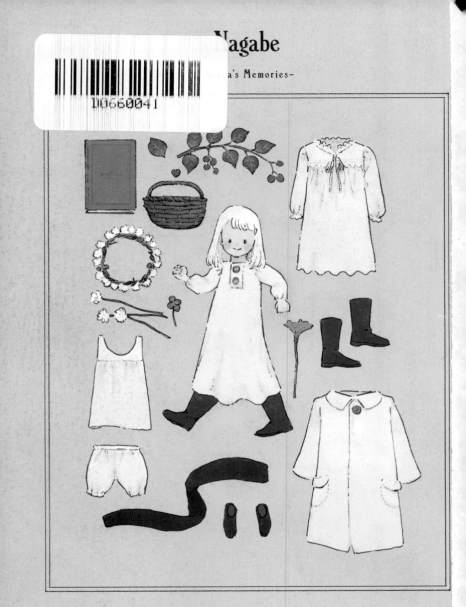

Siúil, a Rún
The Girl from the Other Side

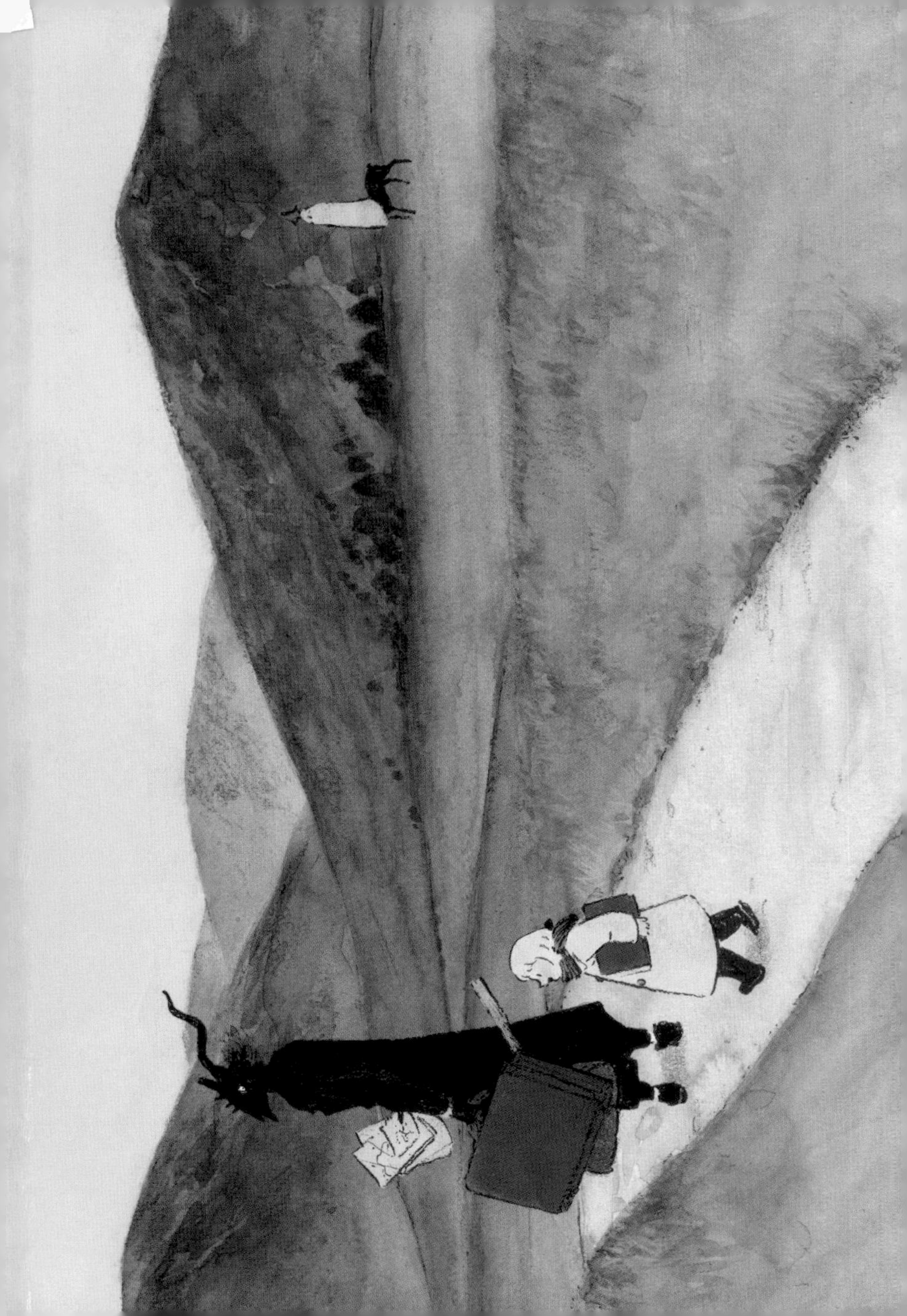

Chapter 26

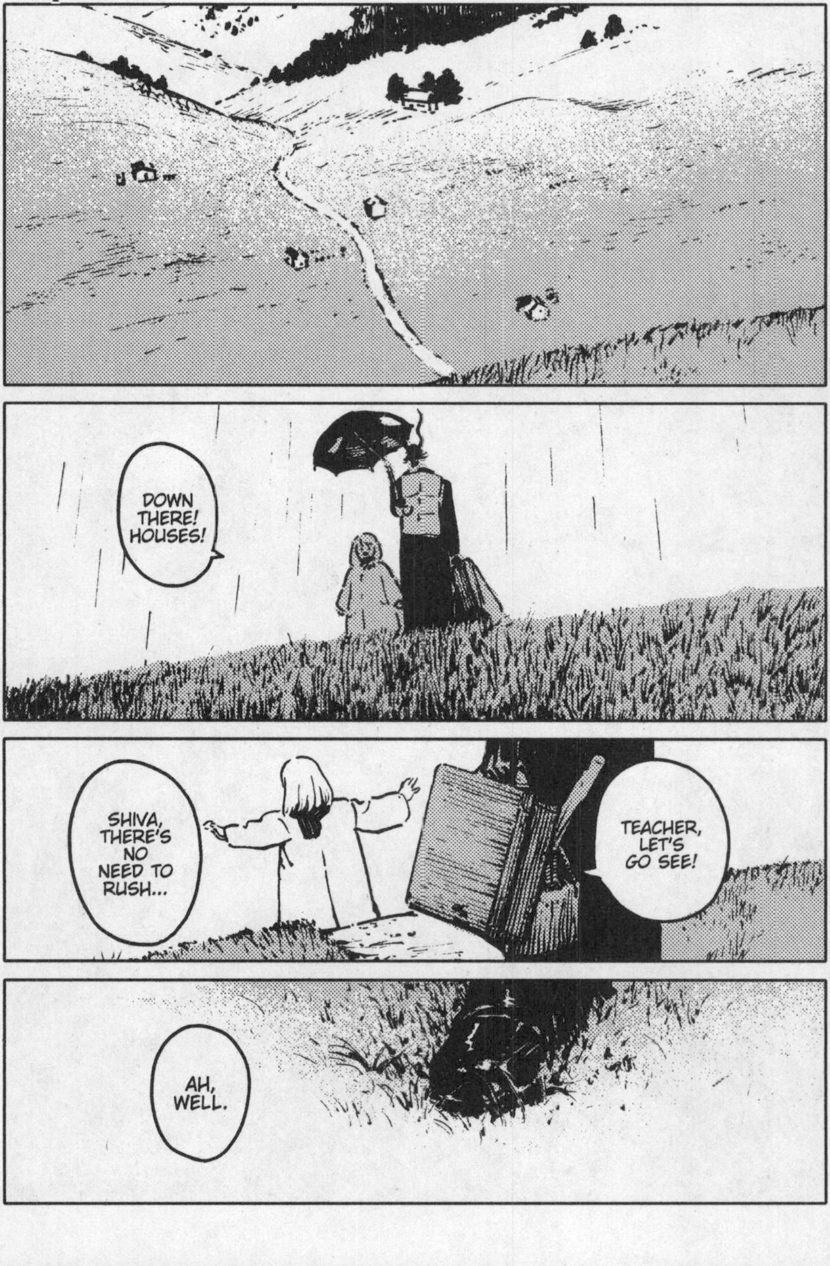
DOWN THERE! HOUSES!
TEACHER, LET'S GO SEE!
SHIVA, THERE'S NO NEED TO RUSH...
AH, WELL.

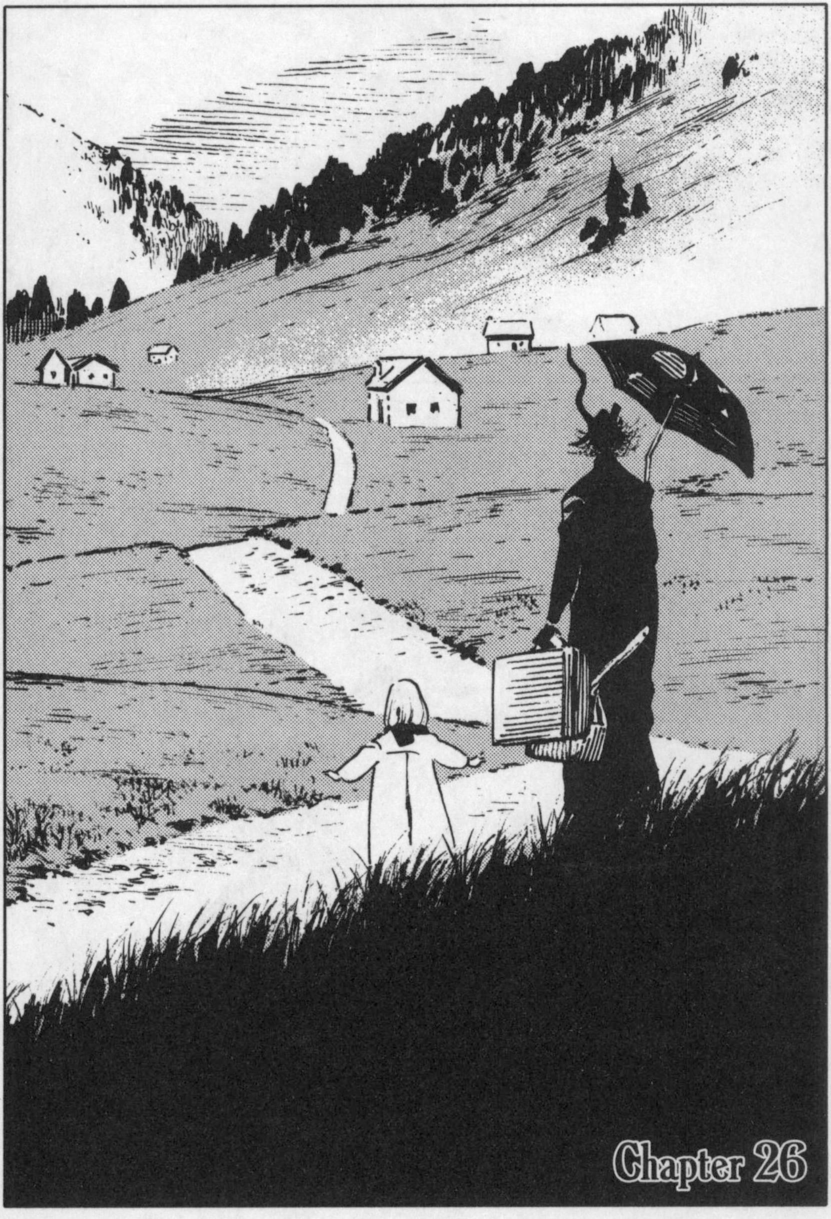
Chapter 26

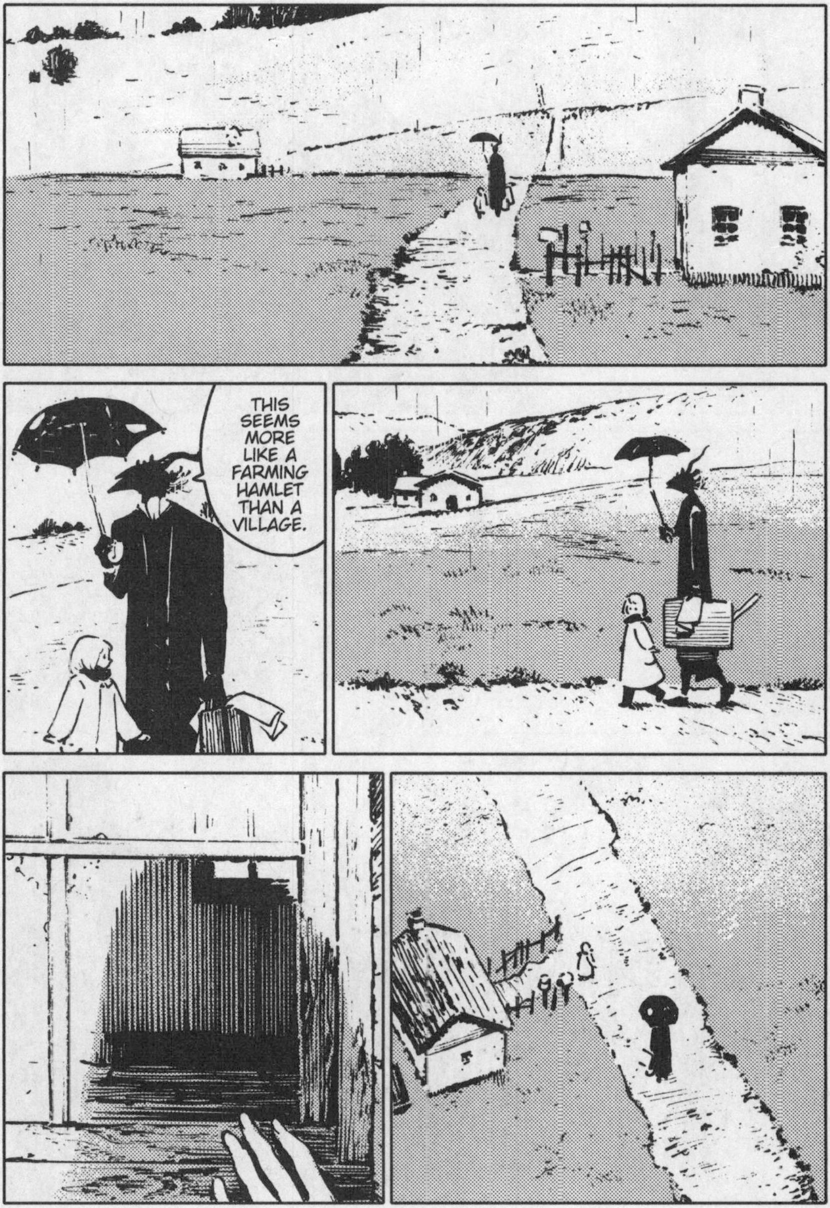
THIS SEEMS MORE LIKE A FARMING HAMLET THAN A VILLAGE.

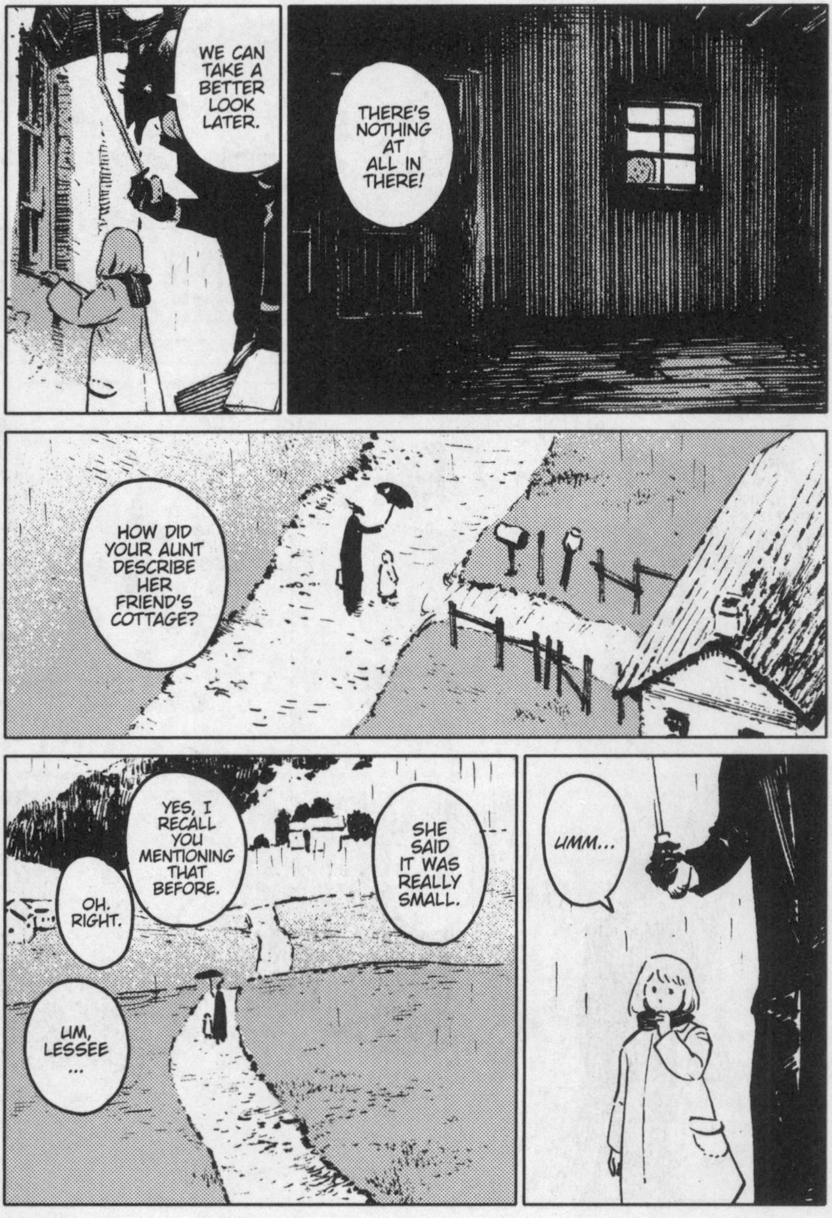
THERE'S NOTHING AT ALL IN THERE!
WE CAN TAKE A BETTER LOOK LATER.
HOW DID YOUR AUNT DESCRIBE HER FRIEND'S COTTAGE?
UMM...
SHE SAID IT WAS REALLY SMALL.
YES, I RECALL YOU MENTIONING THAT BEFORE.
OH. RIGHT.
UM, LESSEE ...

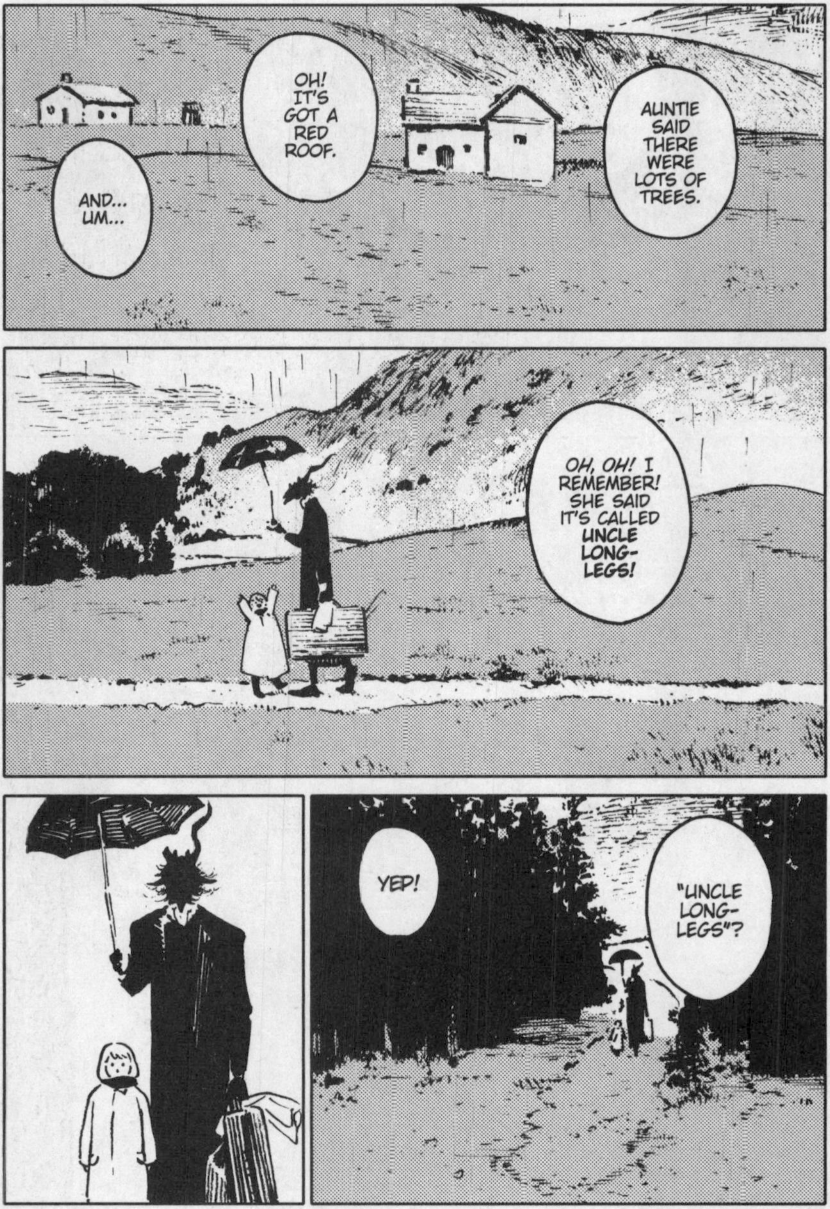
AUNTIE SAID THERE WERE LOTS OF TREES.
OH! IT'S GOT A RED ROOF.
AND... UM...
OH, OH! I REMEMBER! SHE SAID IT'S CALLED **UNCLE LONG-LEGS!**
"UNCLE LONG-LEGS"?
YEP!

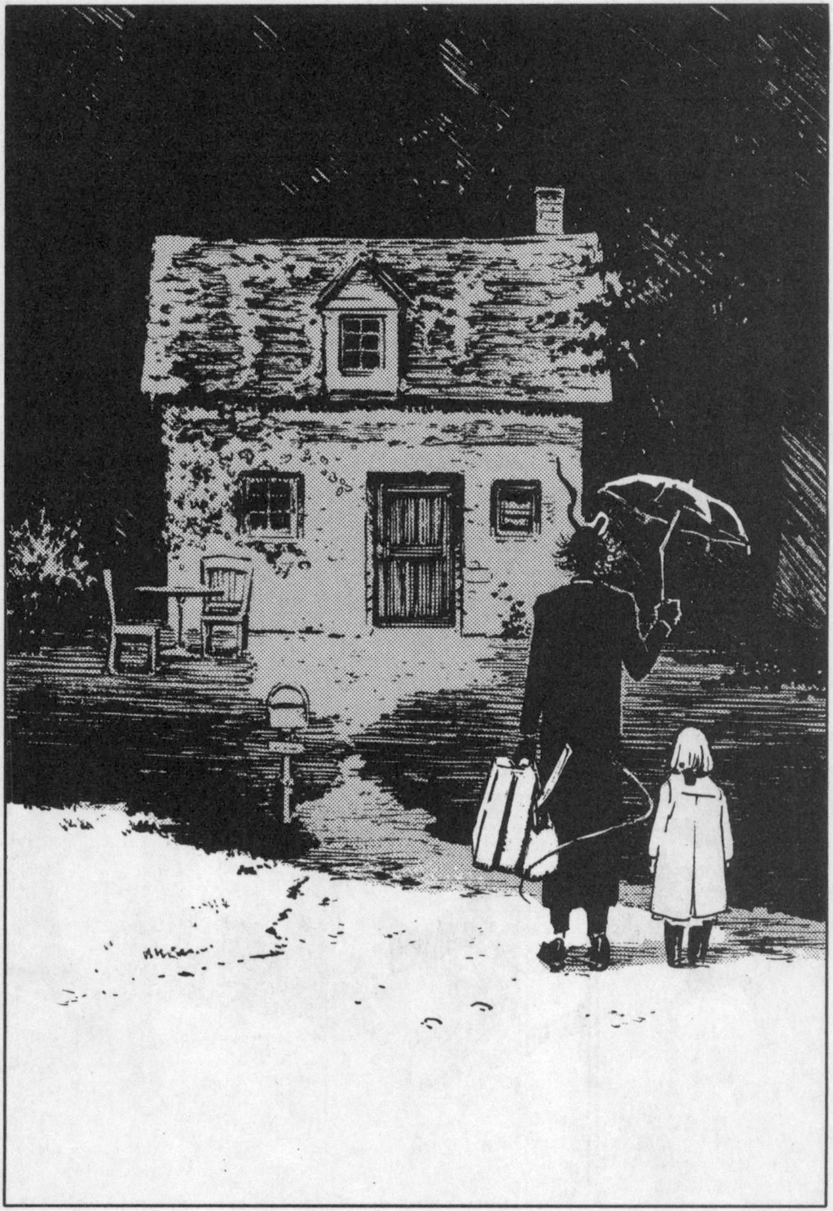

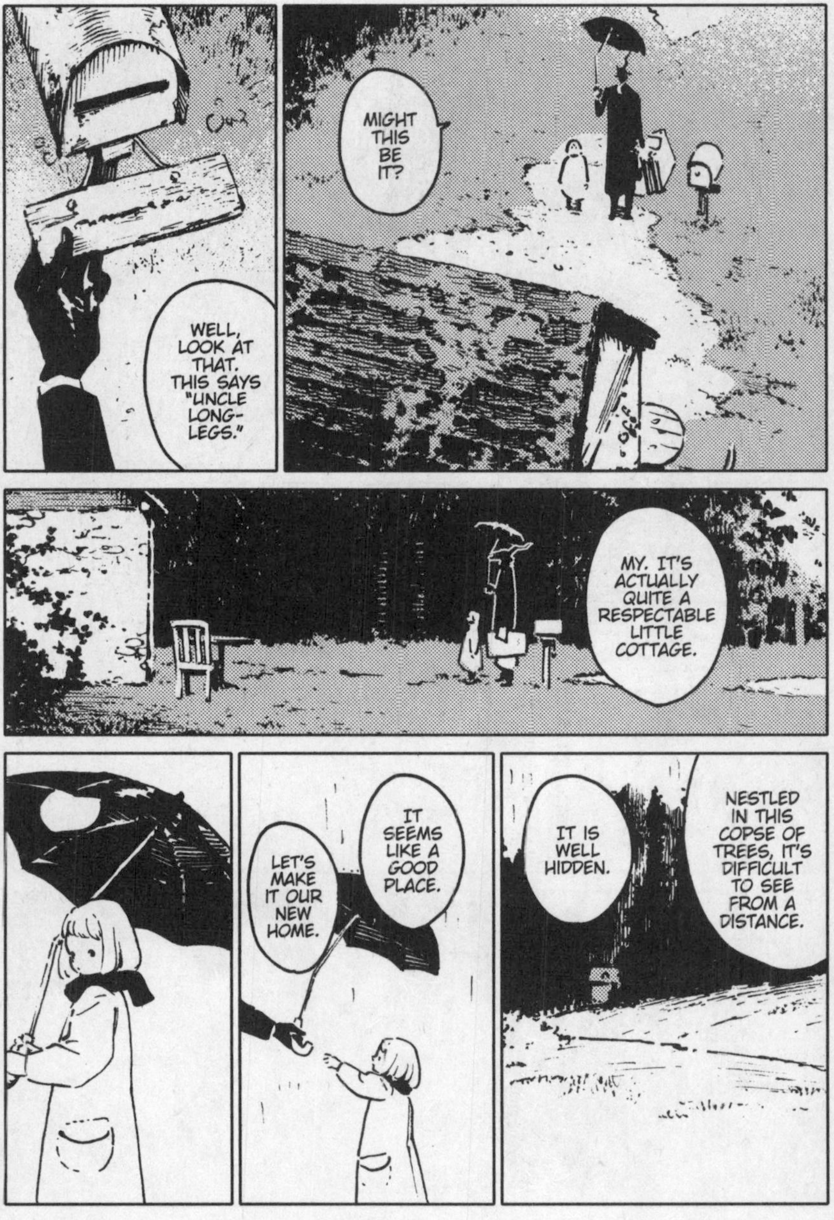
MIGHT THIS BE IT?
WELL, LOOK AT THAT. THIS SAYS "UNCLE LONG-LEGS."
MY. IT'S ACTUALLY QUITE A RESPECTABLE LITTLE COTTAGE.
NESTLED IN THIS COPSE OF TREES, IT'S DIFFICULT TO SEE FROM A DISTANCE.
IT IS WELL HIDDEN.
IT SEEMS LIKE A GOOD PLACE.
LET'S MAKE IT OUR NEW HOME.

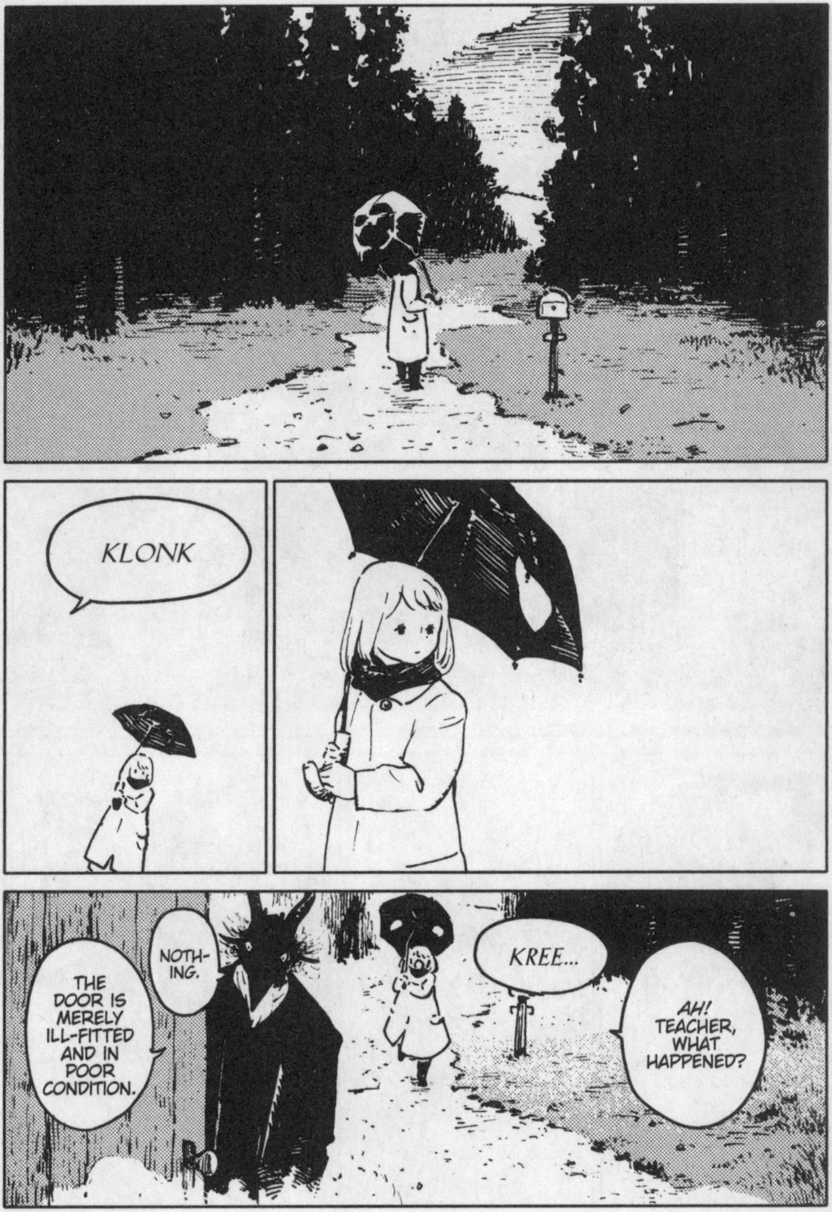
KLONK
AH! TEACHER, WHAT HAPPENED?
KREE...
NOTHING.
THE DOOR IS MERELY ILL-FITTED AND IN POOR CONDITION.

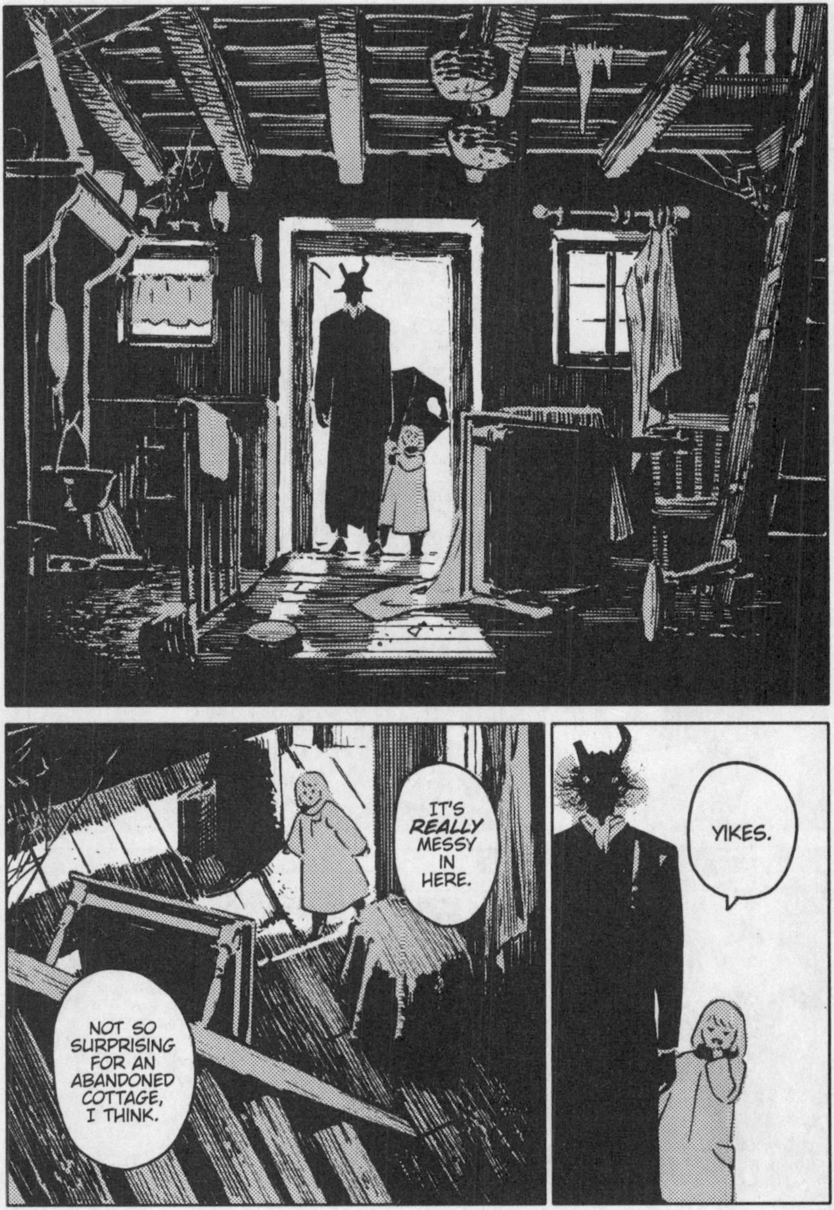
YIKES.
IT'S *REALLY* MESSY IN HERE.
NOT SO SURPRISING FOR AN ABANDONED COTTAGE, I THINK.

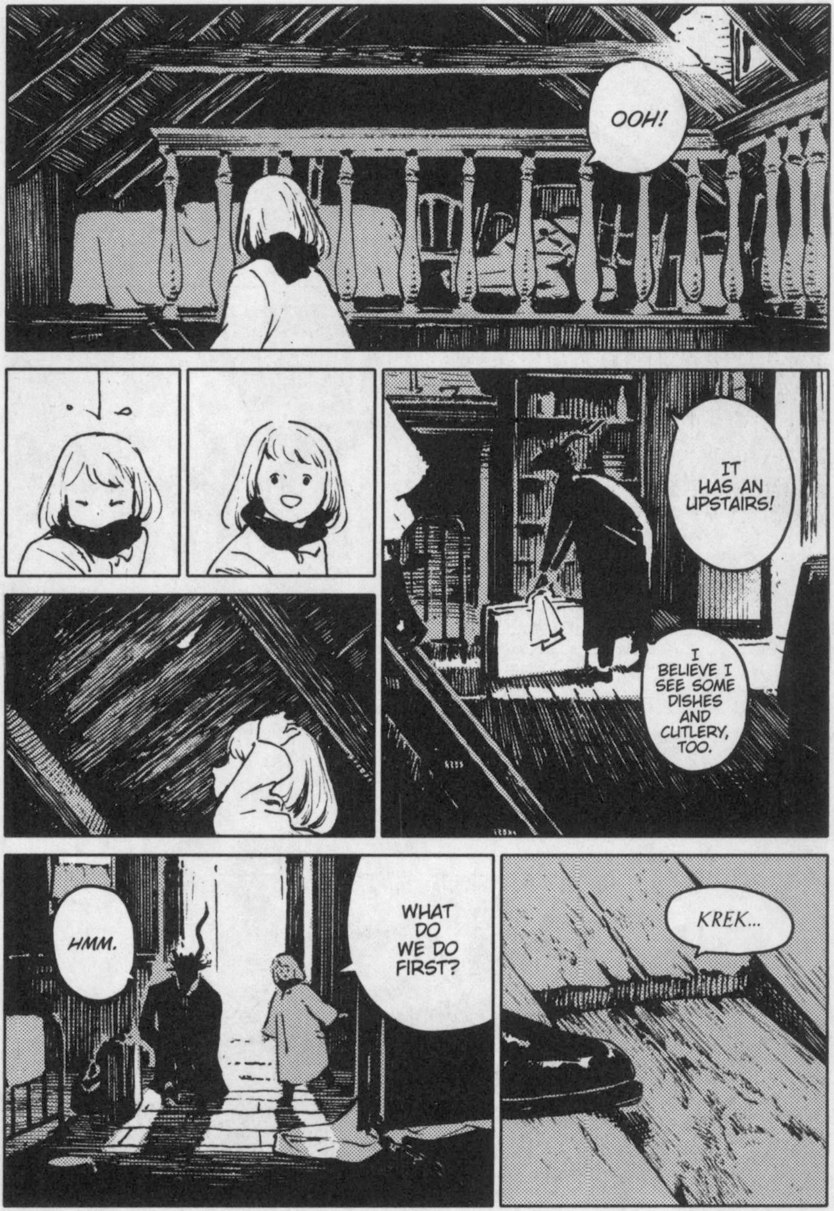
OOH!
IT HAS AN UPSTAIRS!
I BELIEVE I SEE SOME DISHES AND CUTLERY, TOO.
KREK...
WHAT DO WE DO FIRST?
HMM.

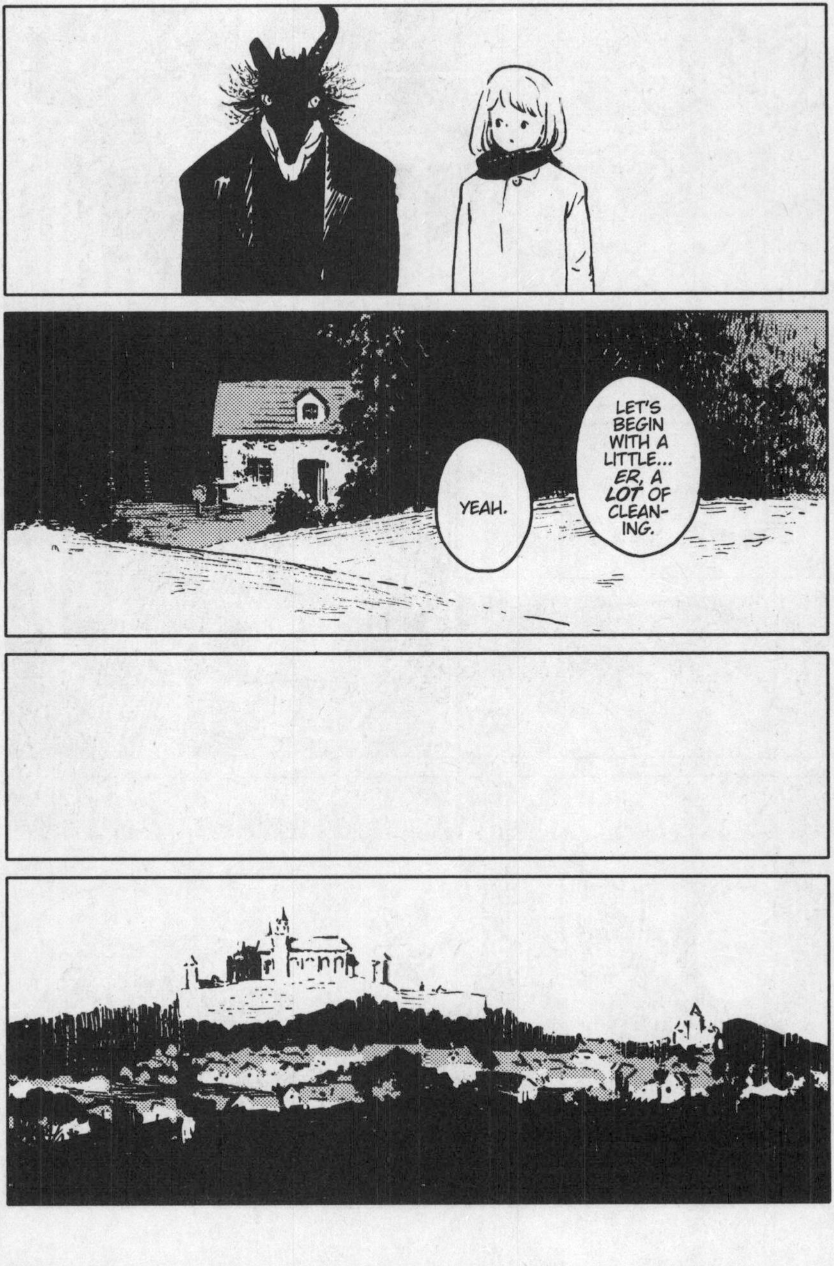
LET'S BEGIN WITH A LITTLE... ER, A LOT OF CLEAN-ING.
YEAH.

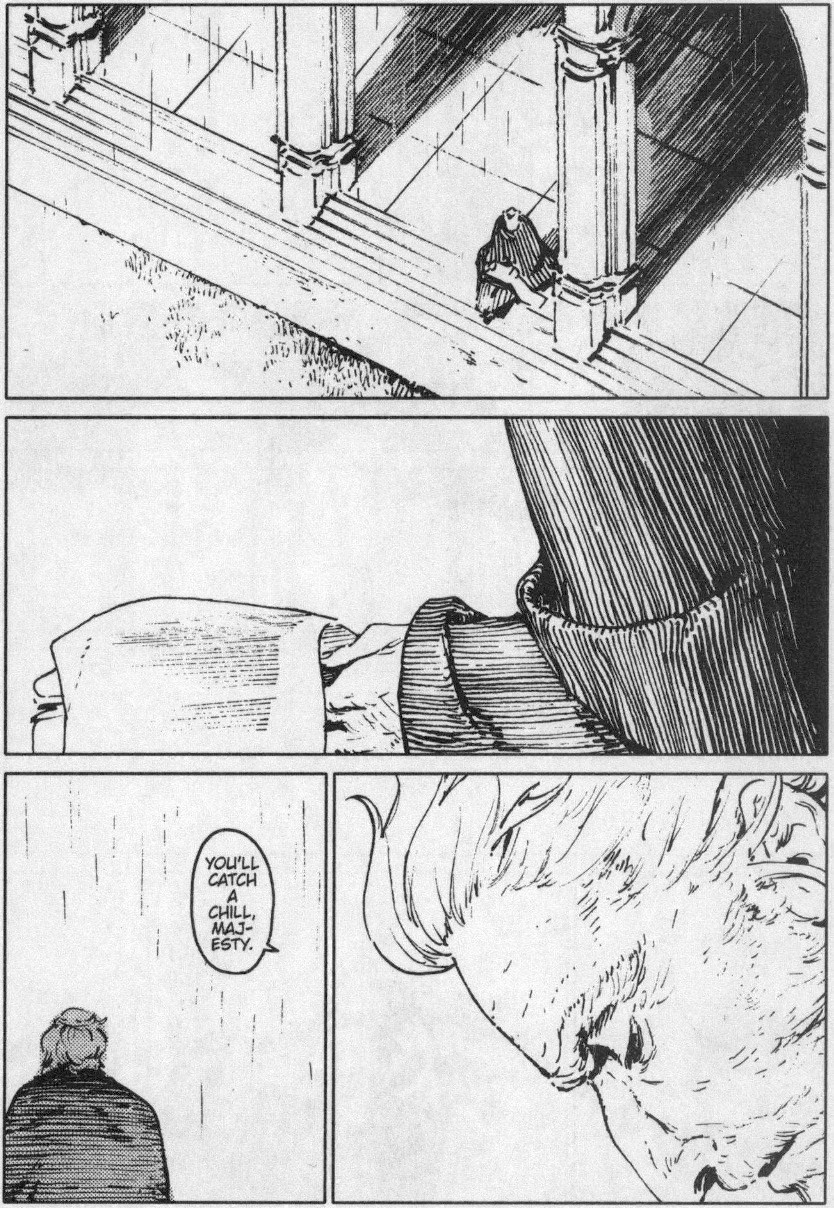
YOU'LL CATCH A CHILL, MAJ-ESTY.

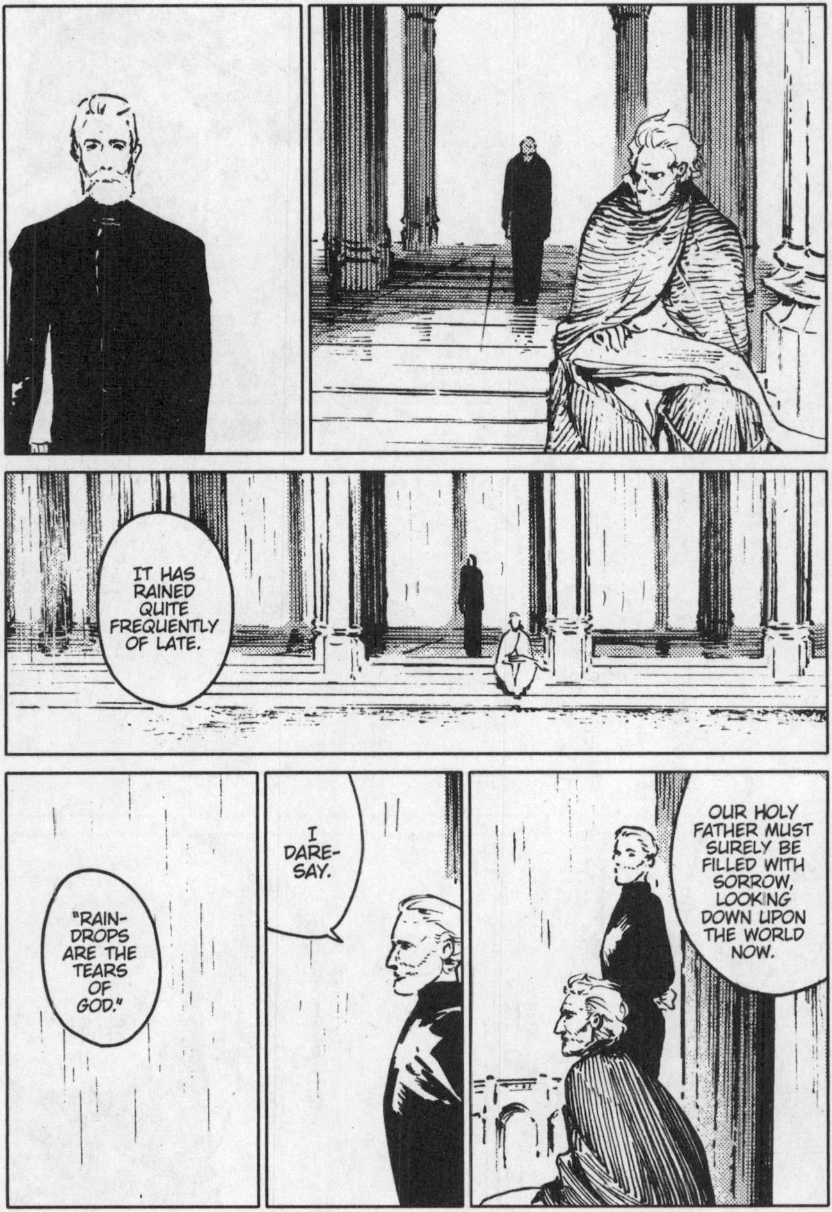
IT HAS RAINED QUITE FREQUENTLY OF LATE.
OUR HOLY FATHER MUST SURELY BE FILLED WITH SORROW, LOOKING DOWN UPON THE WORLD NOW.
I DARE-SAY.
"RAIN-DROPS ARE THE TEARS OF GOD."

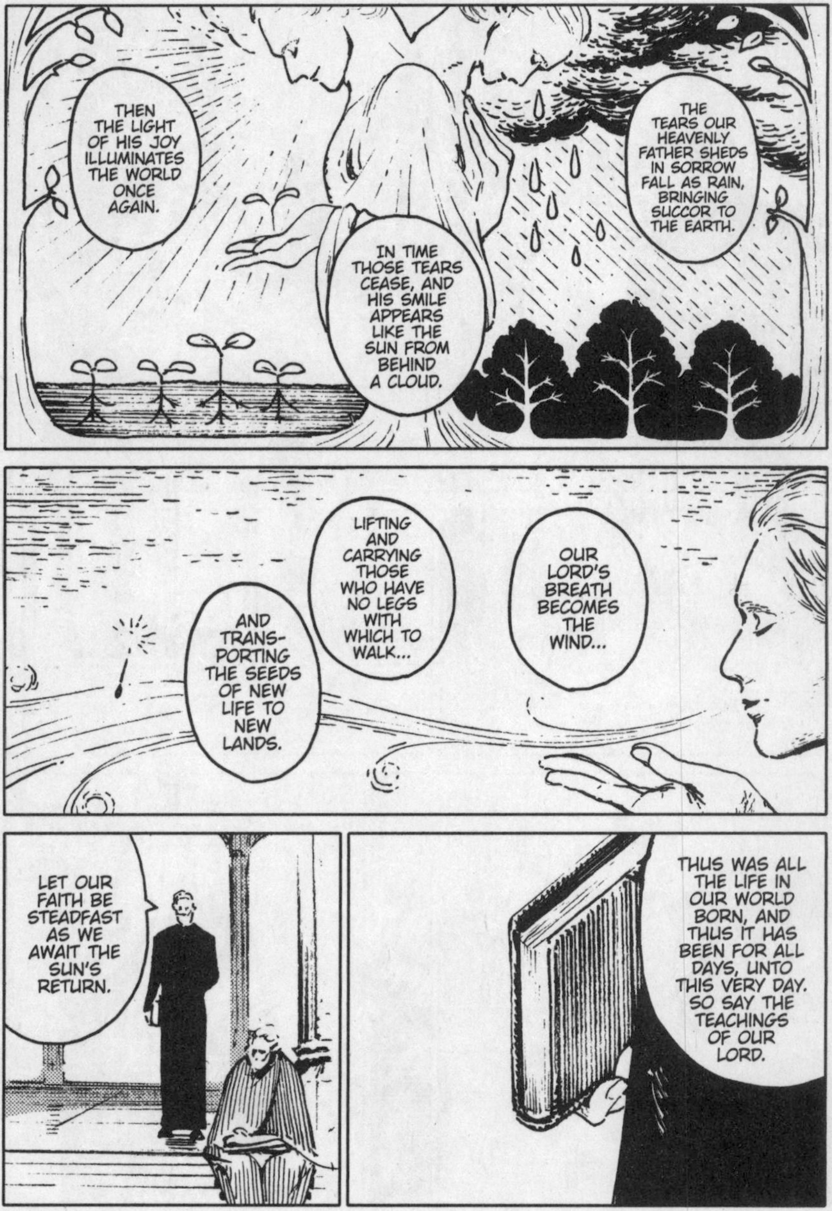
THE TEARS OUR HEAVENLY FATHER SHEDS IN SORROW FALL AS RAIN, BRINGING SUCCOR TO THE EARTH.
IN TIME THOSE TEARS CEASE, AND HIS SMILE APPEARS LIKE THE SUN FROM BEHIND A CLOUD.
THEN THE LIGHT OF HIS JOY ILLUMINATES THE WORLD ONCE AGAIN.
OUR LORD'S BREATH BECOMES THE WIND...
LIFTING AND CARRYING THOSE WHO HAVE NO LEGS WITH WHICH TO WALK...
AND TRANS-PORTING THE SEEDS OF NEW LIFE TO NEW LANDS.
THUS WAS ALL THE LIFE IN OUR WORLD BORN, AND THUS IT HAS BEEN FOR ALL DAYS, UNTO THIS VERY DAY. SO SAY THE TEACHINGS OF OUR LORD.
LET OUR FAITH BE STEADFAST AS WE AWAIT THE SUN'S RETURN.

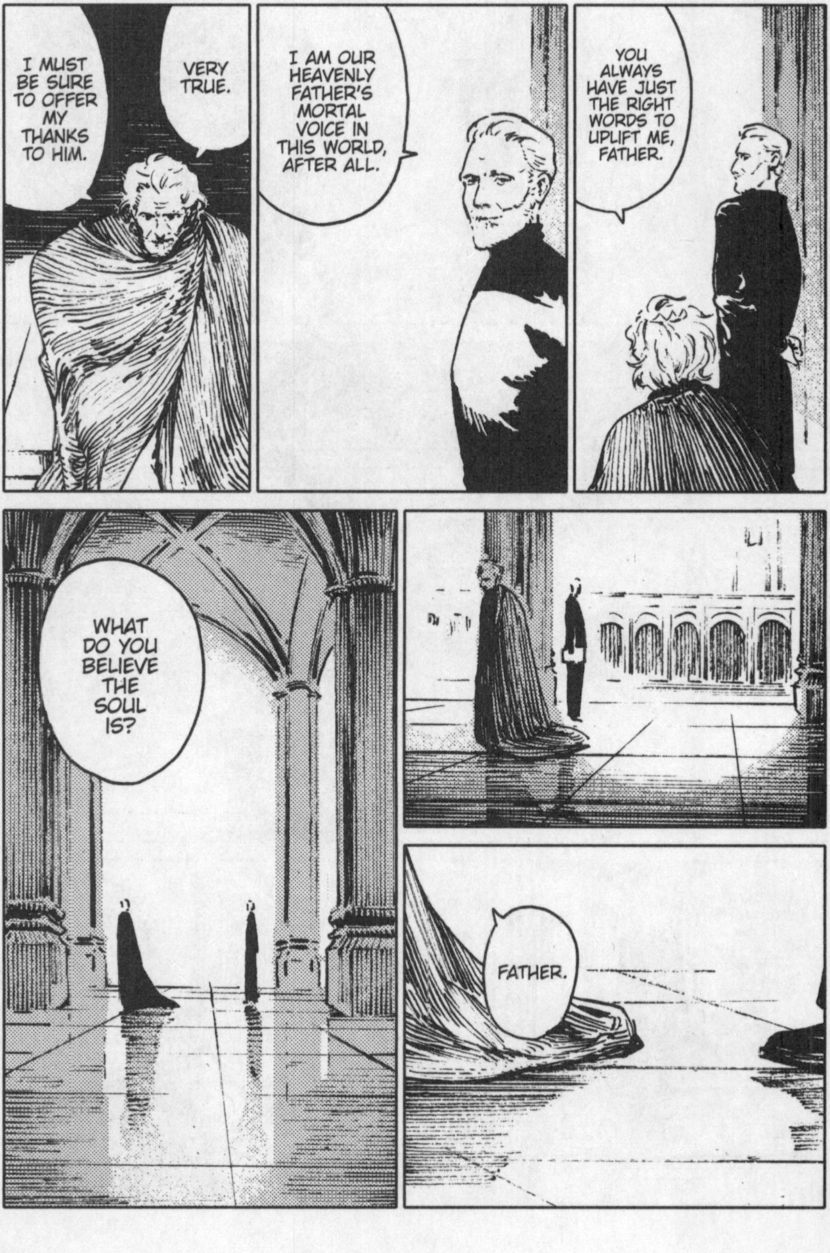
YOU ALWAYS HAVE JUST THE RIGHT WORDS TO UPLIFT ME, FATHER.
I AM OUR HEAVENLY FATHER'S MORTAL VOICE IN THIS WORLD, AFTER ALL.
VERY TRUE.
I MUST BE SURE TO OFFER MY THANKS TO HIM.
FATHER.
WHAT DO YOU BELIEVE THE SOUL IS?

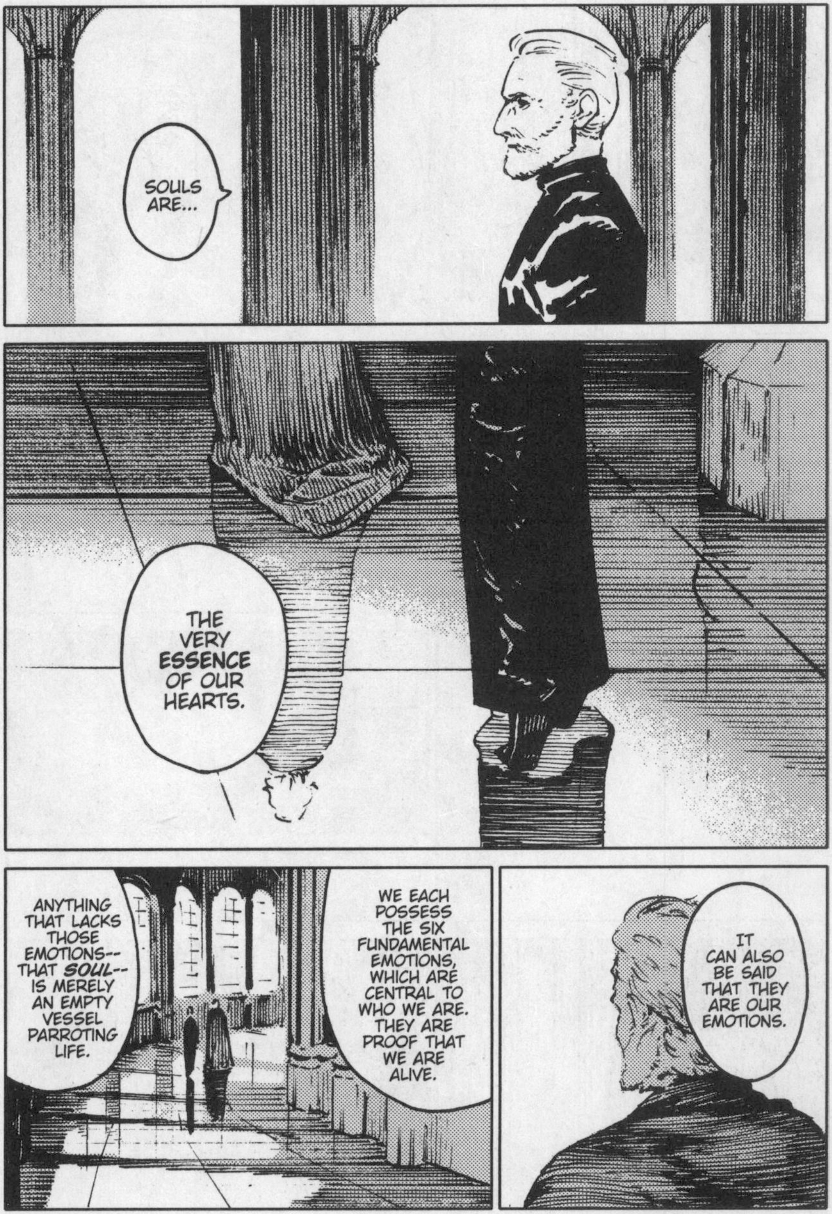
SOULS ARE...
THE VERY ESSENCE OF OUR HEARTS.
IT CAN ALSO BE SAID THAT THEY ARE OUR EMOTIONS.
WE EACH POSSESS THE SIX FUNDAMENTAL EMOTIONS, WHICH ARE CENTRAL TO WHO WE ARE. THEY ARE PROOF THAT WE ARE ALIVE.
ANYTHING THAT LACKS THOSE EMOTIONS-- THAT *SOUL*-- IS MERELY AN EMPTY VESSEL PARROTING LIFE.

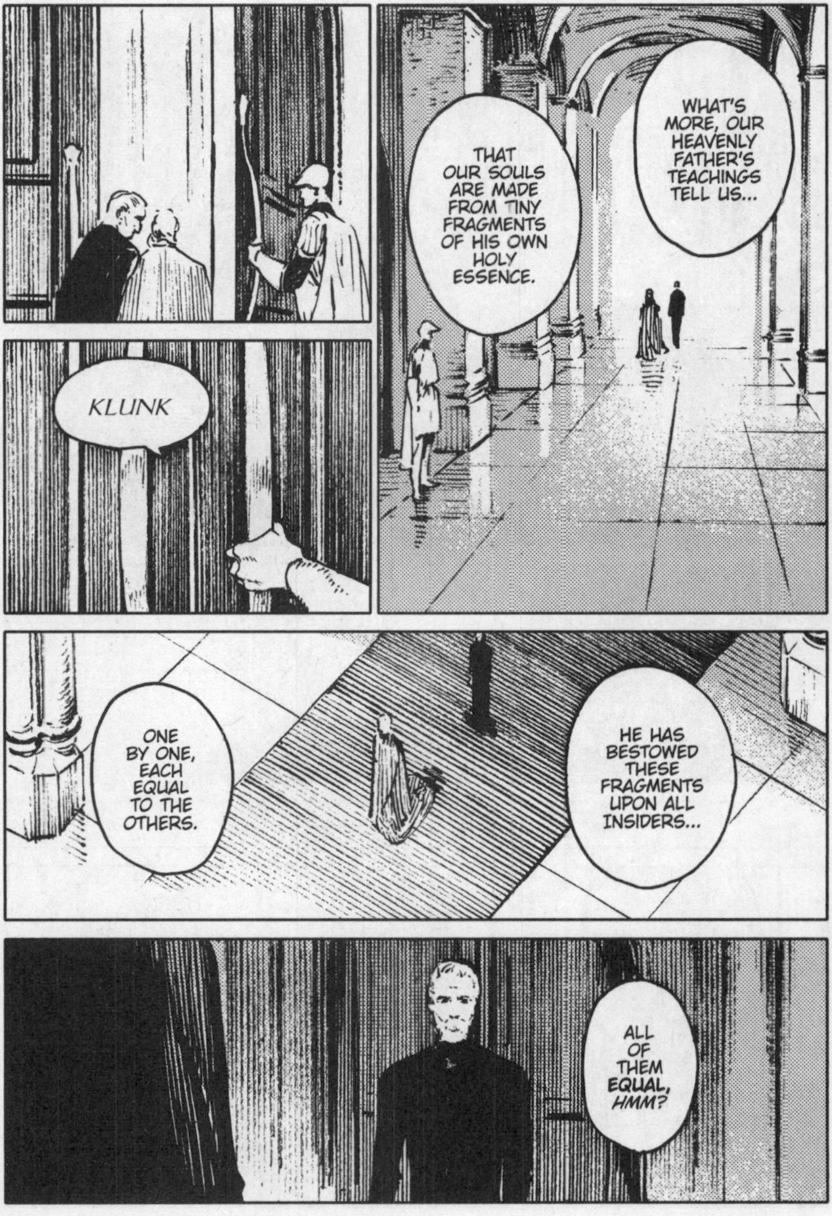
WHAT'S MORE, OUR HEAVENLY FATHER'S TEACHINGS TELL US...
THAT OUR SOULS ARE MADE FROM TINY FRAGMENTS OF HIS OWN HOLY ESSENCE.
KLUNK
HE HAS BESTOWED THESE FRAGMENTS UPON ALL INSIDERS...
ONE BY ONE, EACH EQUAL TO THE OTHERS.
ALL OF THEM EQUAL, *HMM?*

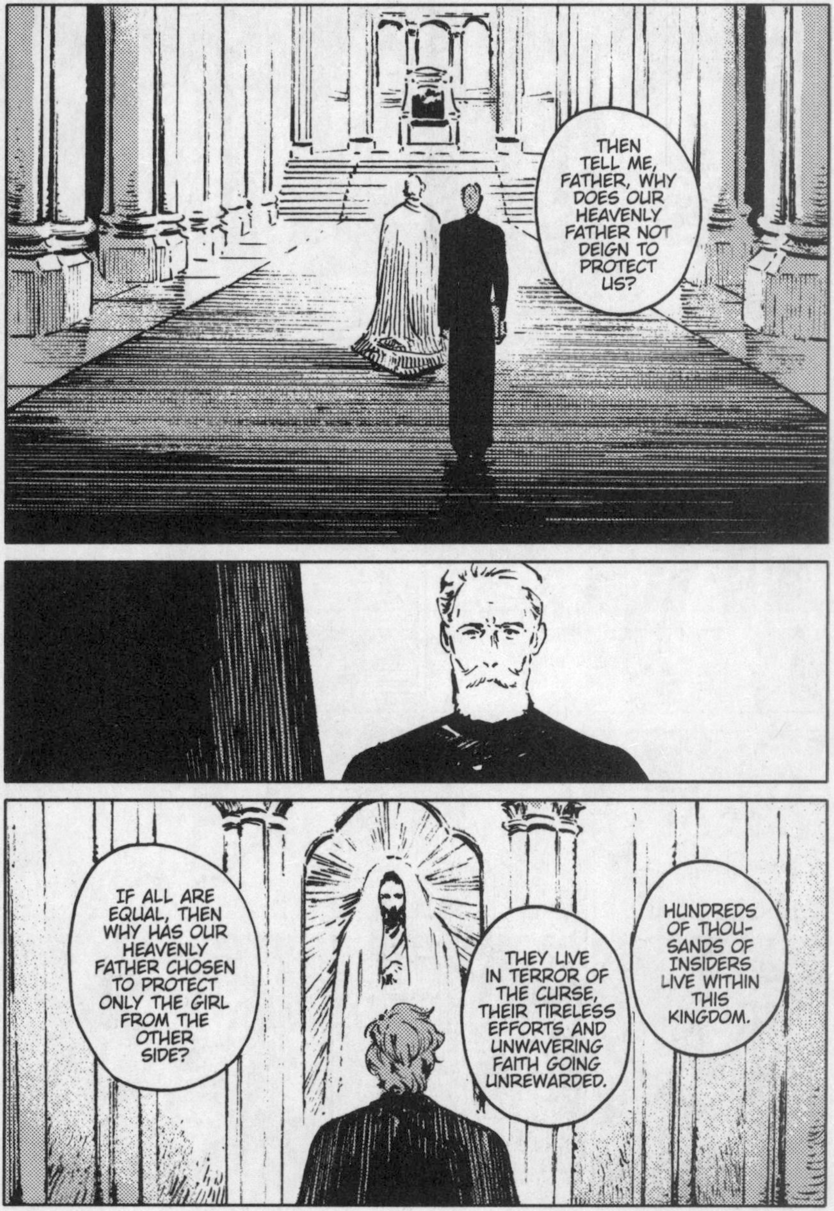
THEN TELL ME, FATHER, WHY DOES OUR HEAVENLY FATHER NOT DEIGN TO PROTECT US?
HUNDREDS OF THOU-SANDS OF INSIDERS LIVE WITHIN THIS KINGDOM.
THEY LIVE IN TERROR OF THE CURSE, THEIR TIRELESS EFFORTS AND UNWAVERING FAITH GOING UNREWARDED.
IF ALL ARE EQUAL, THEN WHY HAS OUR HEAVENLY FATHER CHOSEN TO PROTECT ONLY THE GIRL FROM THE OTHER SIDE?

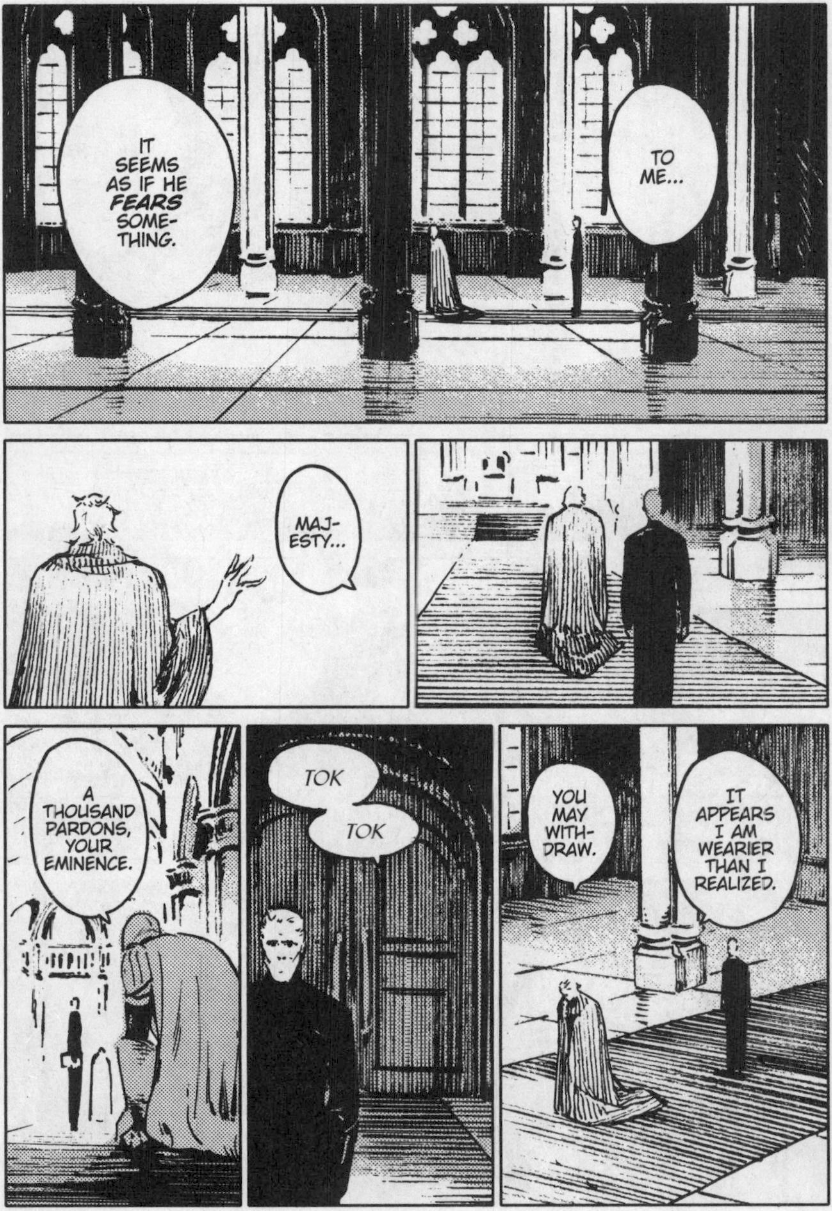
TO ME...
IT SEEMS AS IF HE *FEARS* SOMETHING.
MAJ-ESTY...
IT APPEARS I AM WEARIER THAN I REALIZED.
YOU MAY WITH-DRAW.
TOK
TOK
A THOUSAND PARDONS, YOUR EMINENCE.

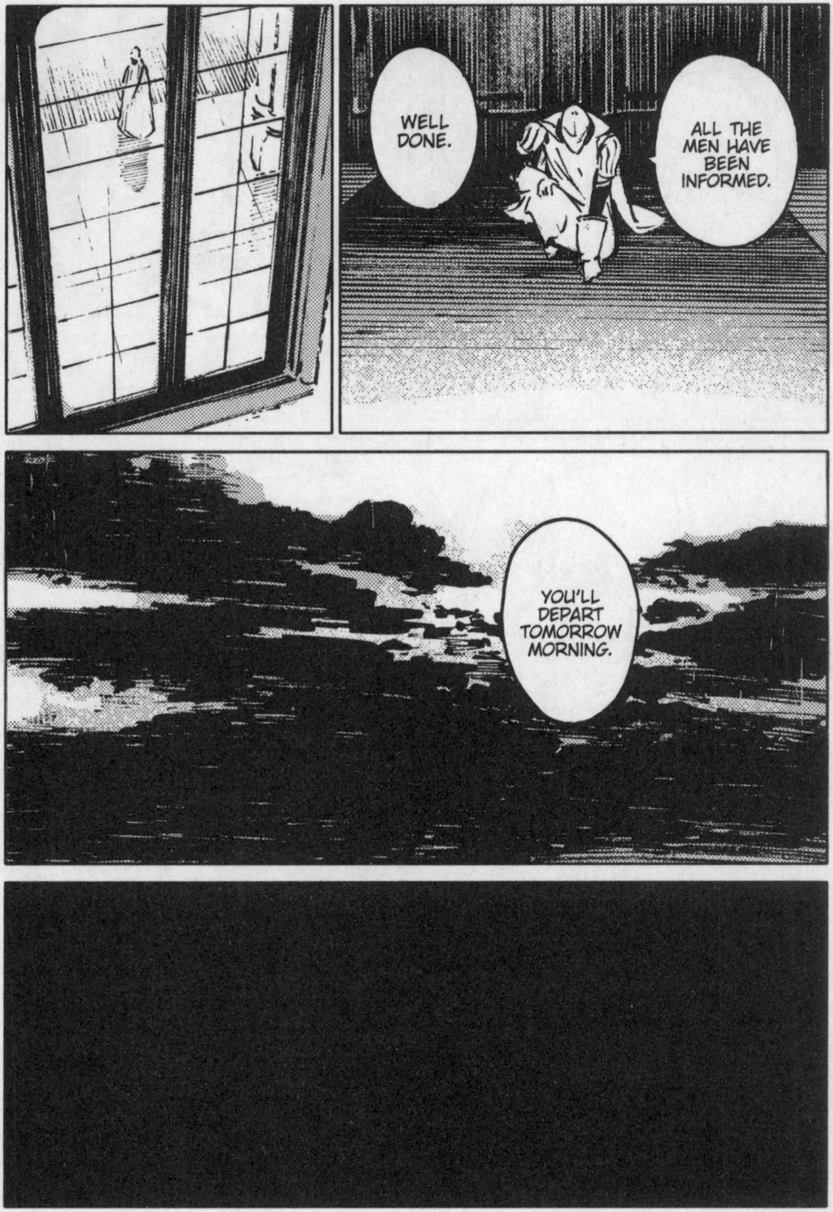
ALL THE MEN HAVE BEEN INFORMED.
WELL DONE.
YOU'LL DEPART TOMORROW MORNING.

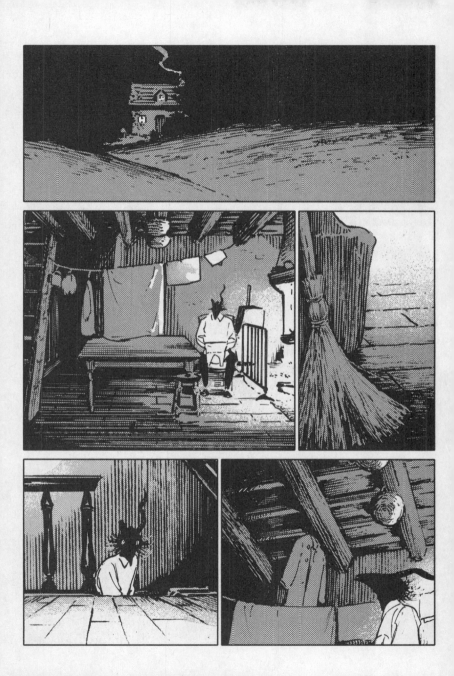

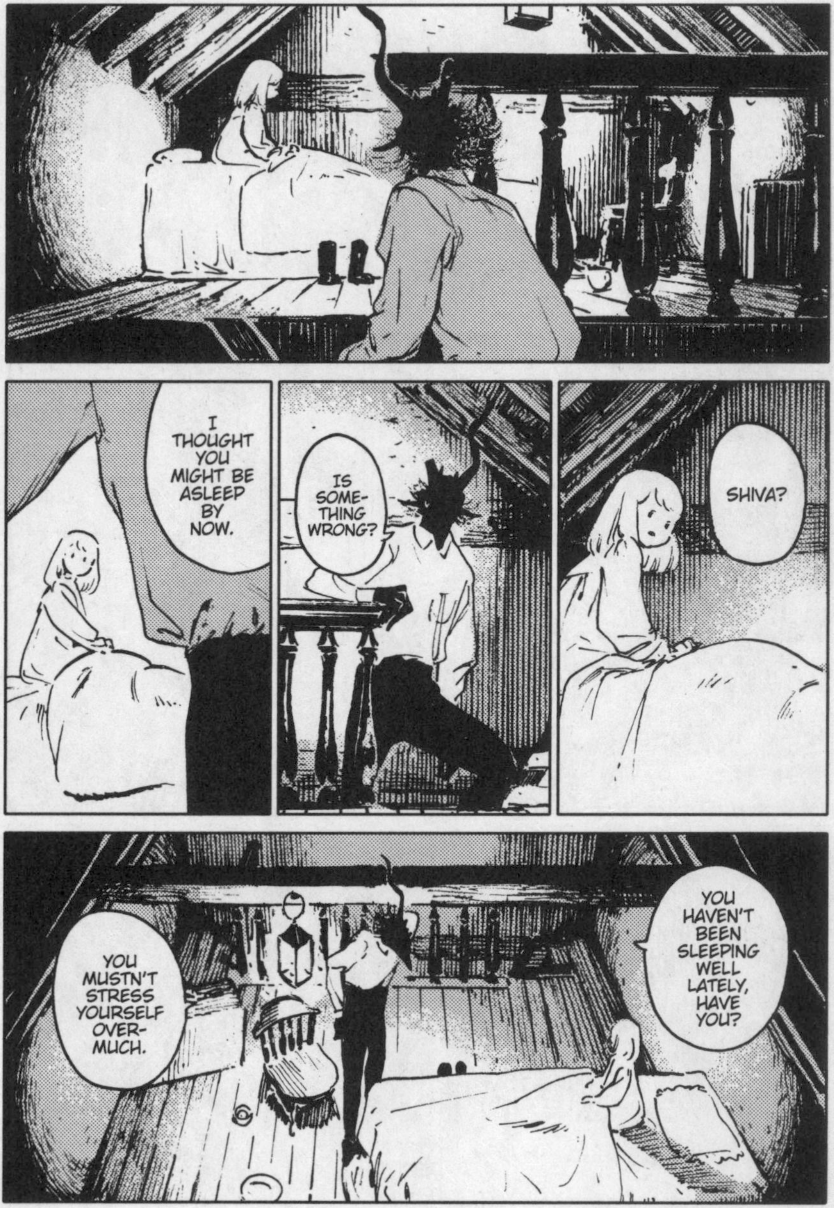
SHIVA?
IS SOMETHING WRONG?
I THOUGHT YOU MIGHT BE ASLEEP BY NOW.
YOU HAVEN'T BEEN SLEEPING WELL LATELY, HAVE YOU?
YOU MUSTN'T STRESS YOURSELF OVERMUCH.

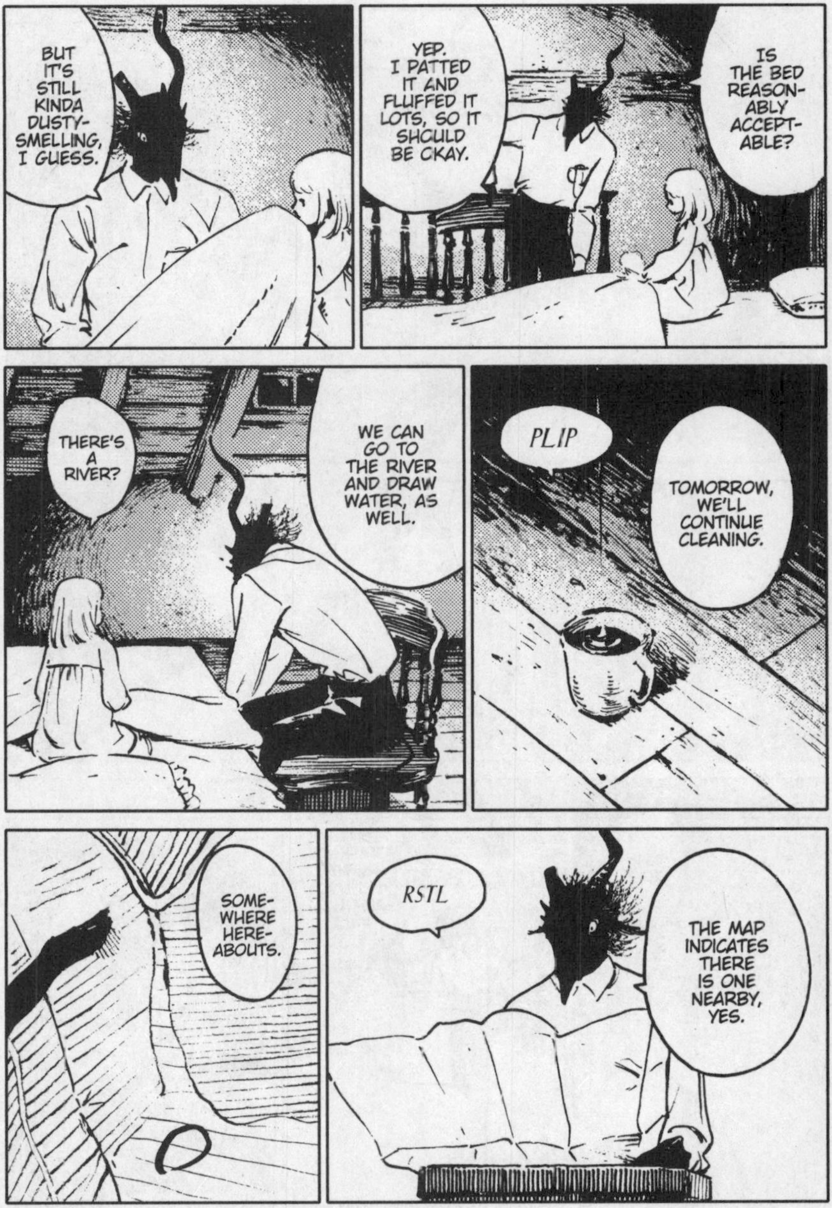
IS THE BED REASONABLY ACCEPTABLE?
YEP. I PATTED IT AND FLUFFED IT LOTS, SO IT SHOULD BE OKAY.
BUT IT'S STILL KINDA DUSTY-SMELLING, I GUESS.
TOMORROW, WE'LL CONTINUE CLEANING.
PLIP
WE CAN GO TO THE RIVER AND DRAW WATER, AS WELL.
THERE'S A RIVER?
THE MAP INDICATES THERE IS ONE NEARBY, YES.
RSTL
SOMEWHERE HEREABOUTS.

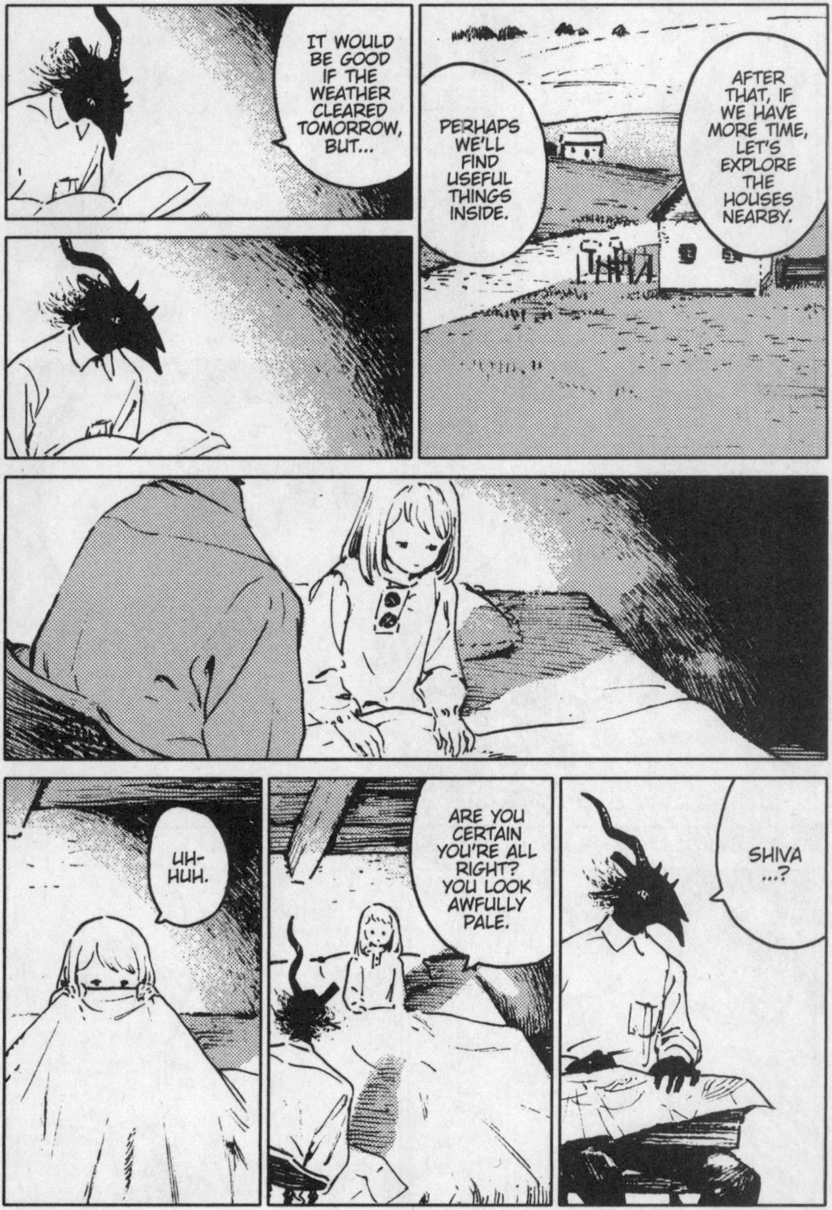
AFTER THAT, IF WE HAVE MORE TIME, LET'S EXPLORE THE HOUSES NEARBY.
PERHAPS WE'LL FIND USEFUL THINGS INSIDE.
IT WOULD BE GOOD IF THE WEATHER CLEARED TOMORROW, BUT...
SHIVA ...?
ARE YOU CERTAIN YOU'RE ALL RIGHT? YOU LOOK AWFULLY PALE.
UH-HUH.

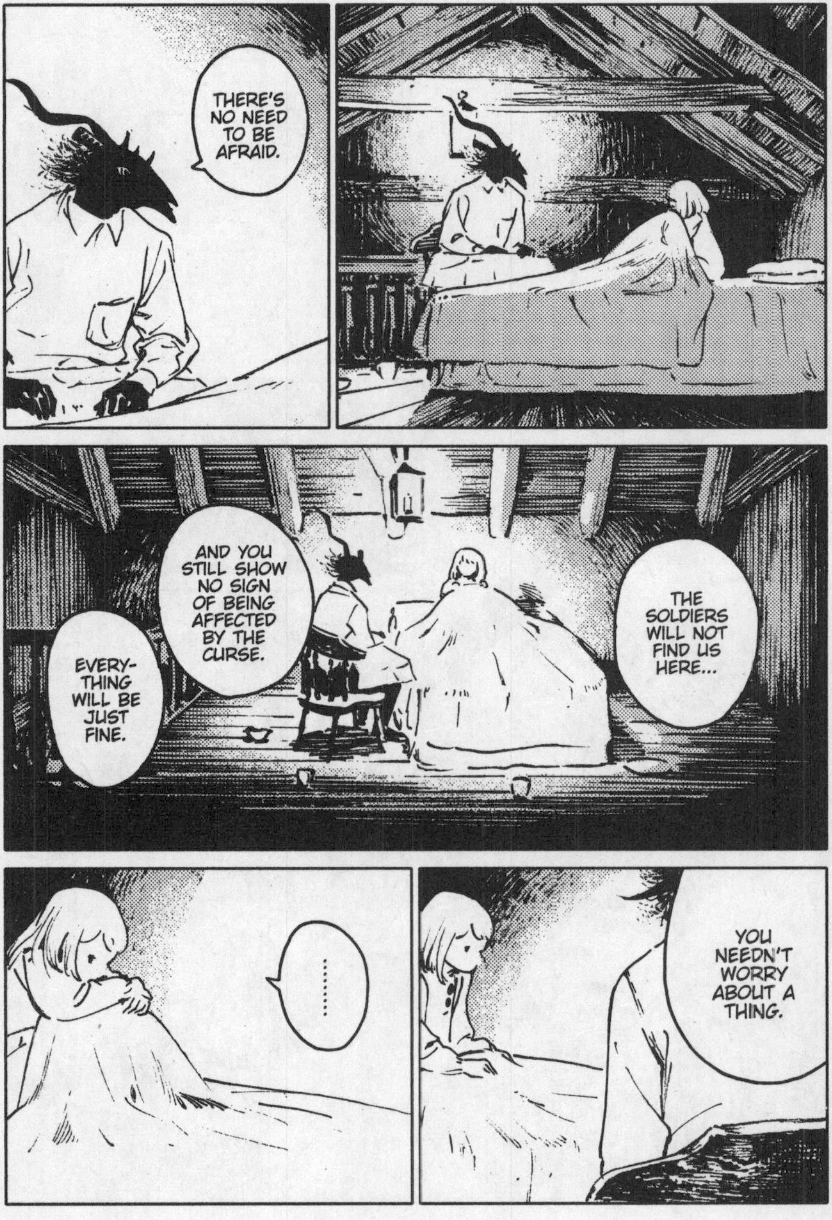
THERE'S NO NEED TO BE AFRAID.
THE SOLDIERS WILL NOT FIND US HERE...
AND YOU STILL SHOW NO SIGN OF BEING AFFECTED BY THE CURSE.
EVERY-THING WILL BE JUST FINE.
YOU NEEDN'T WORRY ABOUT A THING.
......

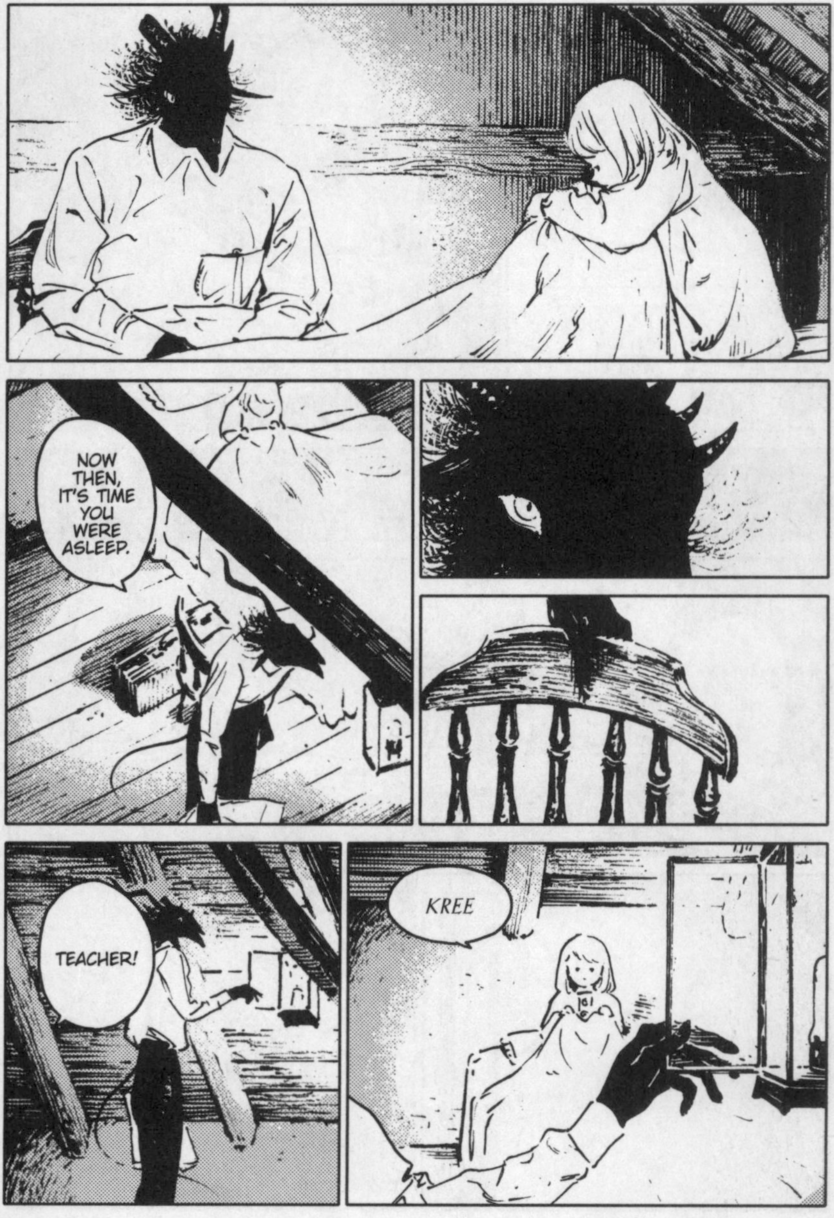
NOW THEN, IT'S TIME YOU WERE ASLEEP.
KREE
TEACHER!

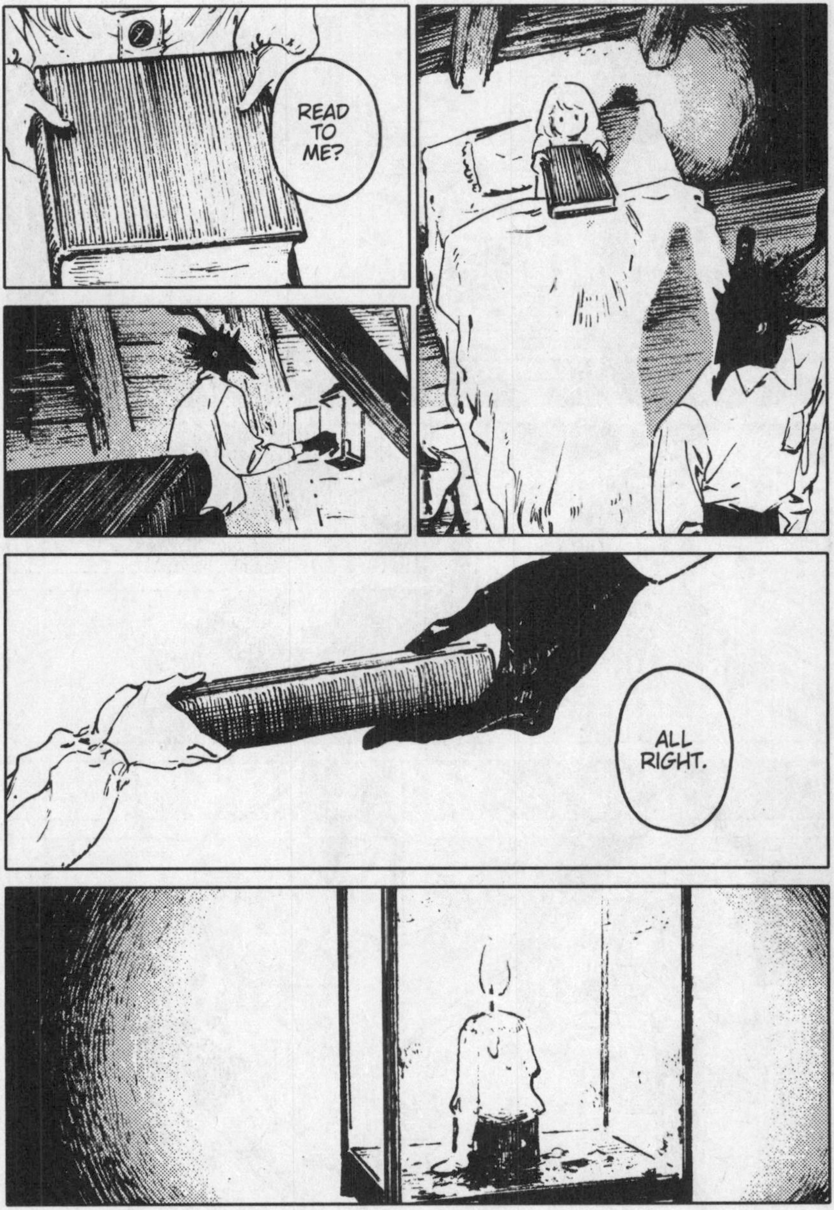
READ TO ME?
ALL RIGHT.

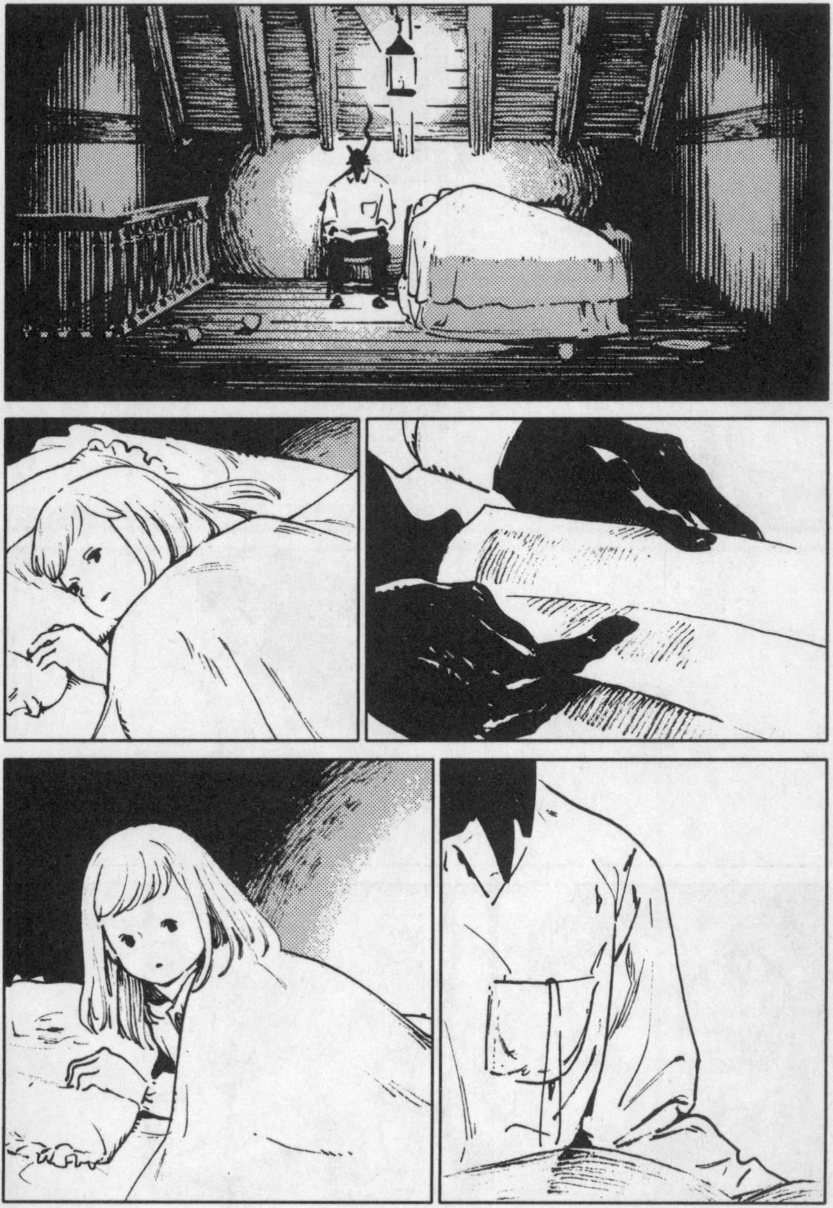

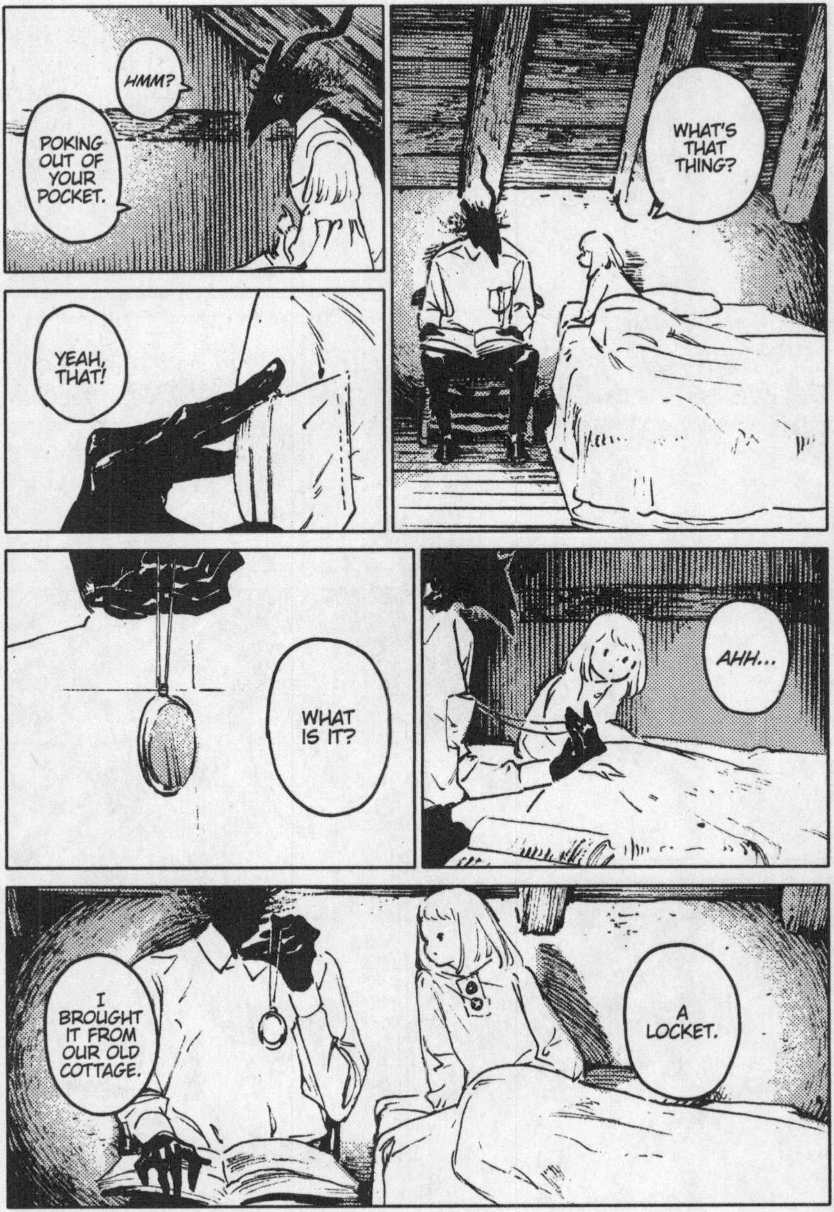

WHAT'S THAT THING?
HMM?
POKING OUT OF YOUR POCKET.
YEAH, THAT!
AHH...
WHAT IS IT?
A LOCKET.
I BROUGHT IT FROM OUR OLD COTTAGE.

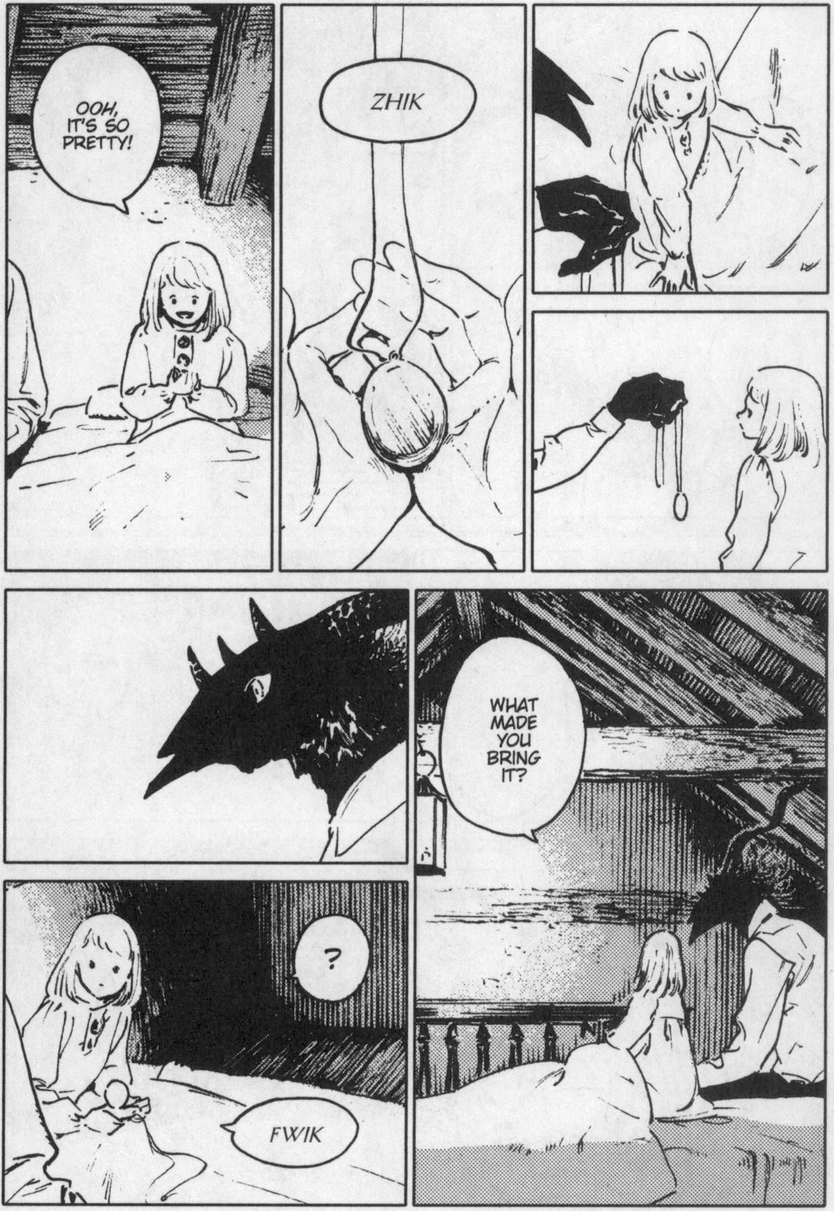
ZHIK
OOH, IT'S SO PRETTY!
WHAT MADE YOU BRING IT?
?
FWIK

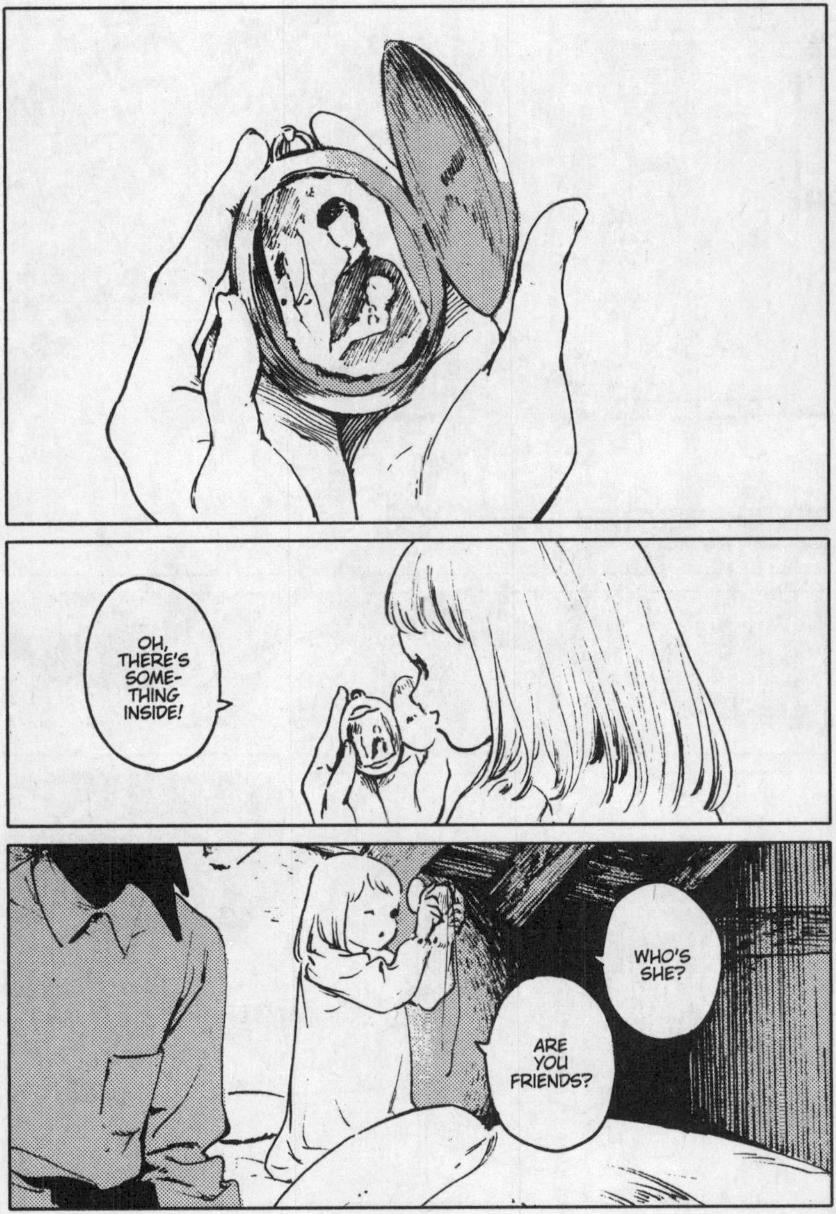
OH, THERE'S SOME-THING INSIDE!
WHO'S SHE?
ARE YOU FRIENDS?

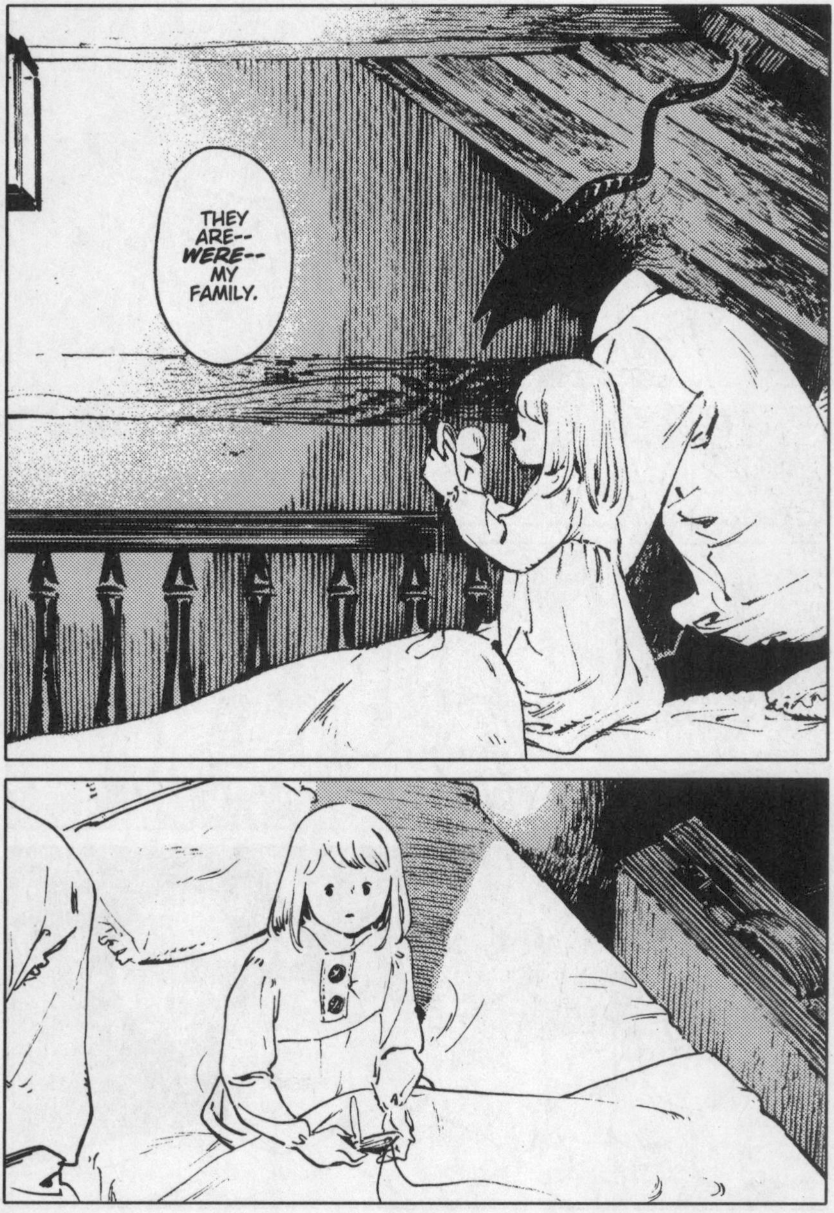
THEY ARE-- *WERE--* MY FAMILY.

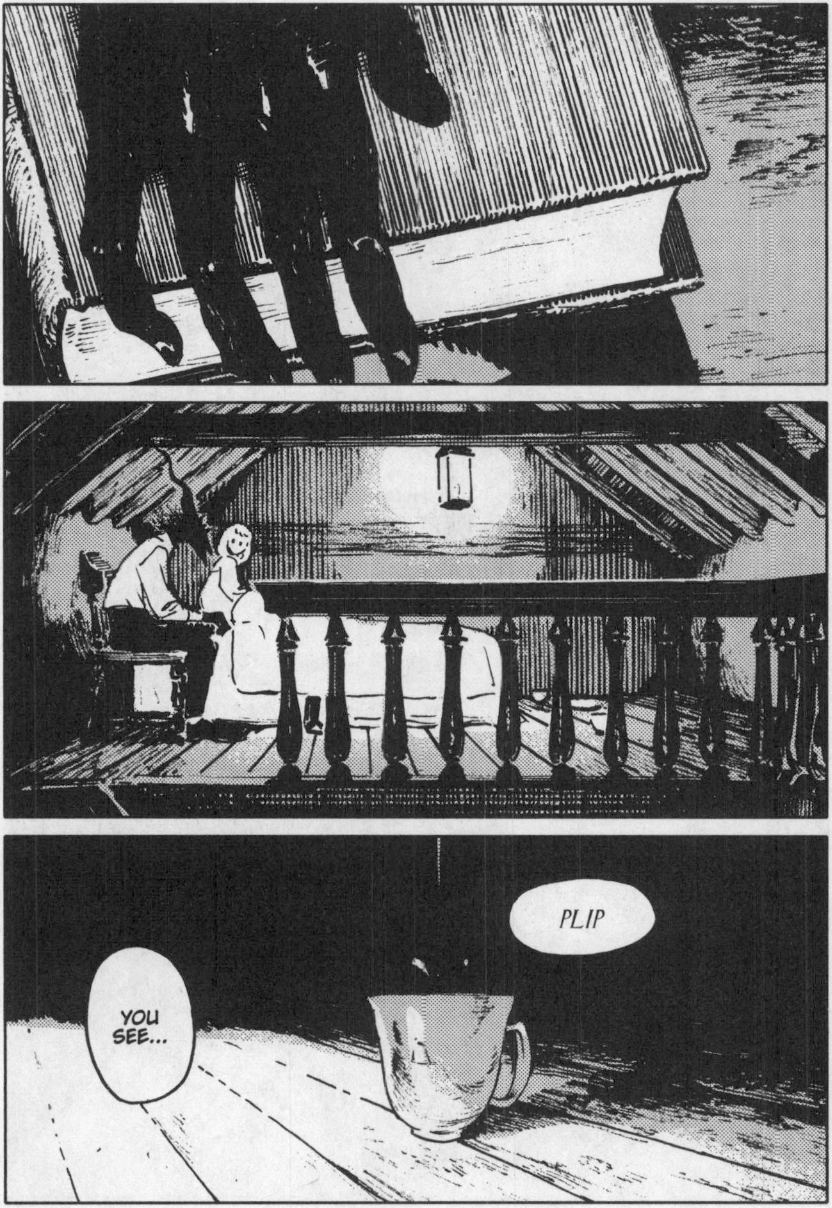
PLIP
YOU SEE...

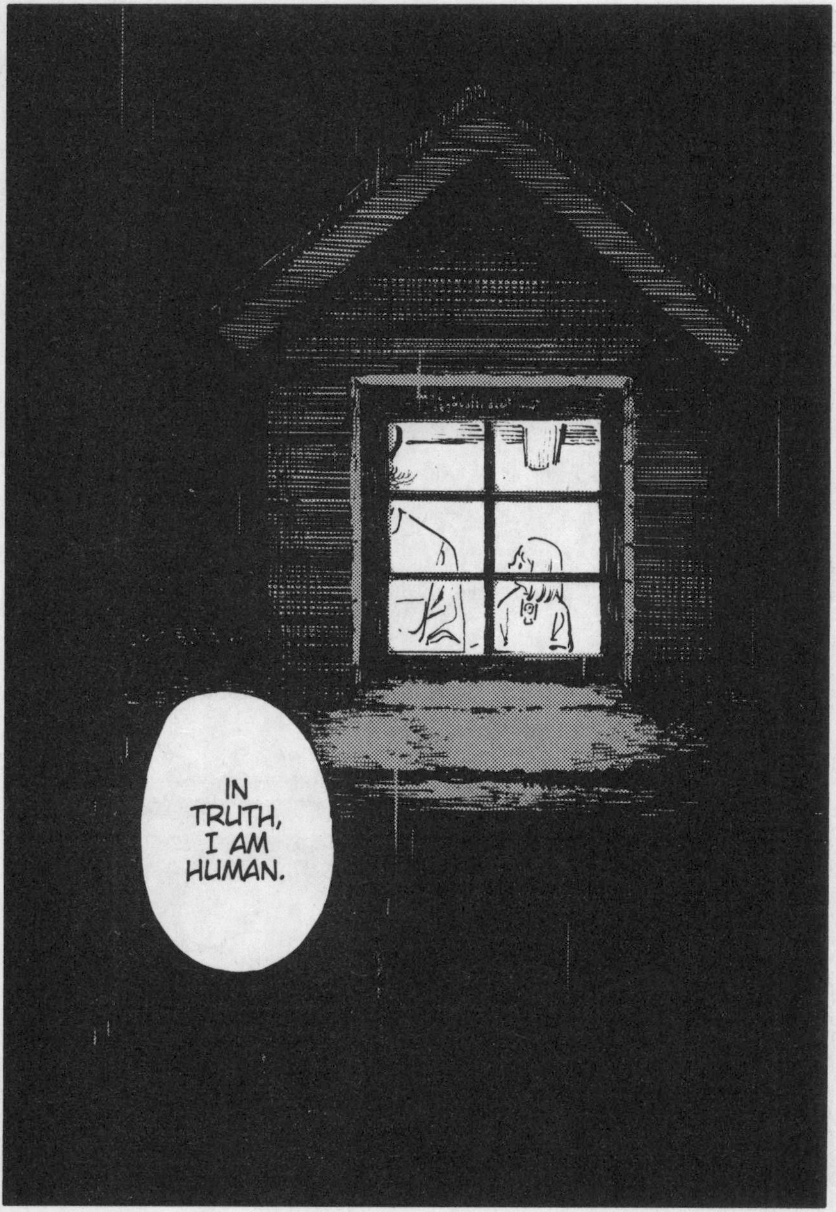
IN TRUTH, I AM HUMAN.

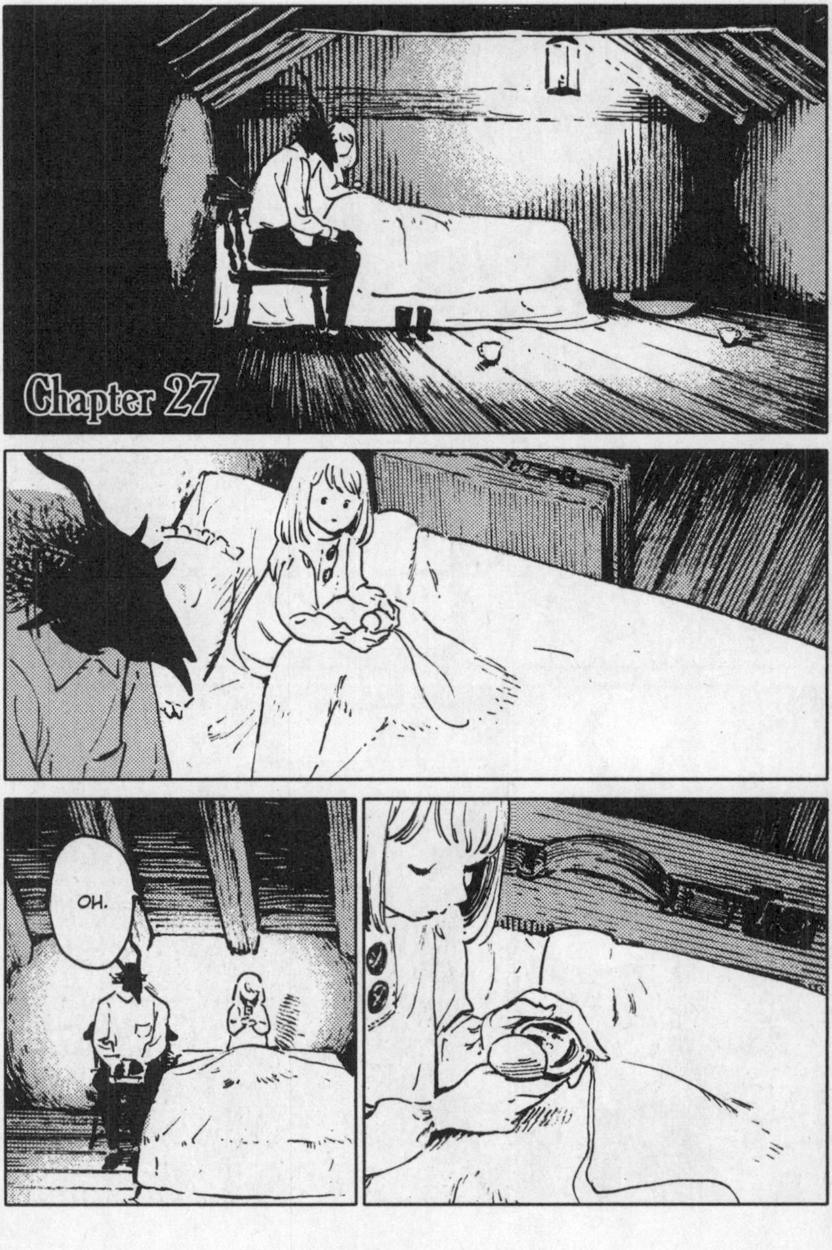
Chapter 27
OH.

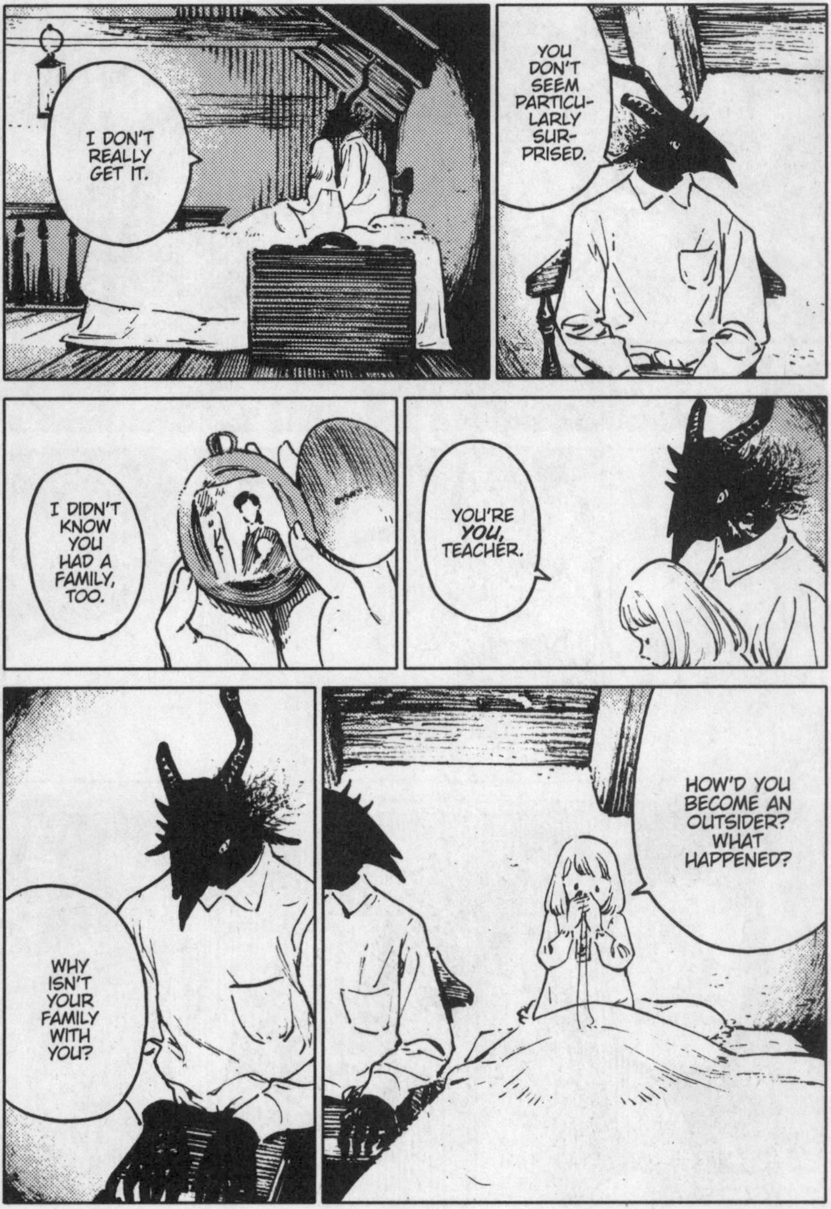
YOU DON'T SEEM PARTICULARLY SURPRISED.
I DON'T REALLY GET IT.
YOU'RE *YOU*, TEACHER.
I DIDN'T KNOW YOU HAD A FAMILY, TOO.
HOW'D YOU BECOME AN OUTSIDER? WHAT HAPPENED?
WHY ISN'T YOUR FAMILY WITH YOU?

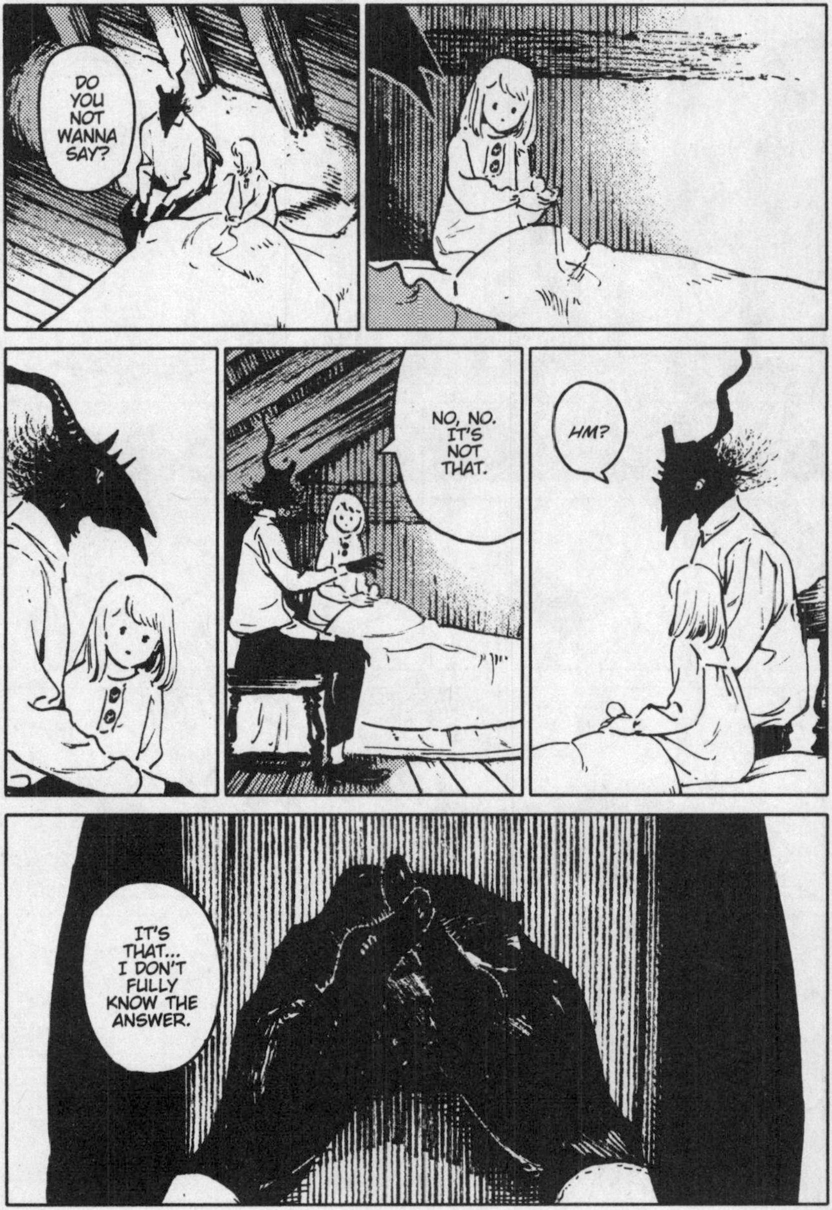
DO YOU NOT WANNA SAY?
HM?
NO, NO. IT'S NOT THAT.
IT'S THAT... I DON'T FULLY KNOW THE ANSWER.

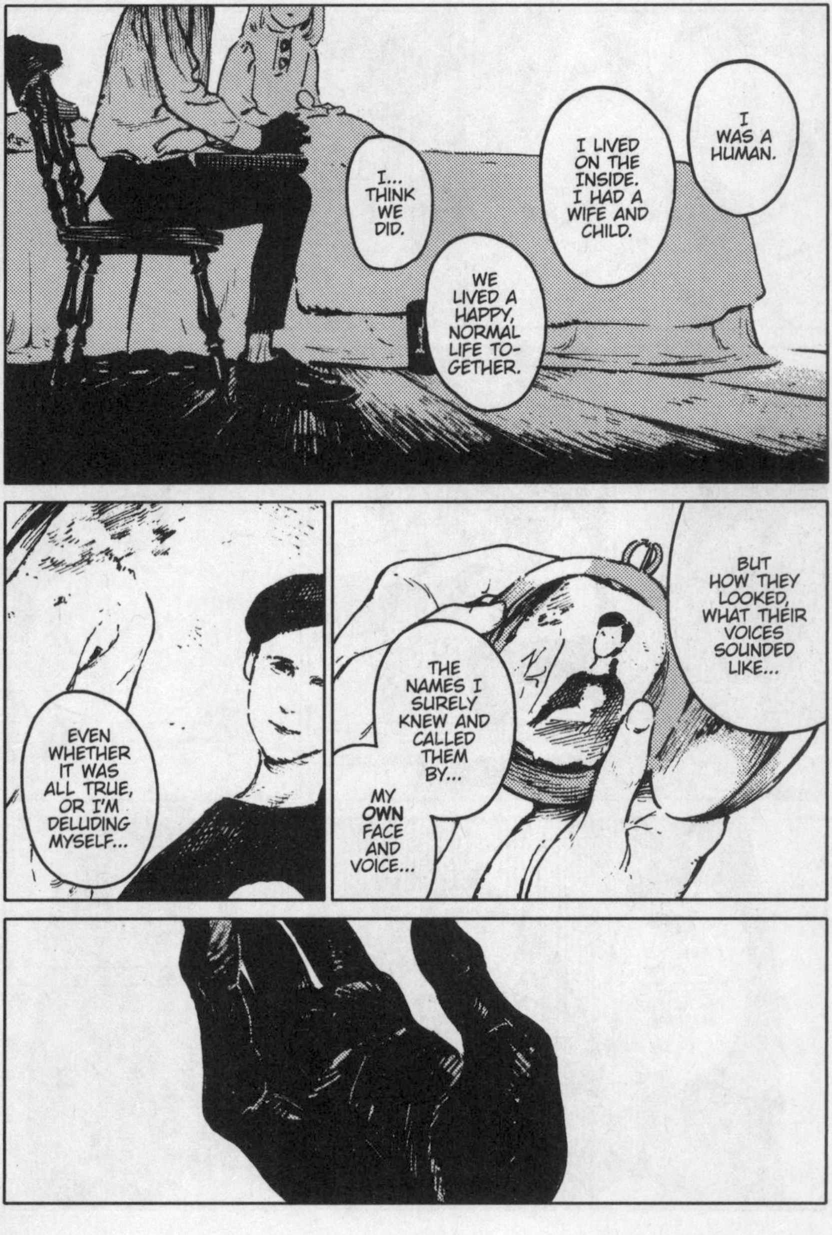
I WAS A HUMAN.
I LIVED ON THE INSIDE. I HAD A WIFE AND CHILD.
WE LIVED A HAPPY, NORMAL LIFE TOGETHER.
I... THINK WE DID.
BUT HOW THEY LOOKED, WHAT THEIR VOICES SOUNDED LIKE...
THE NAMES I SURELY KNEW AND CALLED THEM BY...
MY OWN FACE AND VOICE...
EVEN WHETHER IT WAS ALL TRUE, OR I'M DELUDING MYSELF...

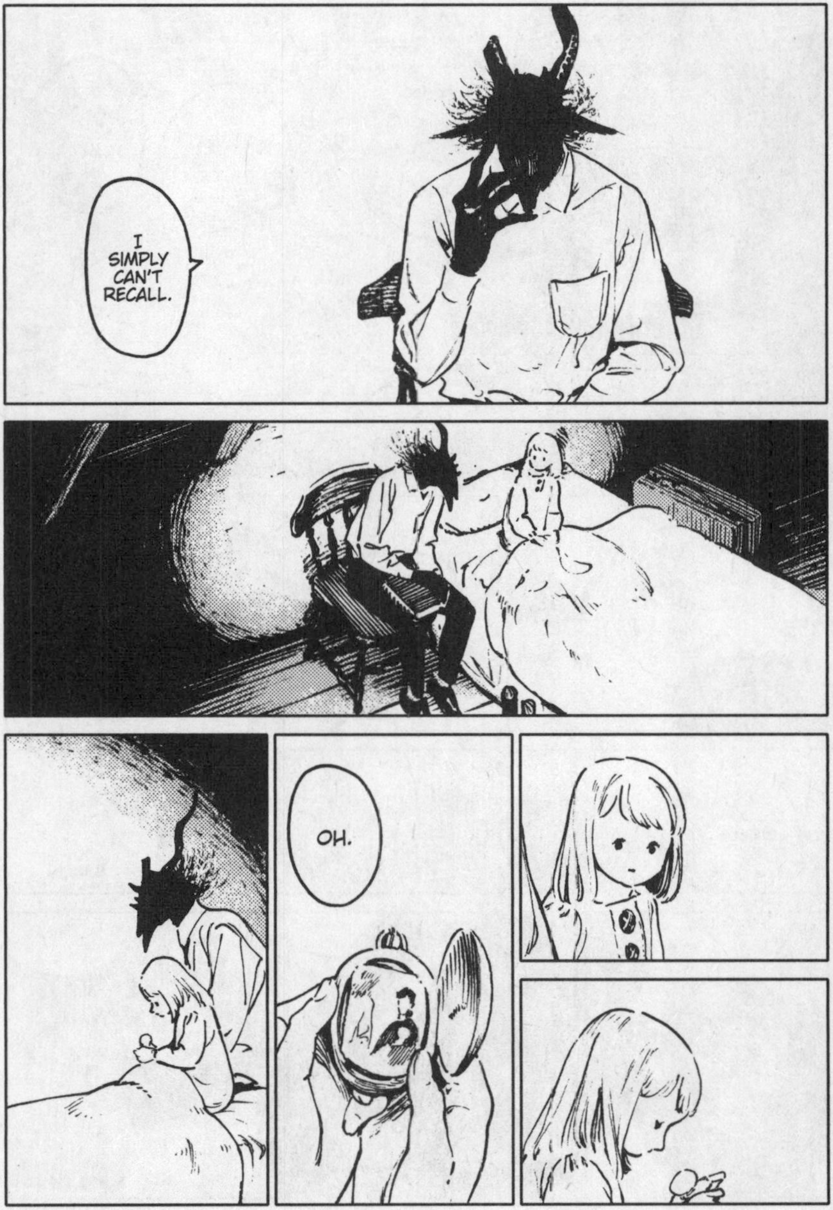
I SIMPLY CAN'T RECALL.
OH.

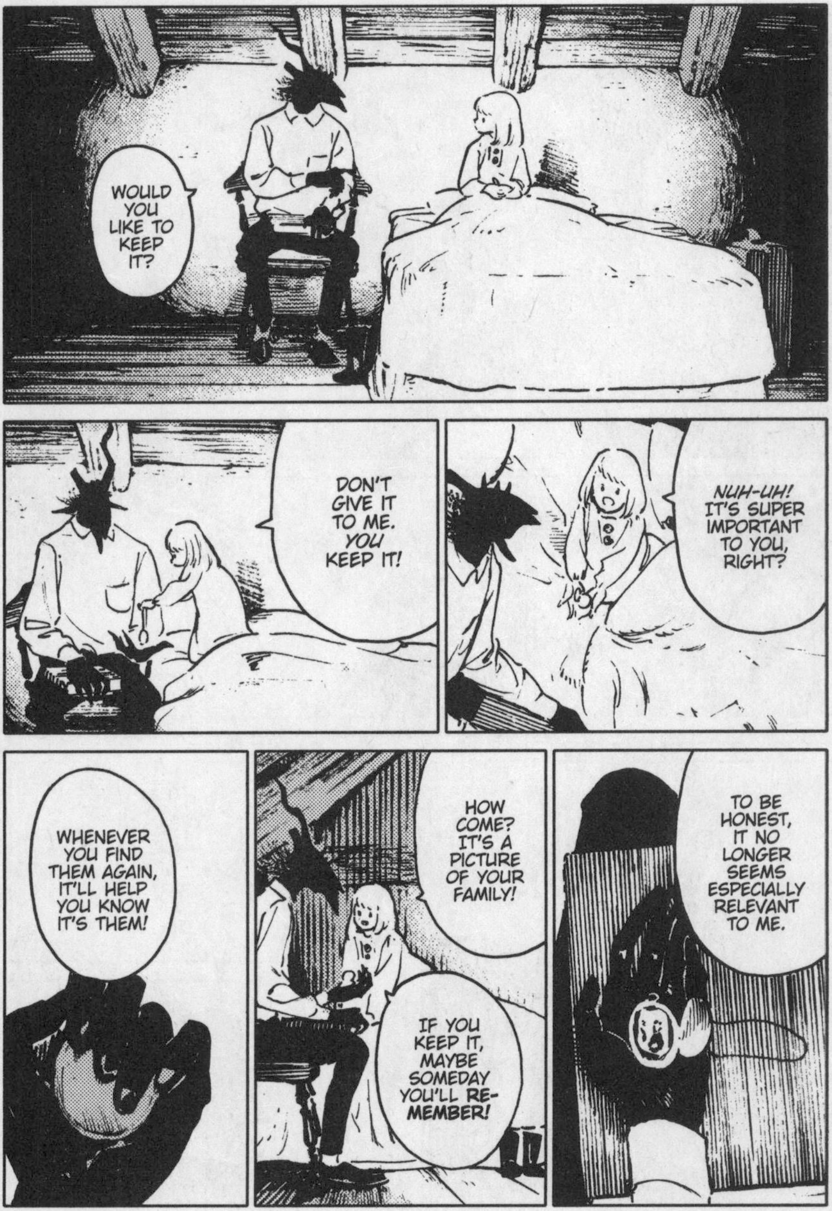
WOULD YOU LIKE TO KEEP IT?
NUH-UH! IT'S SUPER IMPORTANT TO YOU, RIGHT?
DON'T GIVE IT TO ME. *YOU* KEEP IT!
TO BE HONEST, IT NO LONGER SEEMS ESPECIALLY RELEVANT TO ME.
HOW COME? IT'S A PICTURE OF YOUR FAMILY!
IF YOU KEEP IT, MAYBE SOMEDAY YOU'LL RE-MEMBER!
WHENEVER YOU FIND THEM AGAIN, IT'LL HELP YOU KNOW IT'S THEM!

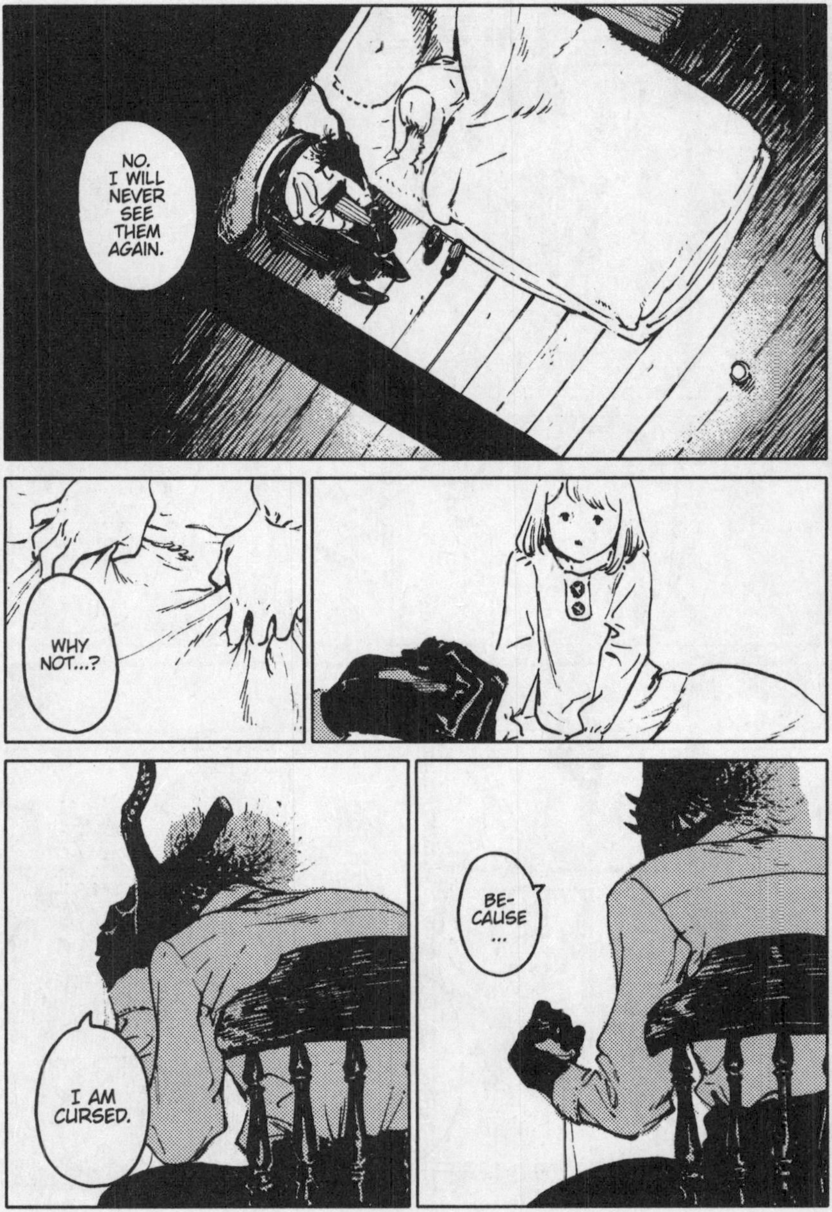
NO. I WILL NEVER SEE THEM AGAIN.
WHY NOT...?
BE-CAUSE ...
I AM CURSED.

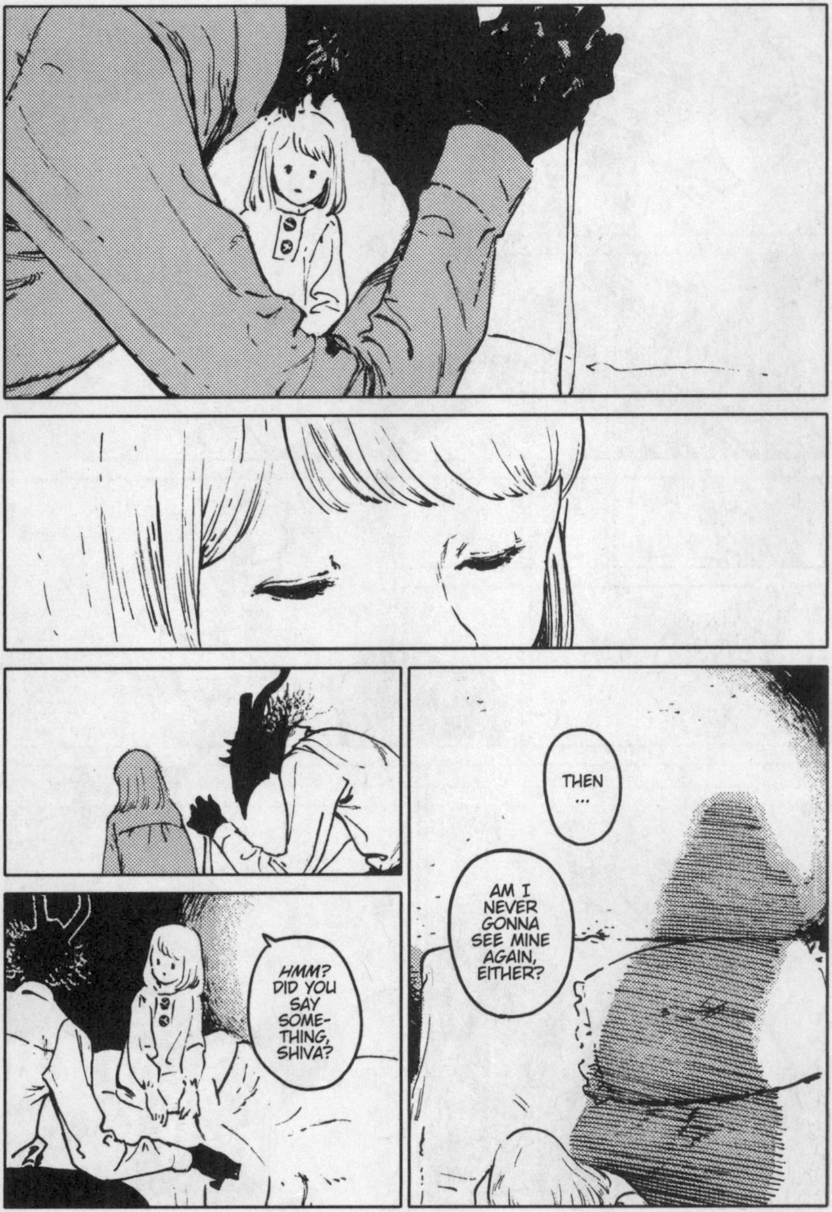
THEN ...
AM I NEVER GONNA SEE MINE AGAIN, EITHER?
HMM? DID YOU SAY SOME-THING, SHIVA?

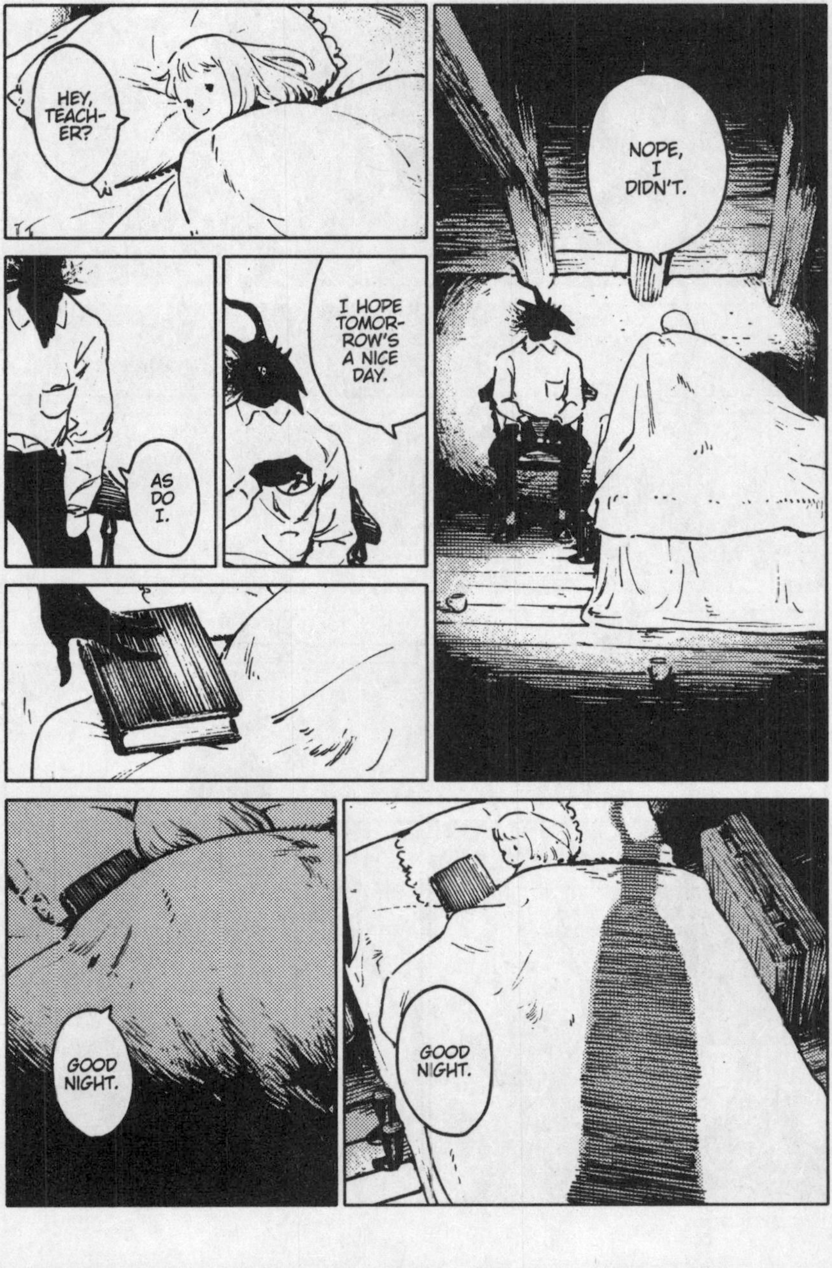
NOPE, I DIDN'T.
HEY, TEACHER?
I HOPE TOMORROW'S A NICE DAY.
AS DO I.
GOOD NIGHT.
GOOD NIGHT.

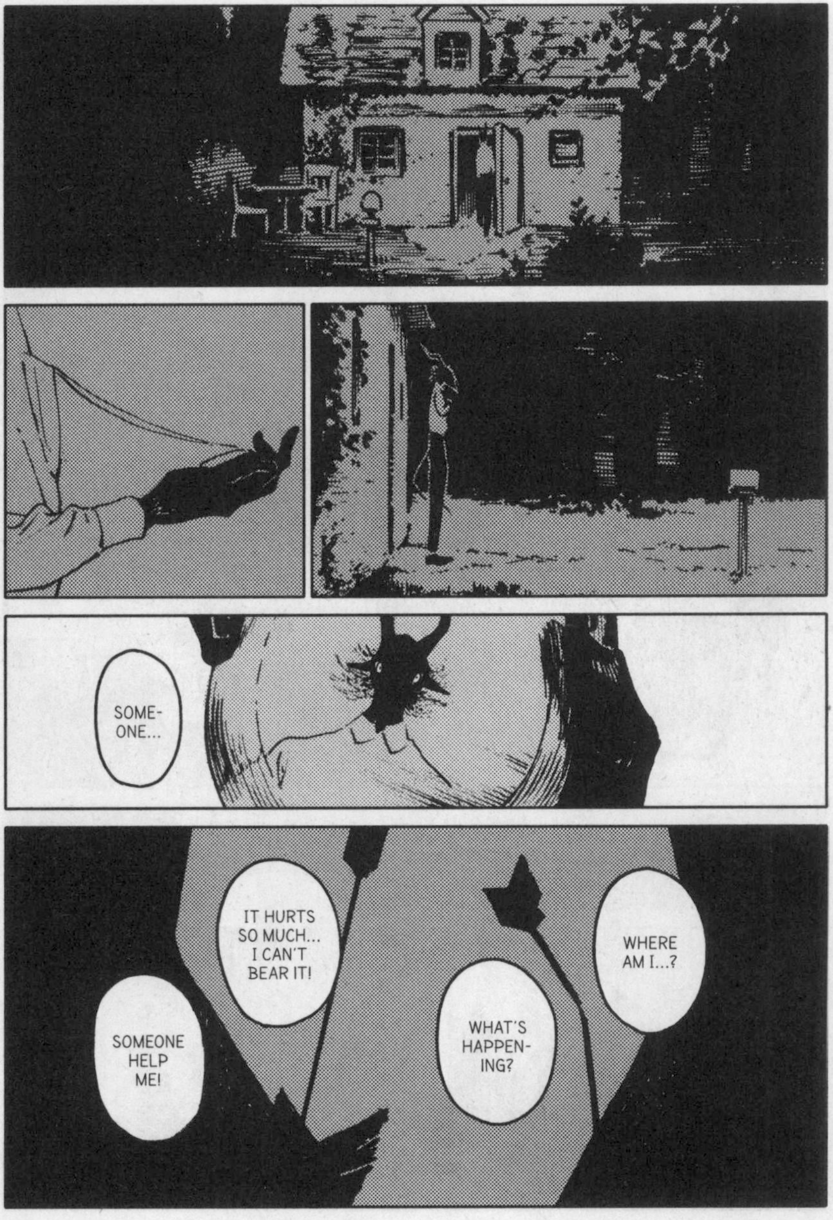
SOME-ONE...
WHERE AM I...?
WHAT'S HAPPEN-ING?
IT HURTS SO MUCH... I CAN'T BEAR IT!
SOMEONE HELP ME!

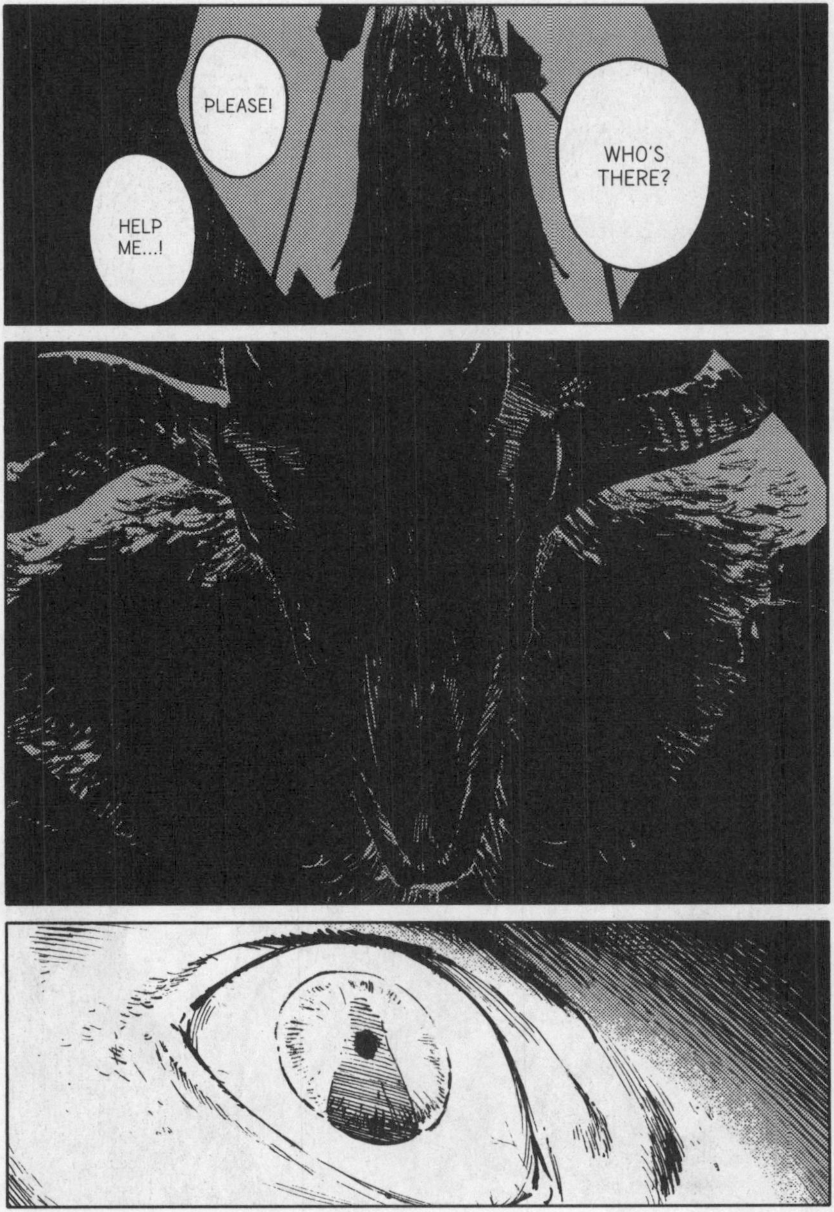
WHO'S THERE?
PLEASE!
HELP ME...!

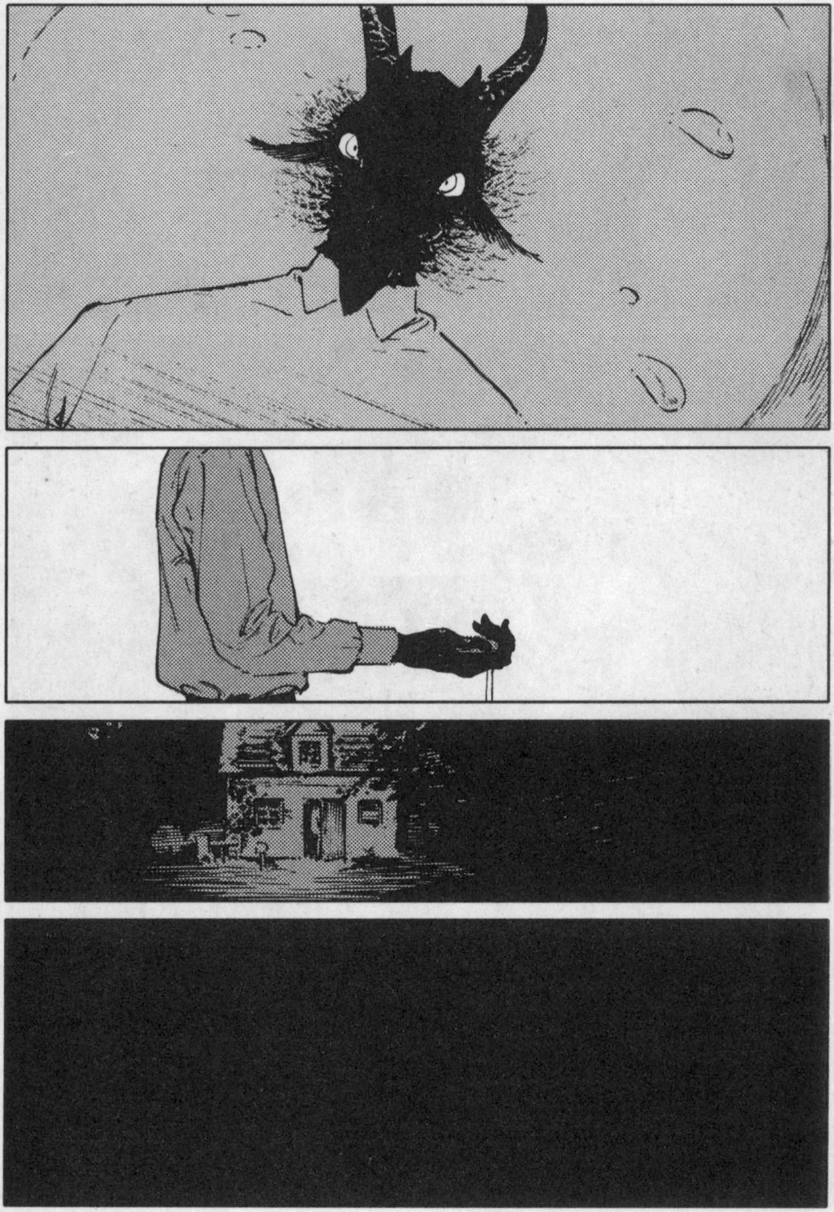

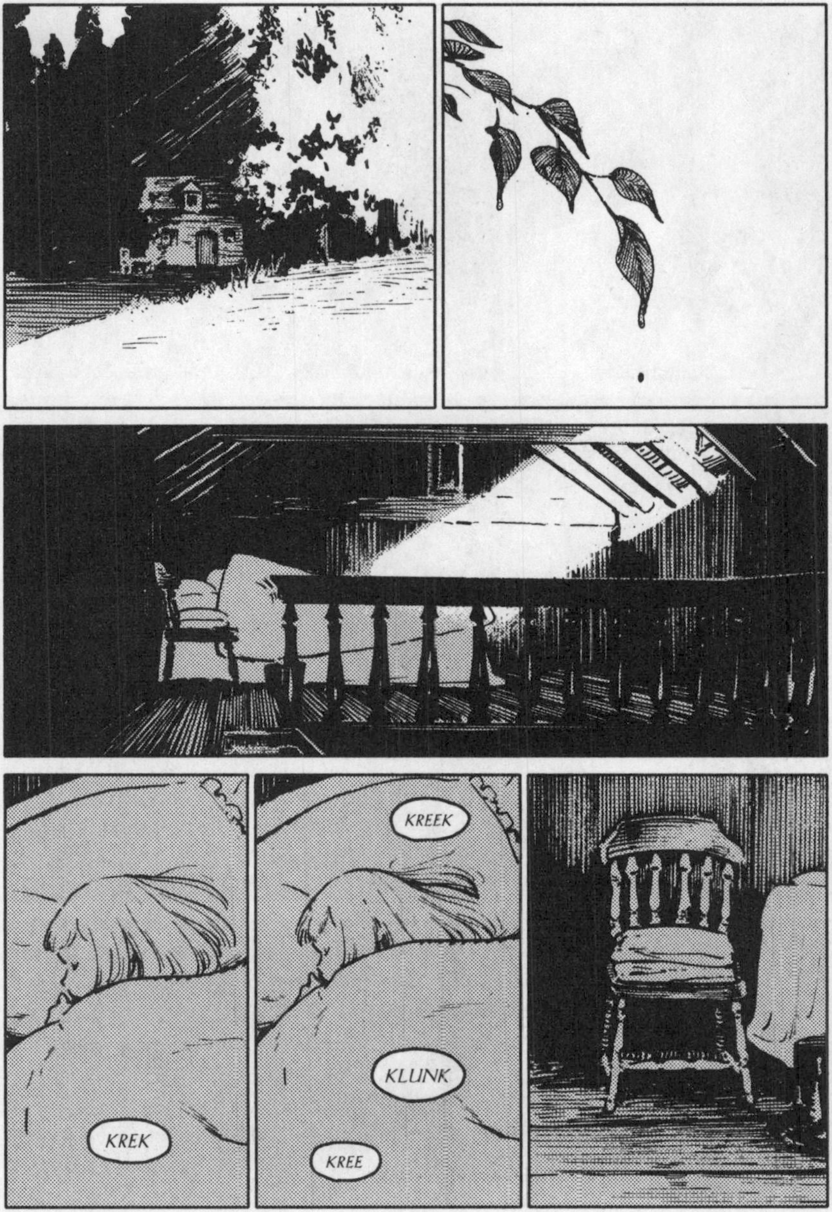
KREK
KREEK
KLUNK
KREE

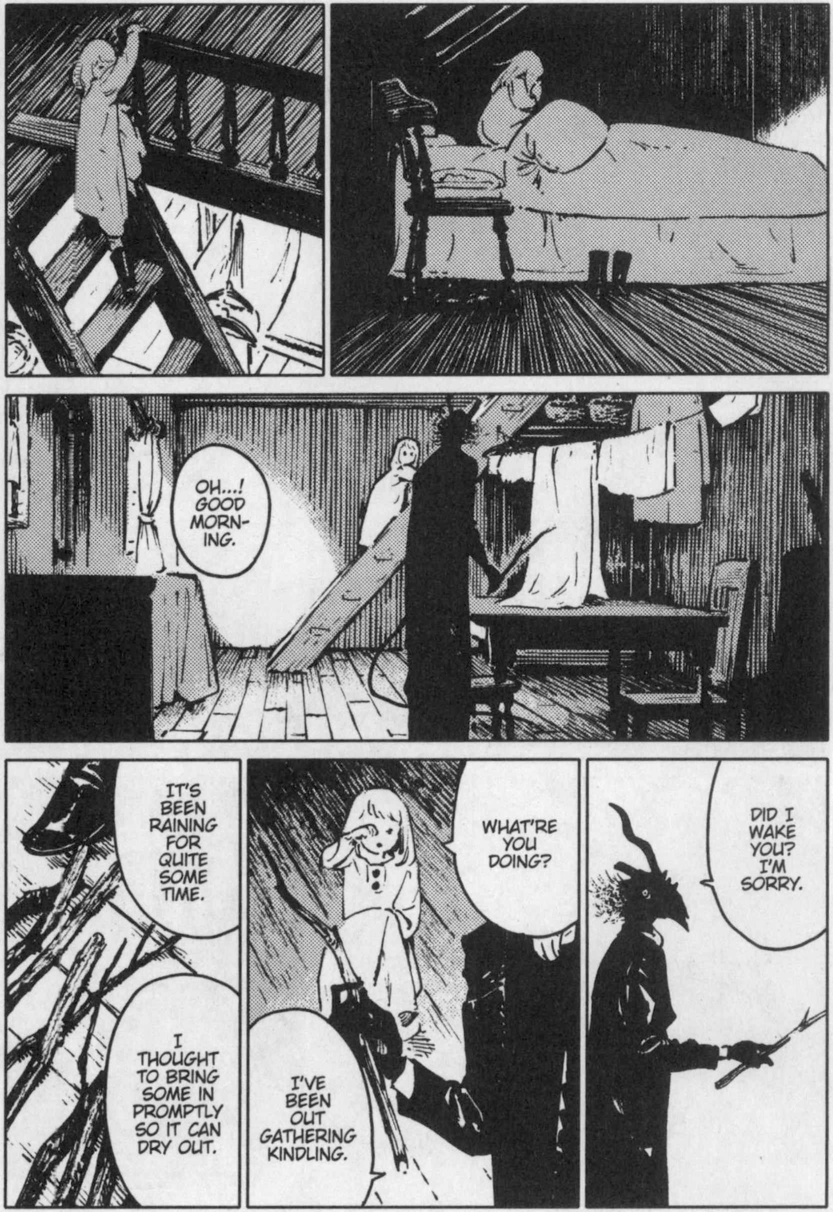
OH...! GOOD MORN-ING.
DID I WAKE YOU? I'M SORRY.
WHAT'RE YOU DOING?
I'VE BEEN OUT GATHERING KINDLING.
IT'S BEEN RAINING FOR QUITE SOME TIME.
I THOUGHT TO BRING SOME IN PROMPTLY SO IT CAN DRY OUT.

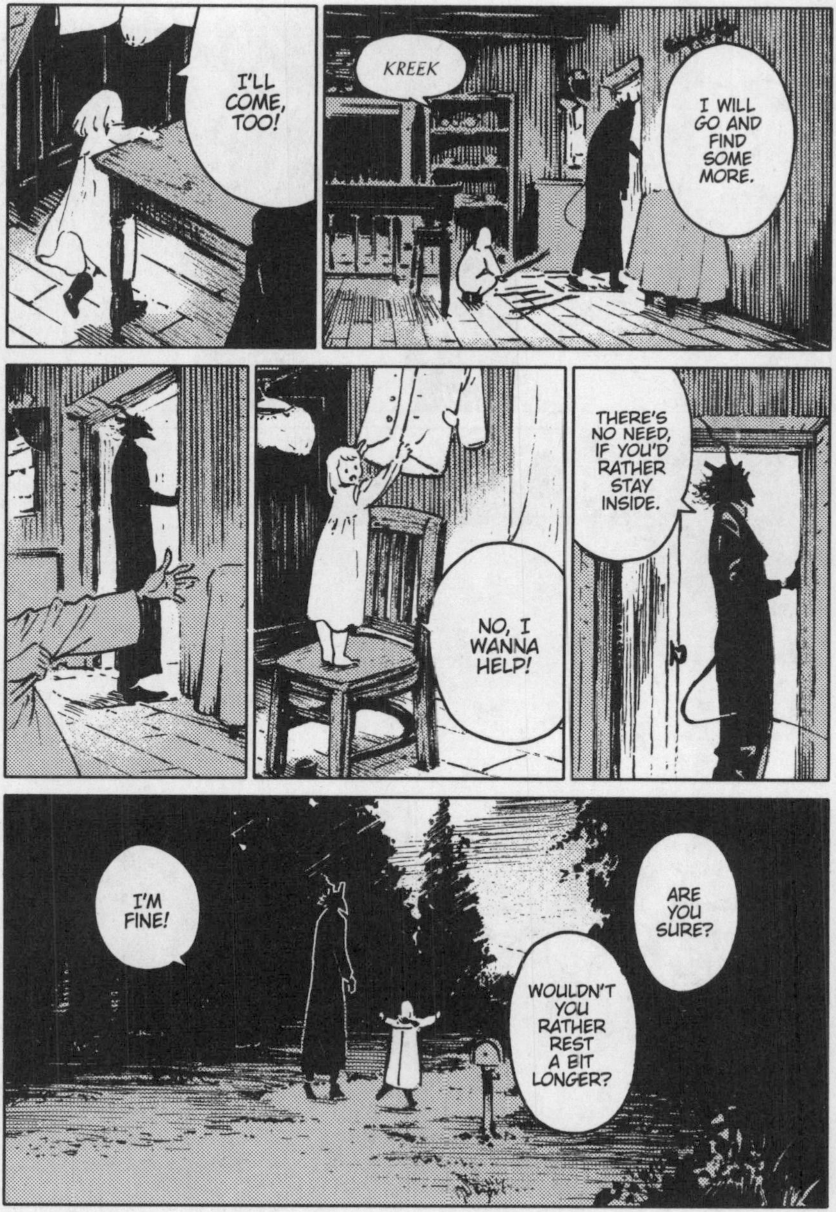
I WILL GO AND FIND SOME MORE.
KREEK
I'LL COME, TOO!
THERE'S NO NEED, IF YOU'D RATHER STAY INSIDE.
NO, I WANNA HELP!
ARE YOU SURE?
WOULDN'T YOU RATHER REST A BIT LONGER?
I'M FINE!

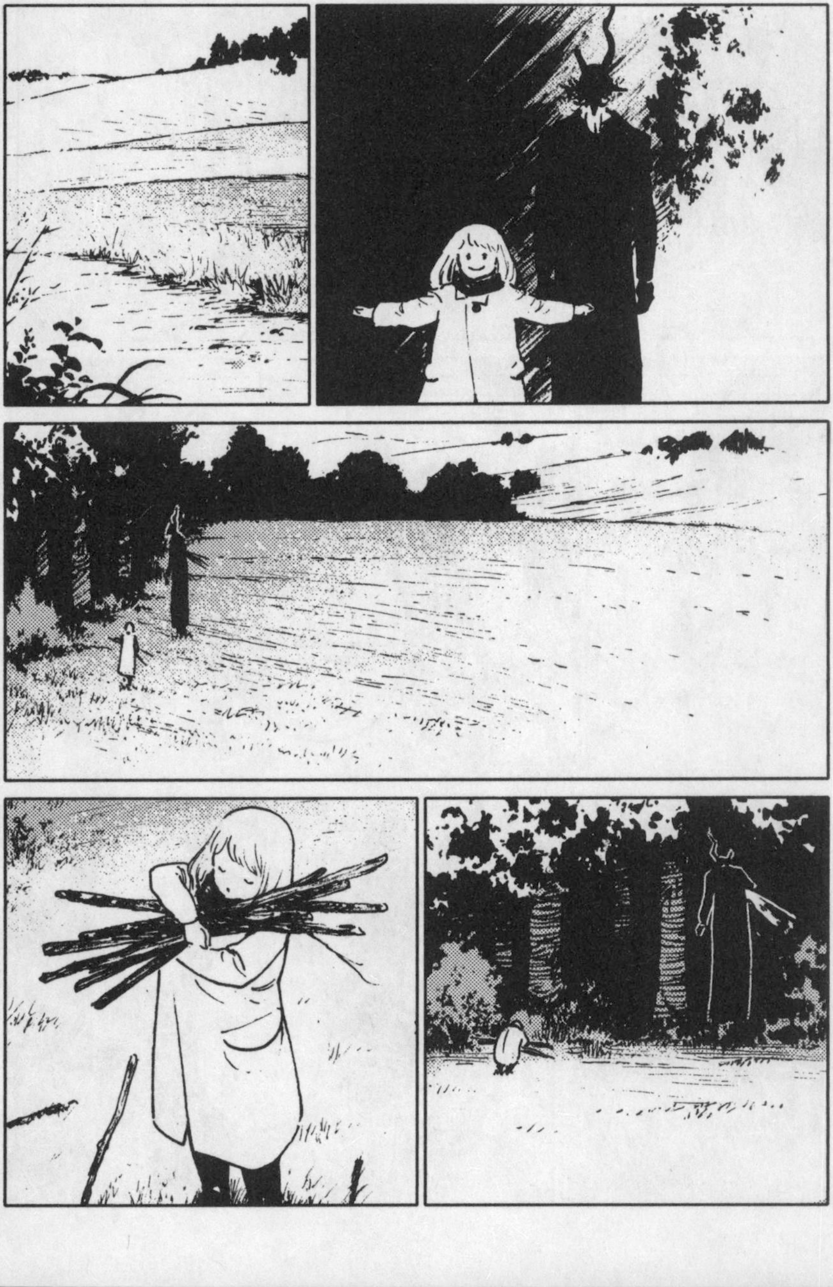

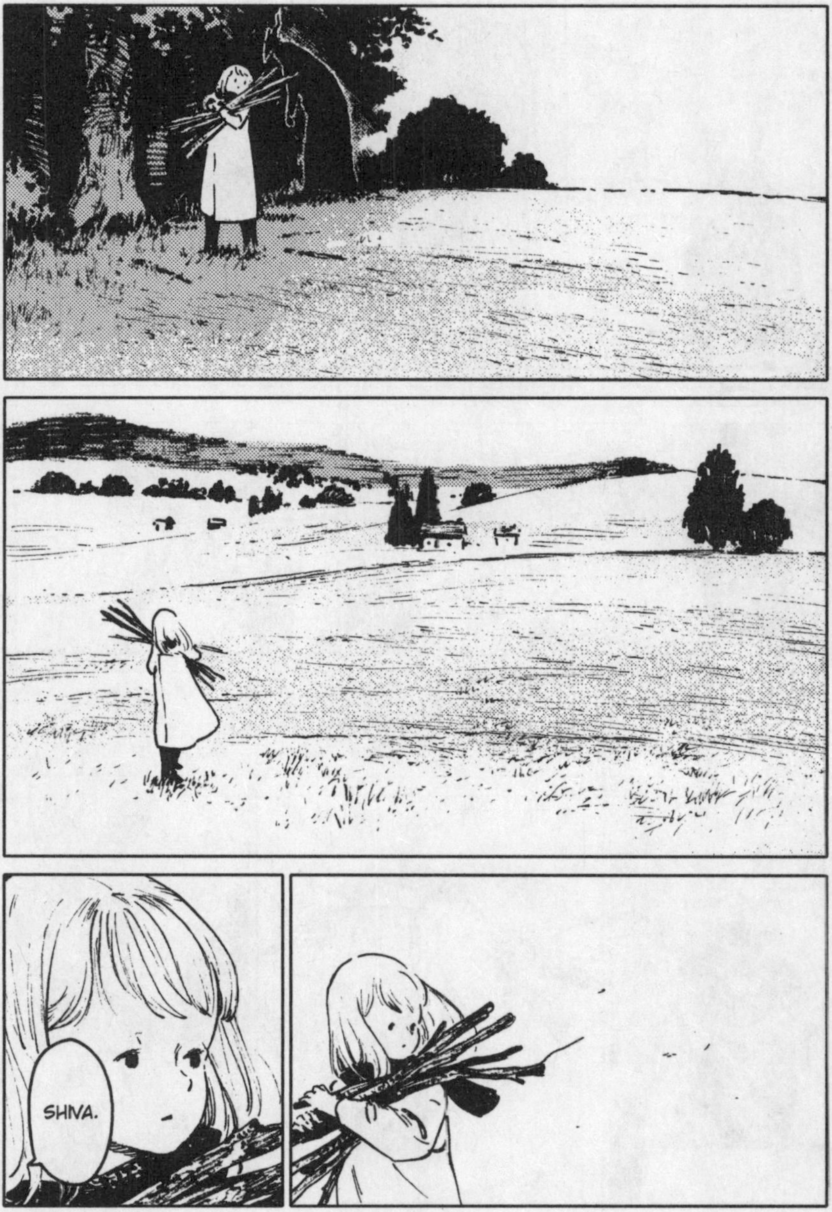
SHIVA.

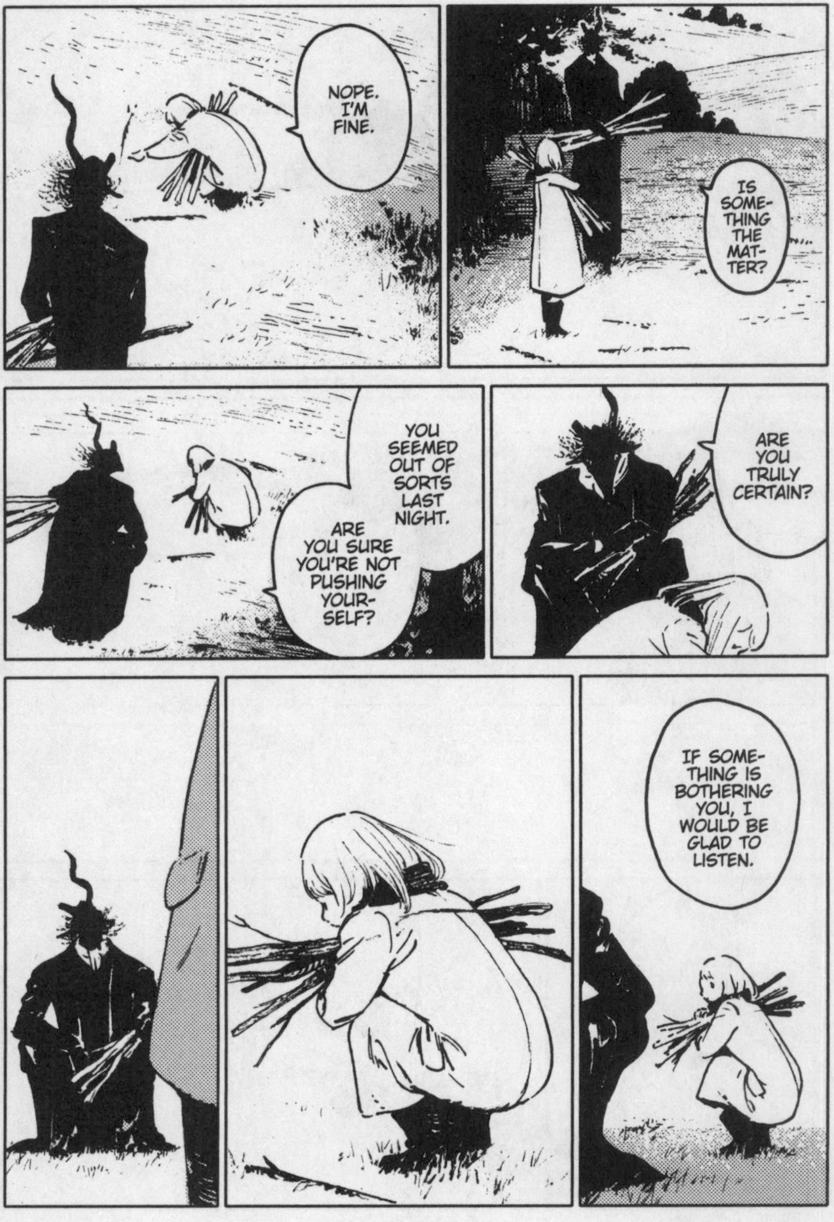
IS SOMETHING THE MATTER?
NOPE. I'M FINE.
ARE YOU TRULY CERTAIN?
YOU SEEMED OUT OF SORTS LAST NIGHT.
ARE YOU SURE YOU'RE NOT PUSHING YOURSELF?
IF SOMETHING IS BOTHERING YOU, I WOULD BE GLAD TO LISTEN.

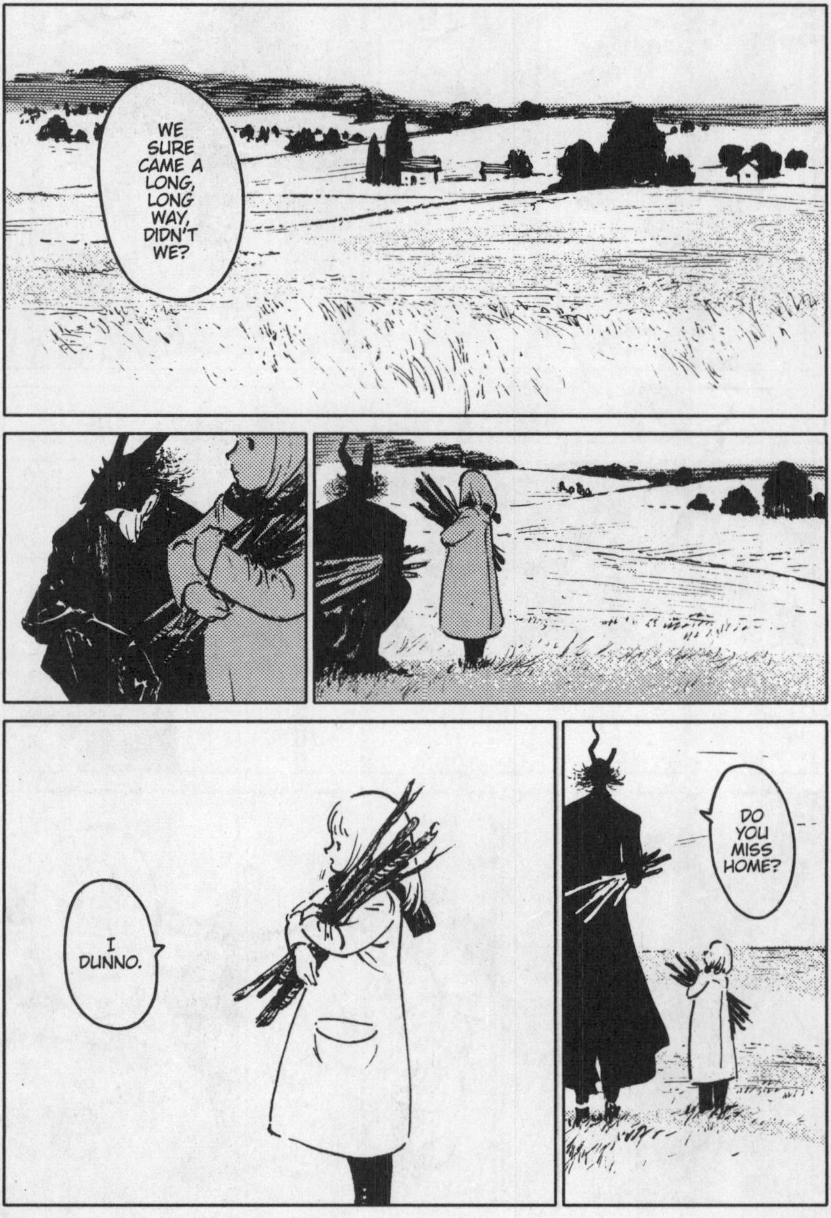
WE SURE CAME A LONG, LONG WAY, DIDN'T WE?
DO YOU MISS HOME?
I DUNNO.

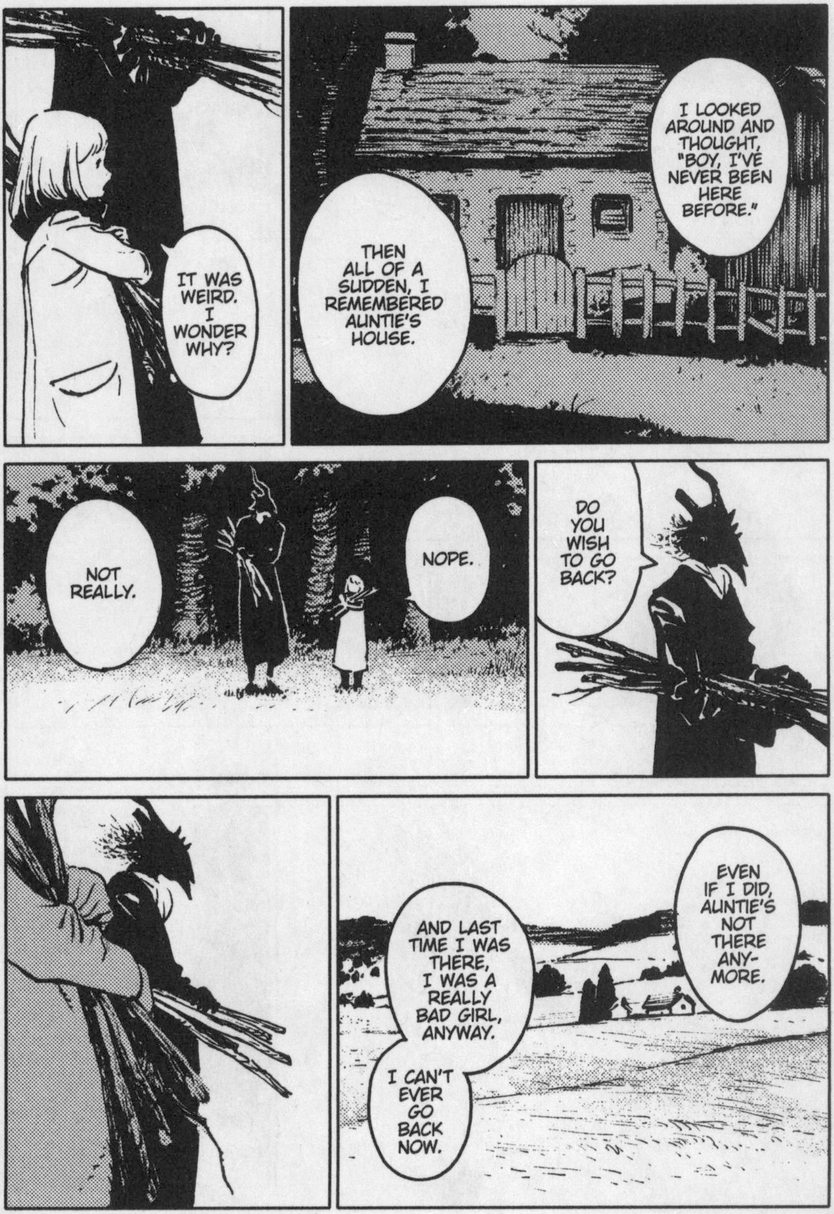
I LOOKED AROUND AND THOUGHT, "BOY, I'VE NEVER BEEN HERE BEFORE."
THEN ALL OF A SUDDEN, I REMEMBERED AUNTIE'S HOUSE.
IT WAS WEIRD. I WONDER WHY?
DO YOU WISH TO GO BACK?
NOPE.
NOT REALLY.
EVEN IF I DID, AUNTIE'S NOT THERE ANY-MORE.
AND LAST TIME I WAS THERE, I WAS A REALLY BAD GIRL, ANYWAY.
I CAN'T EVER GO BACK NOW.

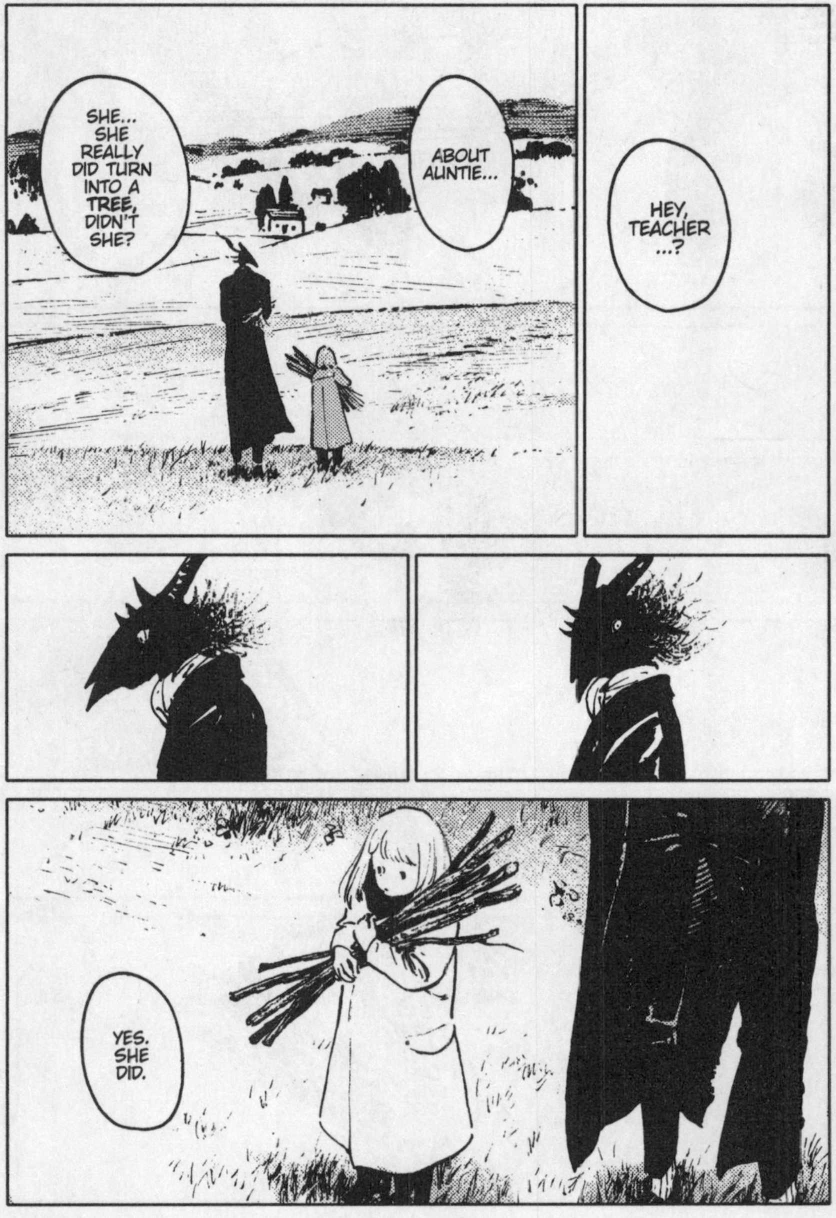
HEY, TEACHER ...?
ABOUT AUNTIE...
SHE... SHE REALLY DID TURN INTO A TREE, DIDN'T SHE?
YES. SHE DID.

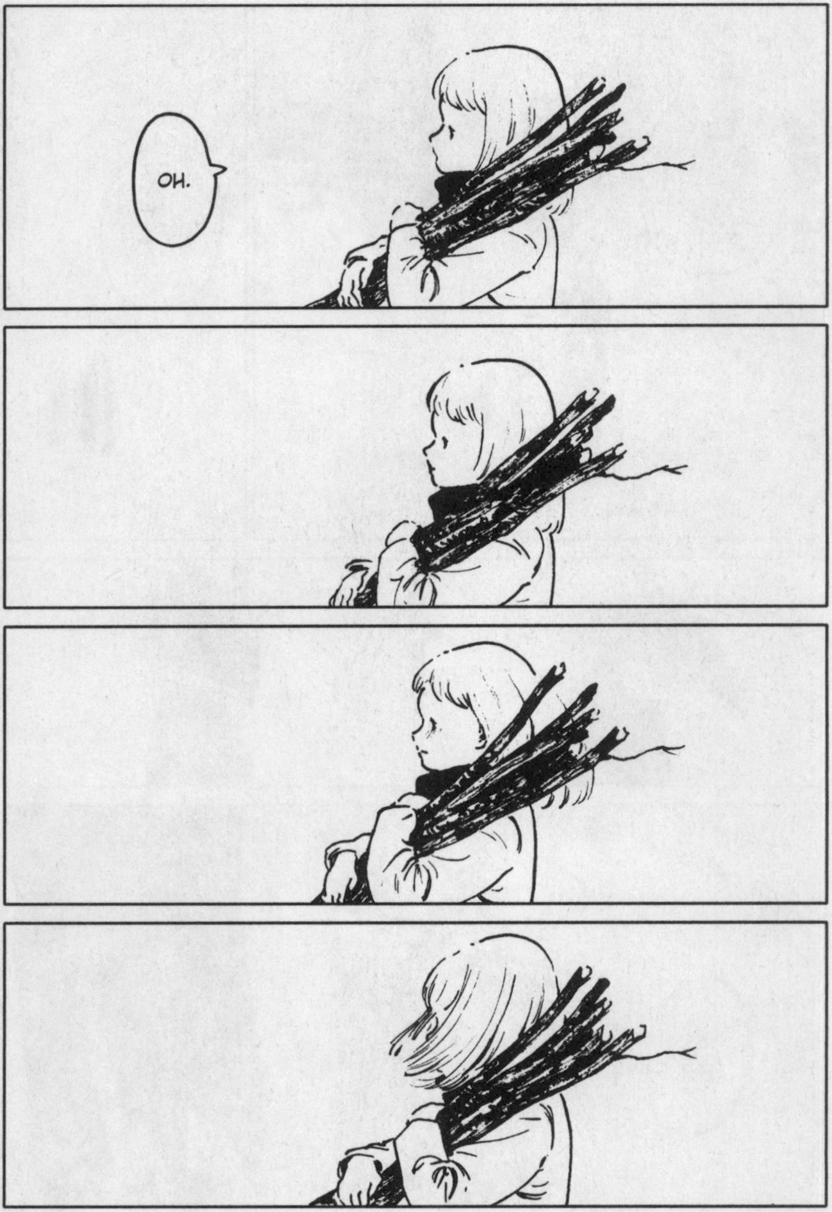
OH.

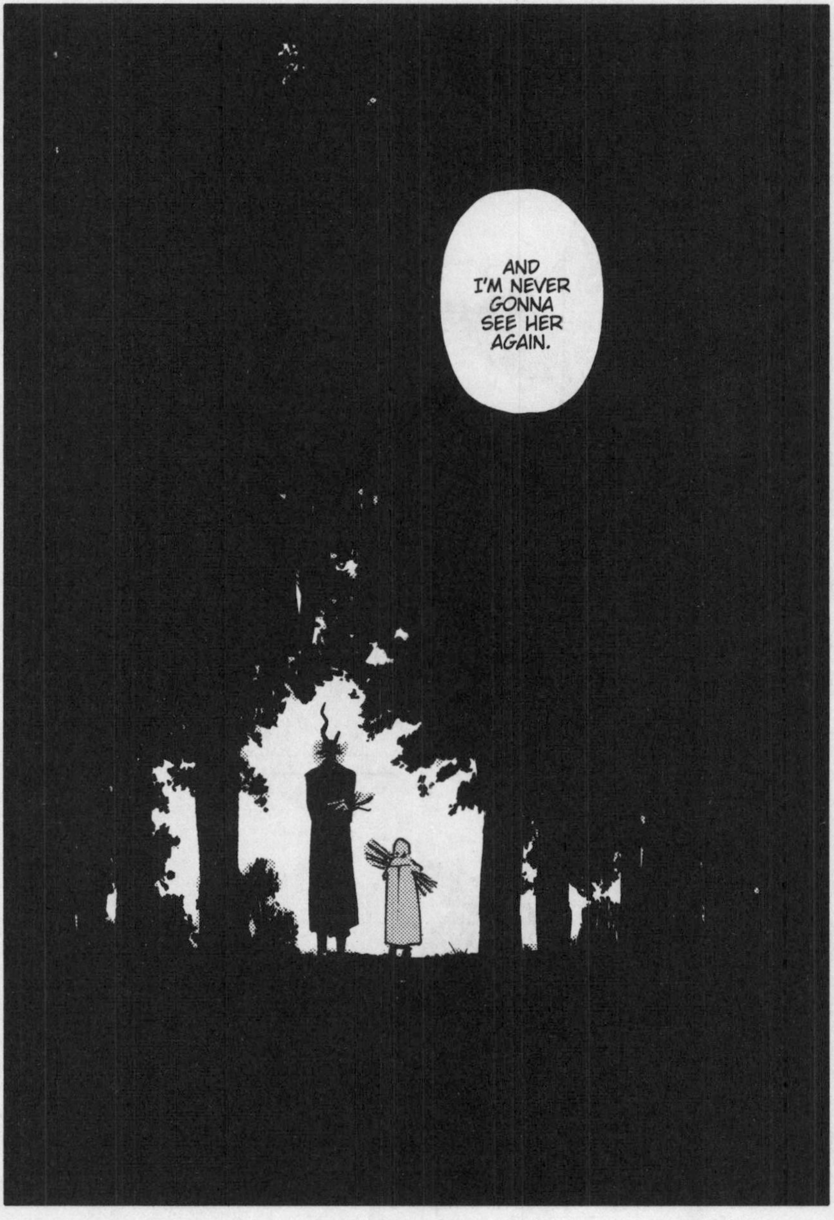
AND I'M NEVER GONNA SEE HER AGAIN.

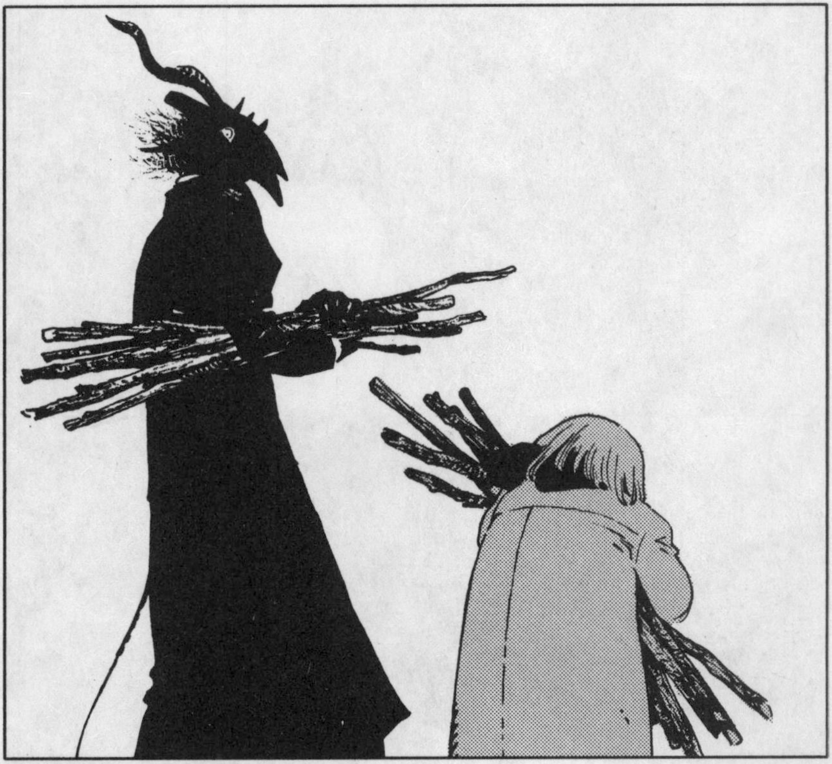
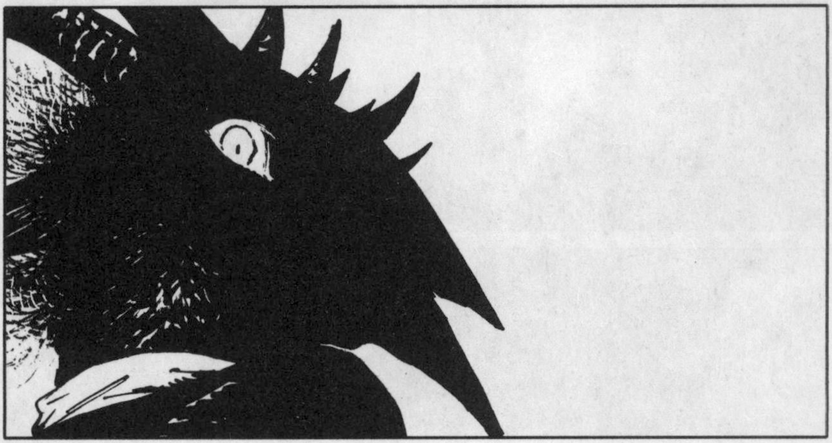

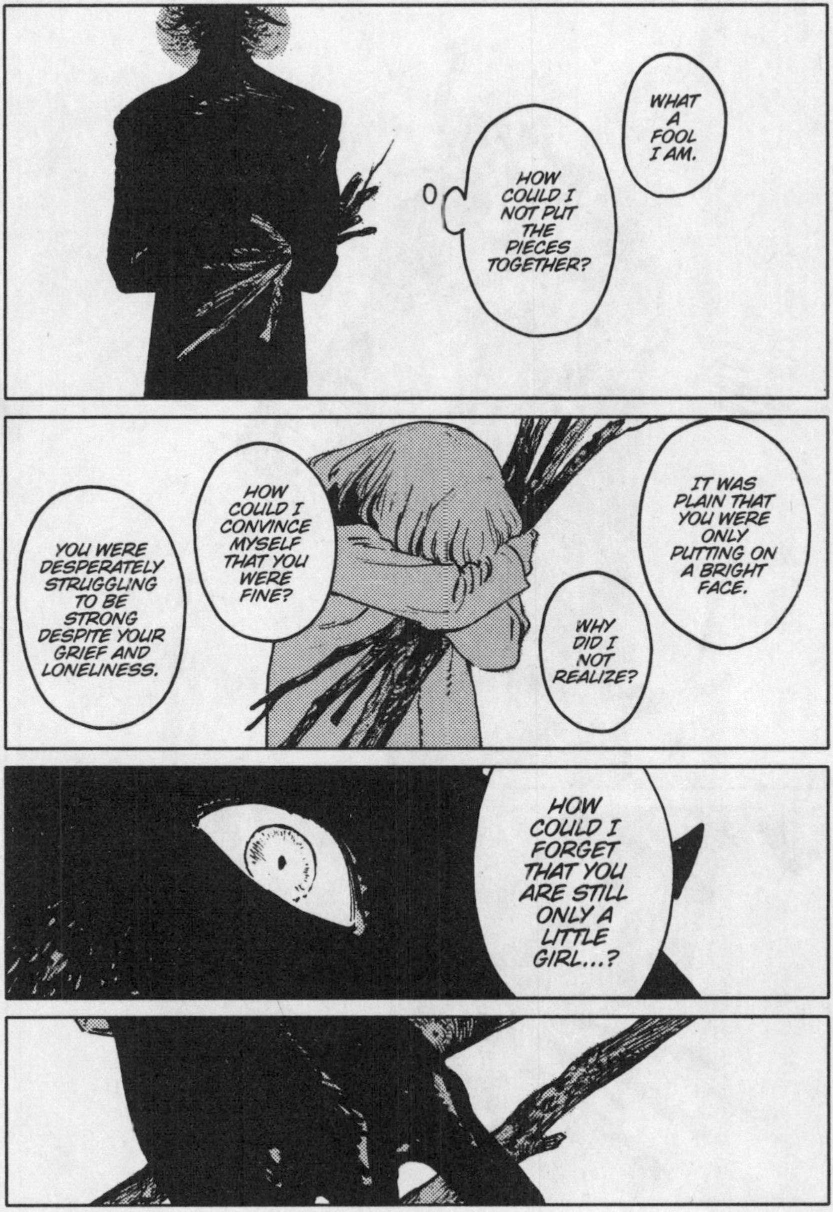
WHAT A FOOL I AM.
HOW COULD I NOT PUT THE PIECES TOGETHER?
IT WAS PLAIN THAT YOU WERE ONLY PUTTING ON A BRIGHT FACE.
WHY DID I NOT REALIZE?
HOW COULD I CONVINCE MYSELF THAT YOU WERE FINE?
YOU WERE DESPERATELY STRUGGLING TO BE STRONG DESPITE YOUR GRIEF AND LONELINESS.
HOW COULD I FORGET THAT YOU ARE STILL ONLY A LITTLE GIRL...?

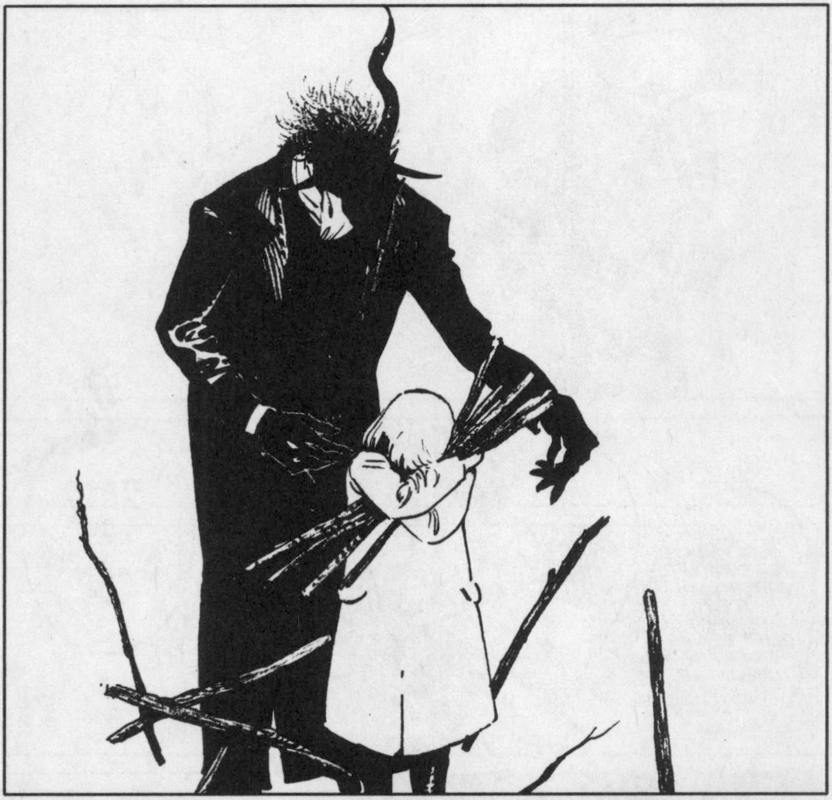
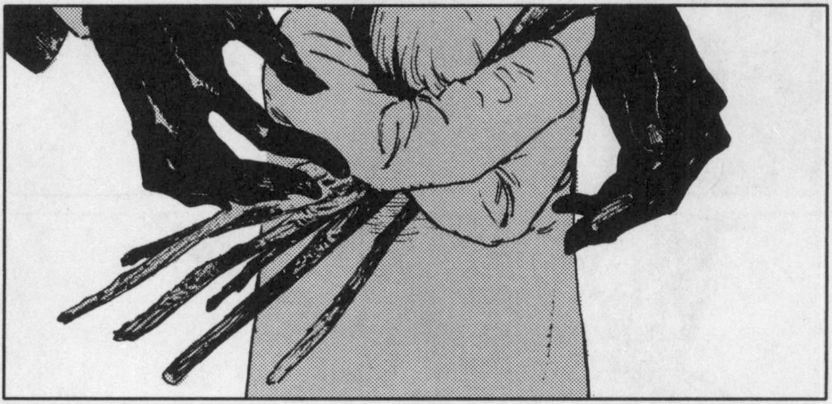

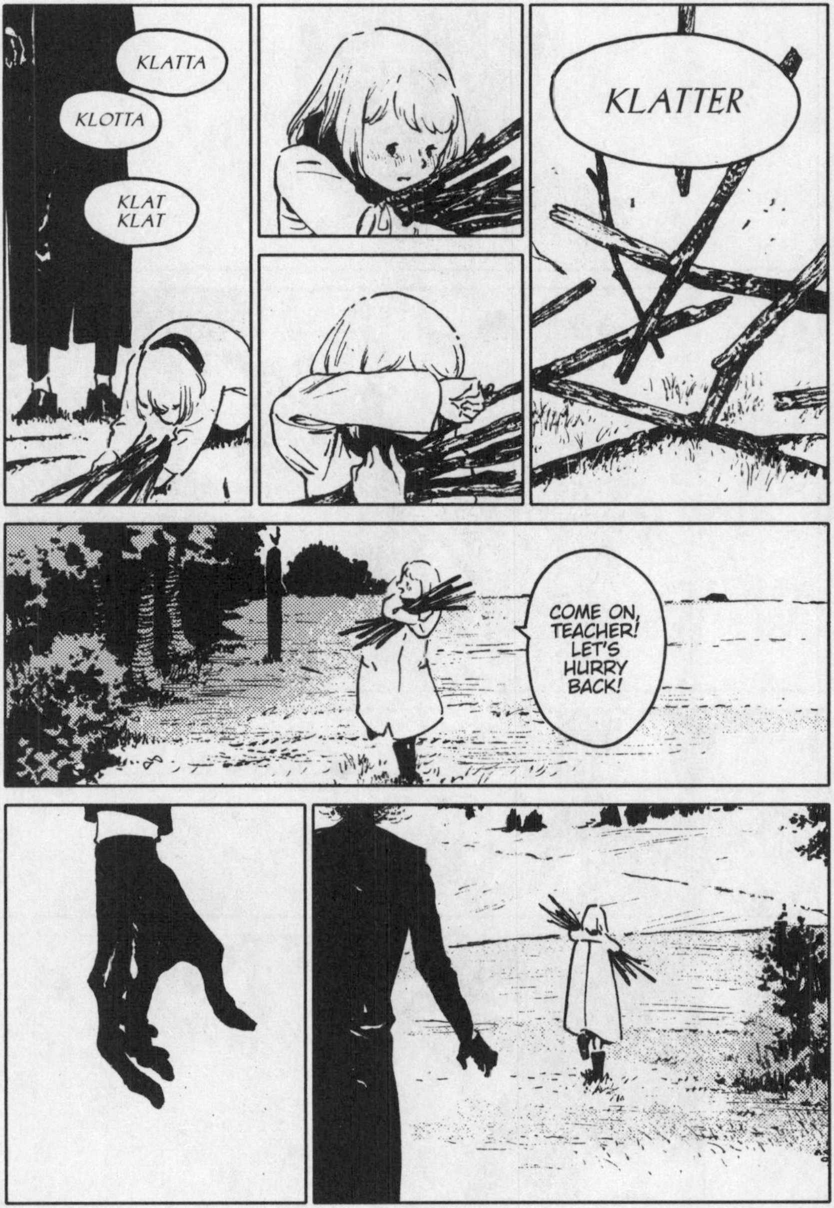
KLATTER
KLATTA
KLOTTA
KLAT KLAT
COME ON, TEACHER! LET'S HURRY BACK!

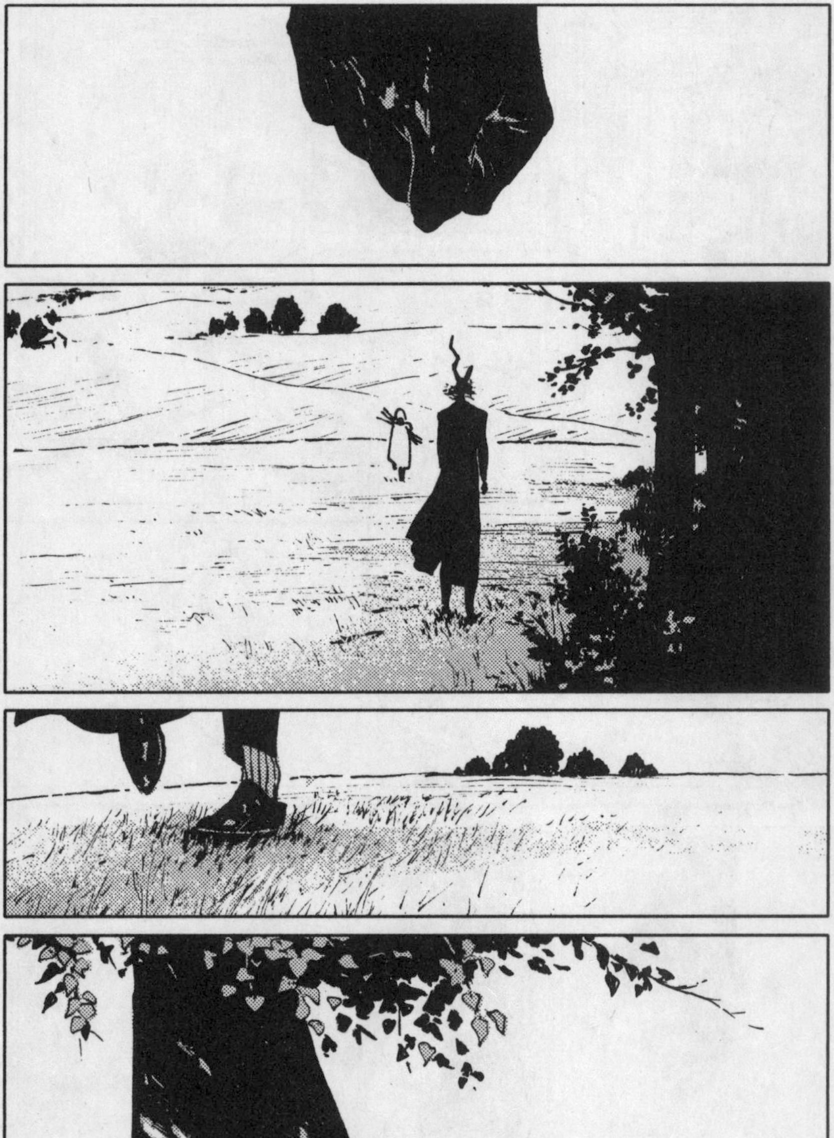

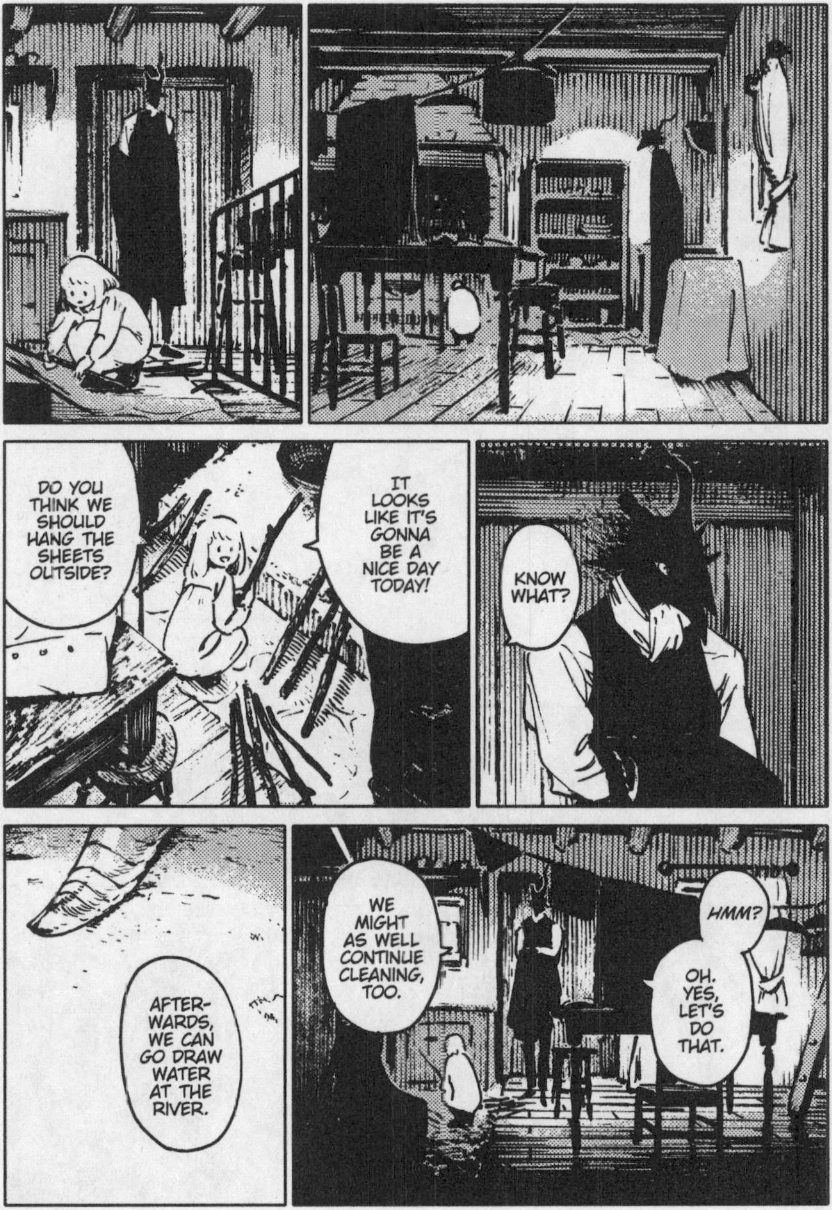
KNOW WHAT?
IT LOOKS LIKE IT'S GONNA BE A NICE DAY TODAY!
DO YOU THINK WE SHOULD HANG THE SHEETS OUTSIDE?
HMM?
OH. YES, LET'S DO THAT.
WE MIGHT AS WELL CONTINUE CLEANING, TOO.
AFTER-WARDS, WE CAN GO DRAW WATER AT THE RIVER.

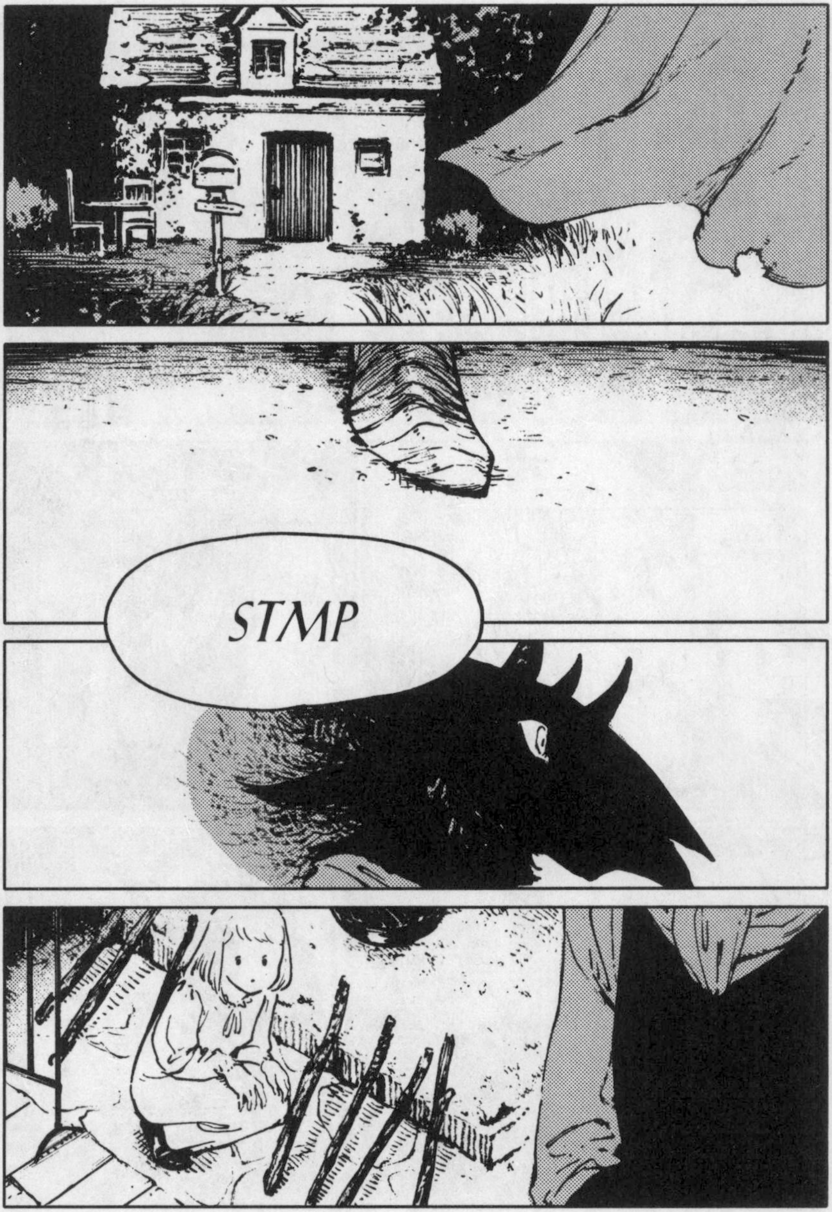
STMP

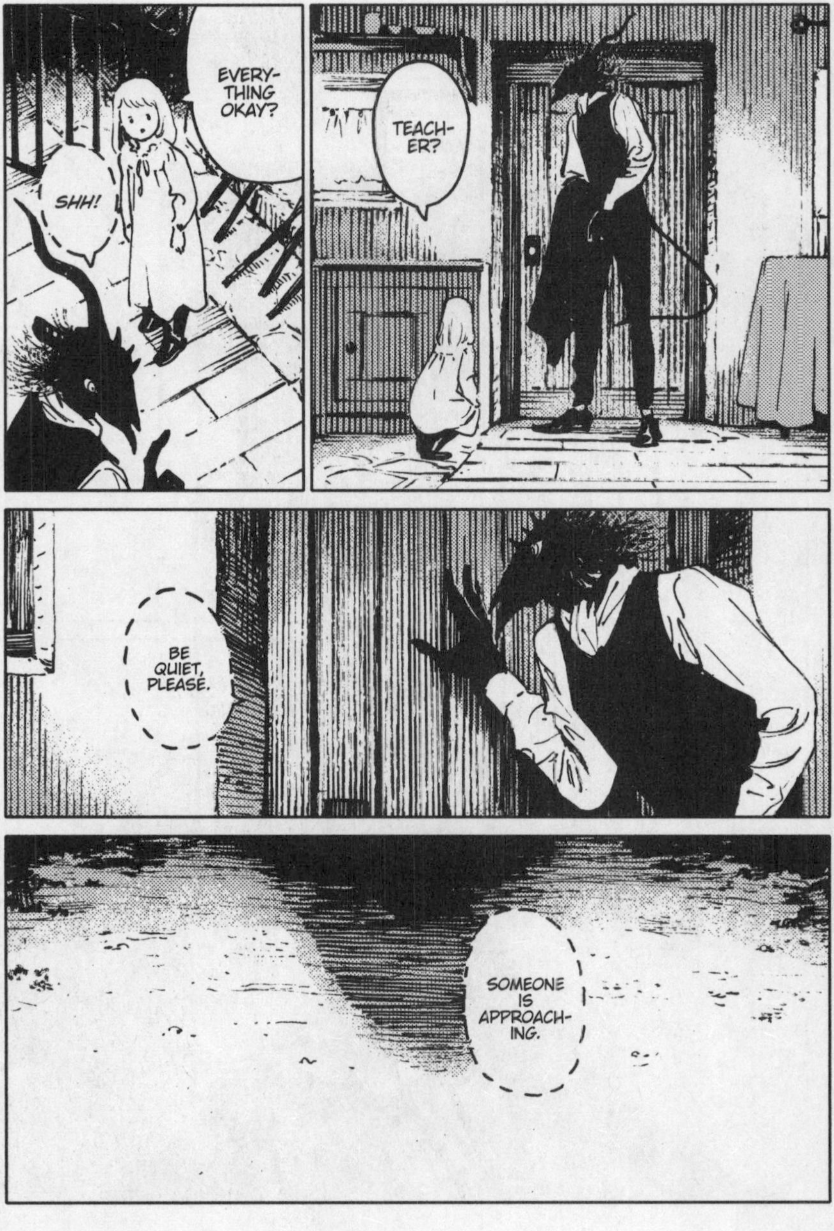
TEACHER?
EVERYTHING OKAY?
SHH!
BE QUIET, PLEASE.
SOMEONE IS APPROACHING.

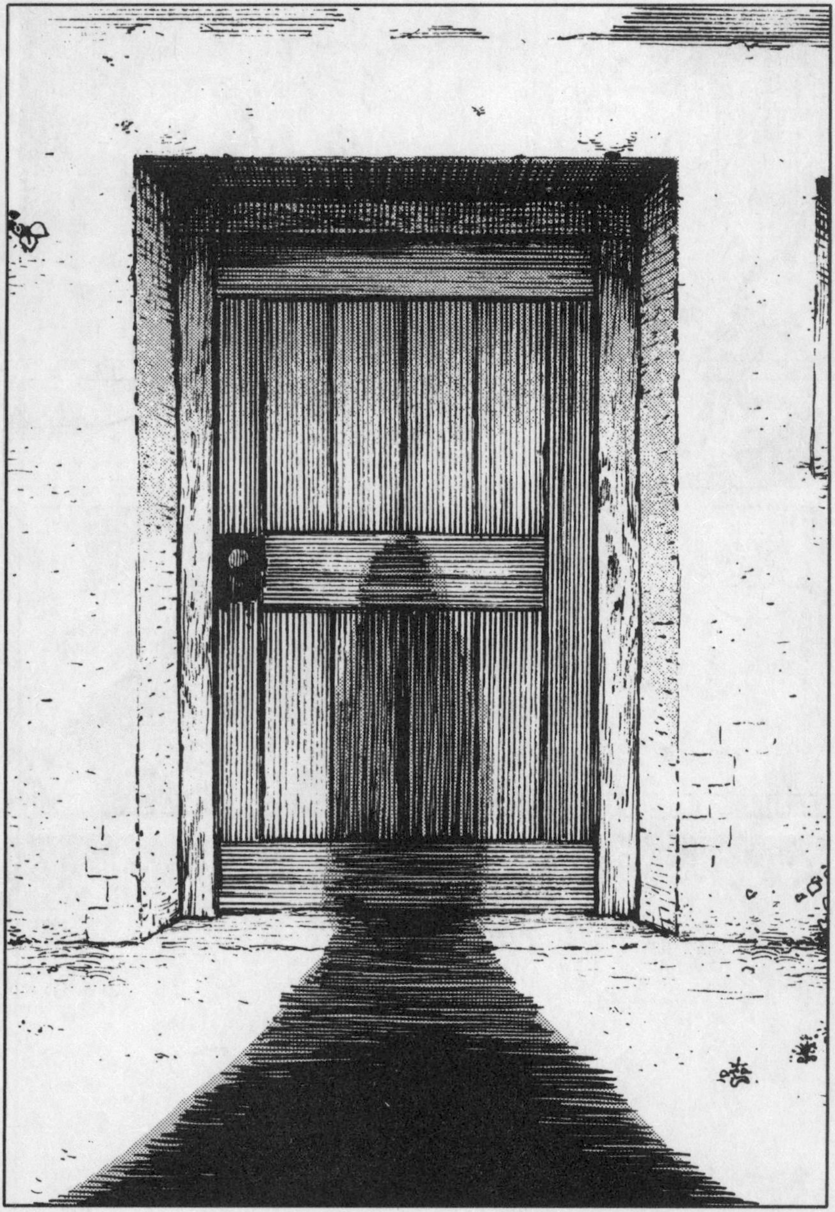

Chapter 28

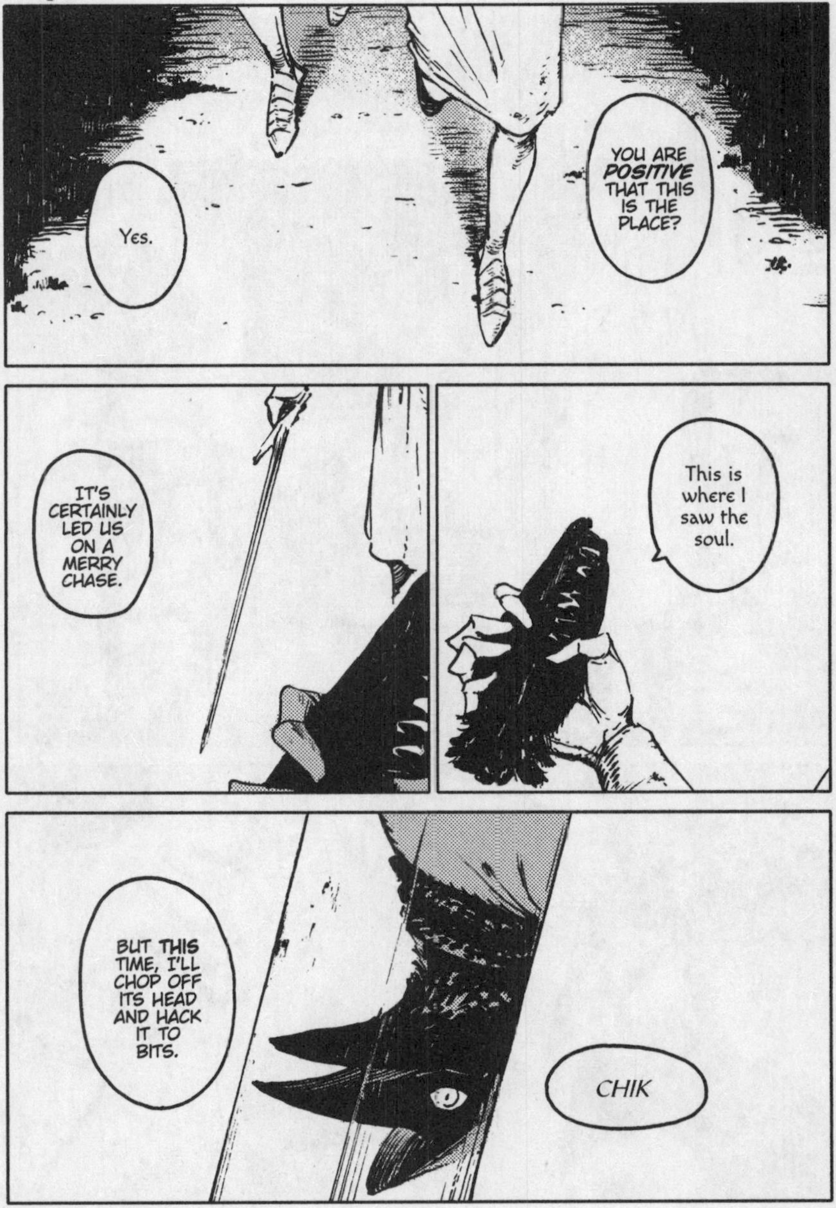
YOU ARE *POSITIVE* THAT THIS IS THE PLACE?
Yes.
This is where I saw the soul.
IT'S CERTAINLY LED US ON A MERRY CHASE.
BUT THIS TIME, I'LL CHOP OFF ITS HEAD AND HACK IT TO BITS.
CHIK

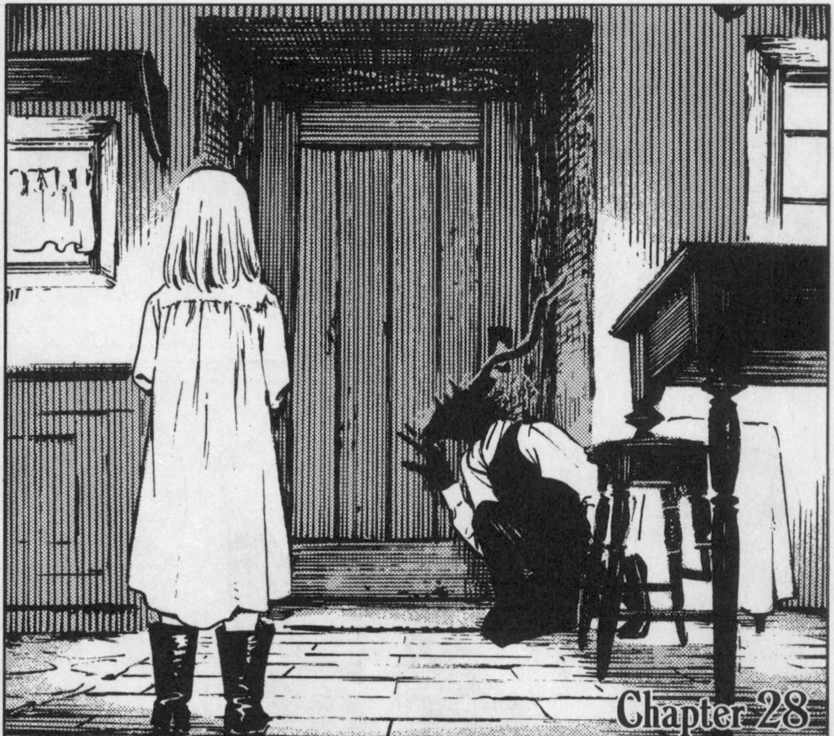
Chapter 28

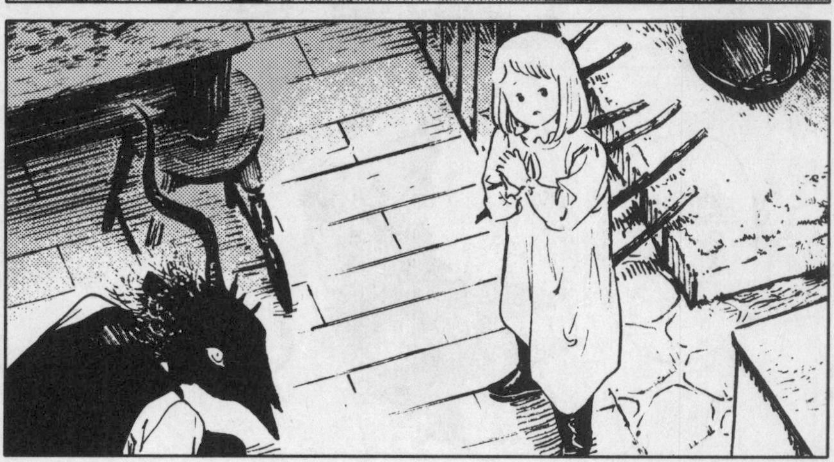

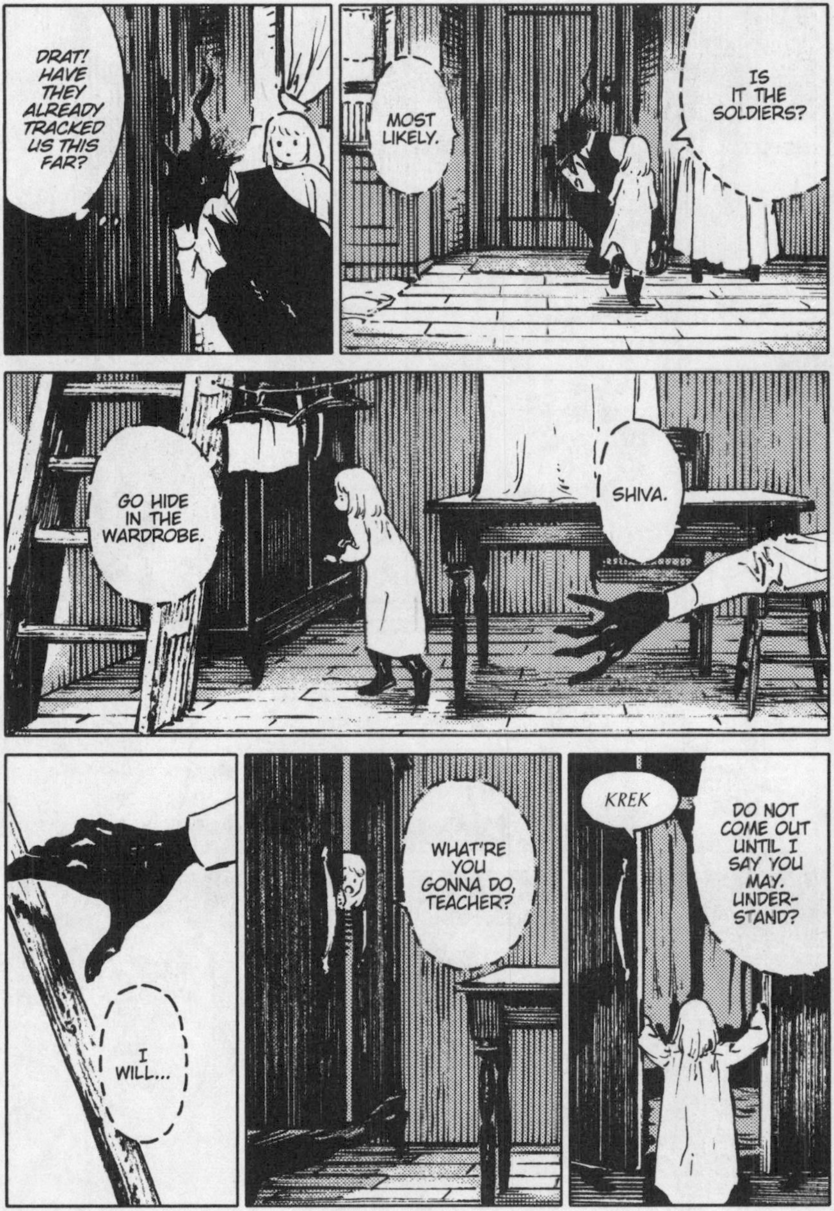
IS IT THE SOLDIERS?
MOST LIKELY.
DRAT! HAVE THEY ALREADY TRACKED US THIS FAR?
SHIVA.
GO HIDE IN THE WARDROBE.
DO NOT COME OUT UNTIL I SAY YOU MAY. UNDER-STAND?
KREK
WHAT'RE YOU GONNA DO, TEACHER?
I WILL...

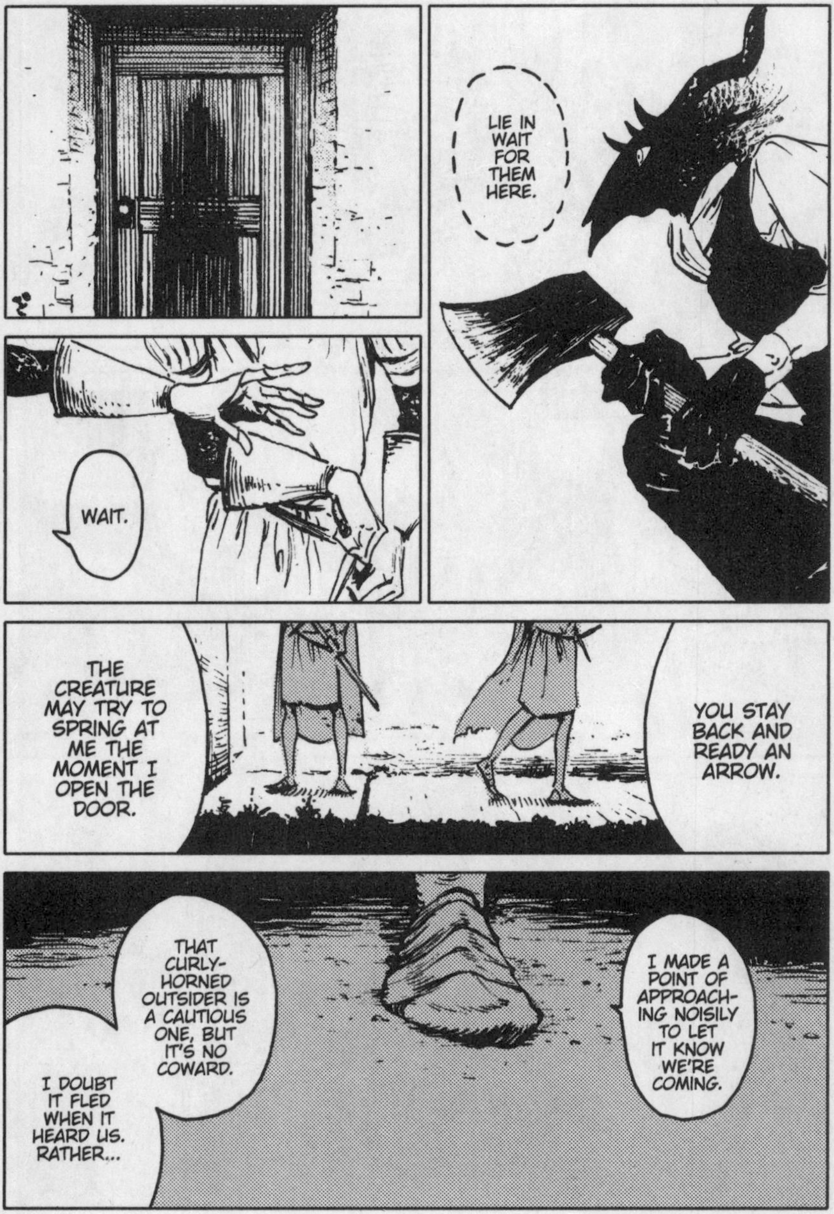
LIE IN WAIT FOR THEM HERE.
WAIT.
THE CREATURE MAY TRY TO SPRING AT ME THE MOMENT I OPEN THE DOOR.
YOU STAY BACK AND READY AN ARROW.
I MADE A POINT OF APPROACH-ING NOISILY TO LET IT KNOW WE'RE COMING.
THAT CURLY-HORNED OUTSIDER IS A CAUTIOUS ONE, BUT IT'S NO COWARD.
I DOUBT IT FLED WHEN IT HEARD US. RATHER...

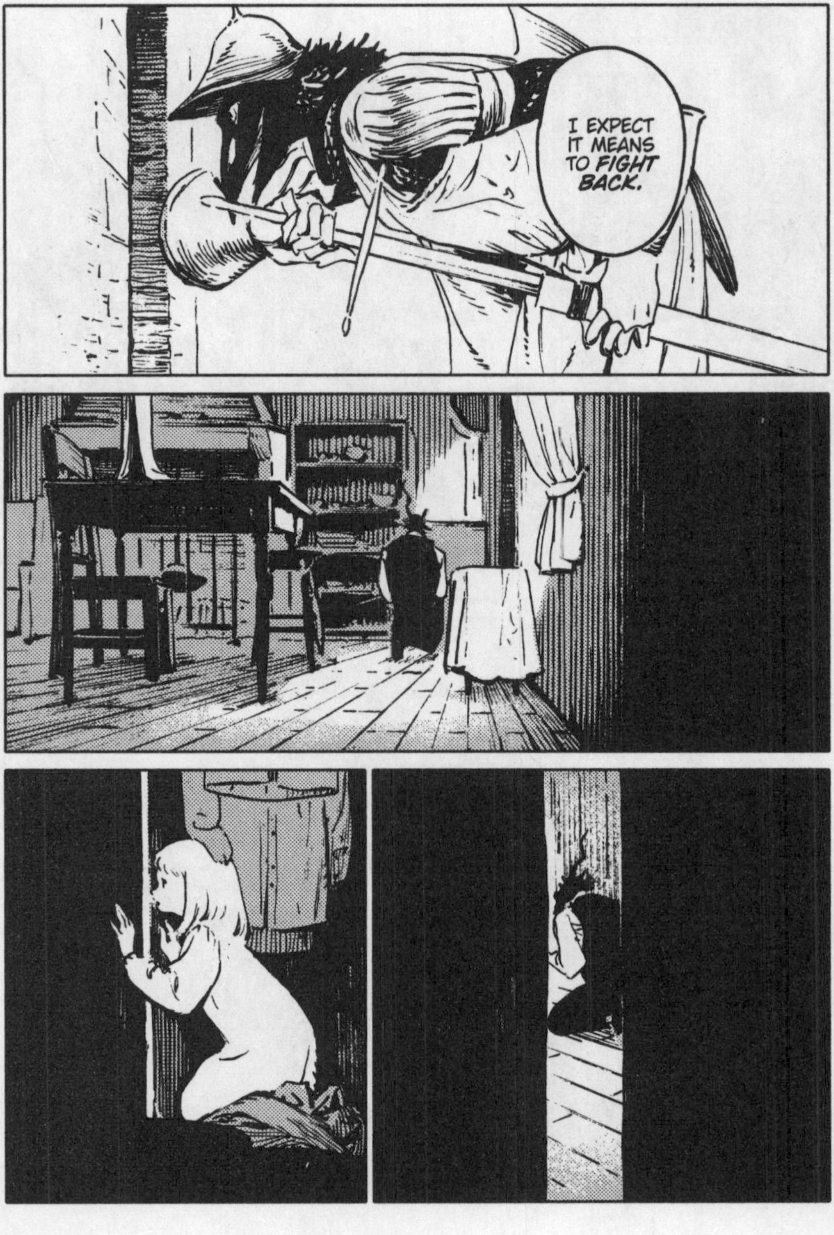
I EXPECT IT MEANS TO FIGHT BACK.

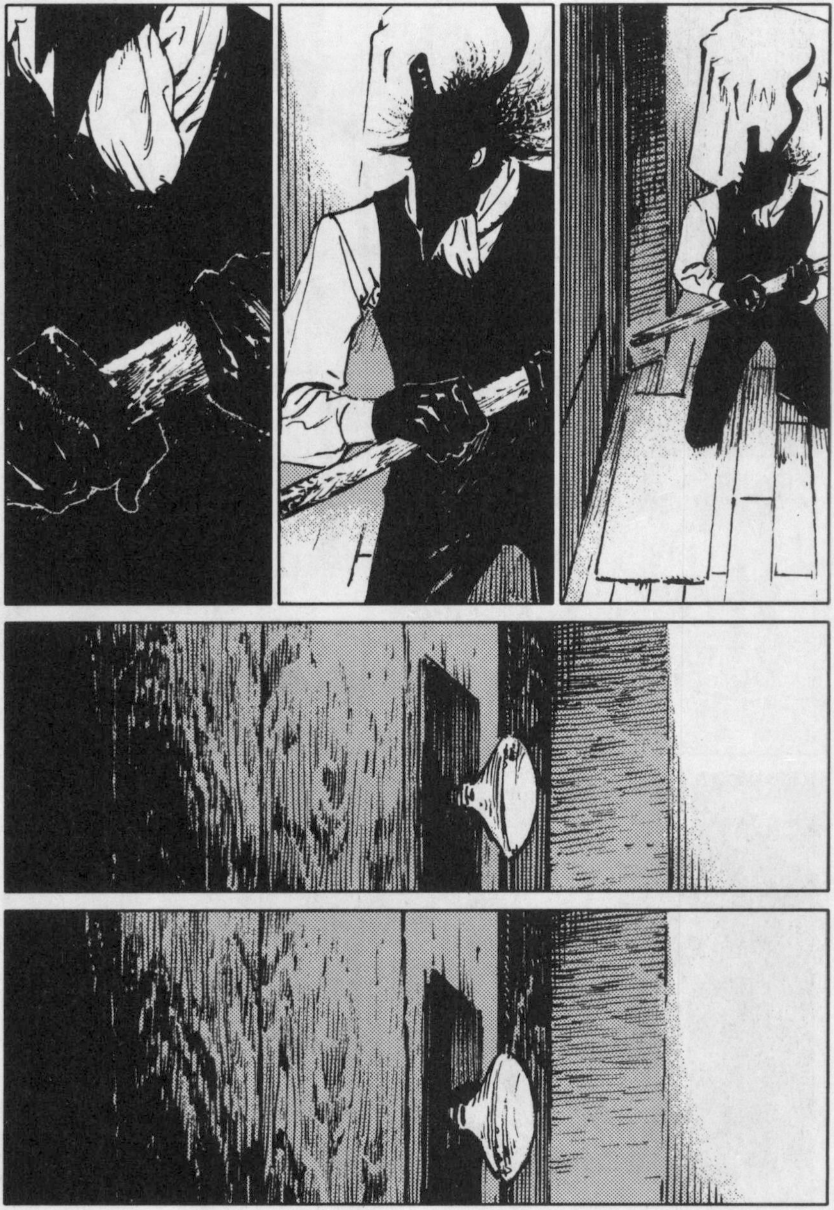

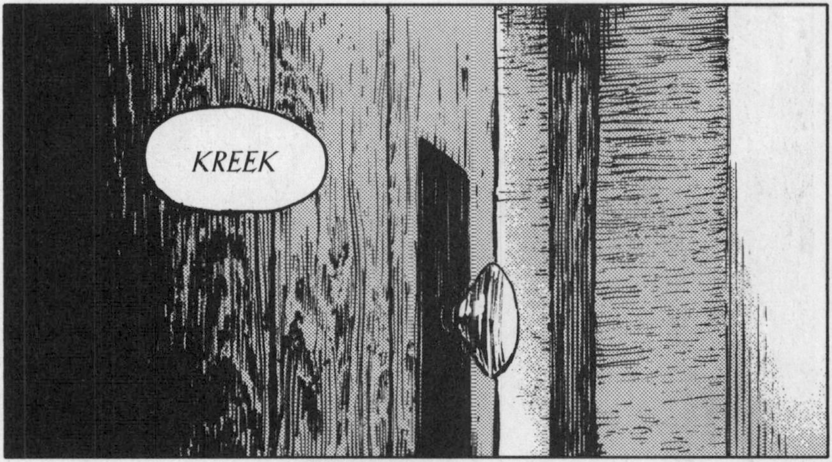
KREEK
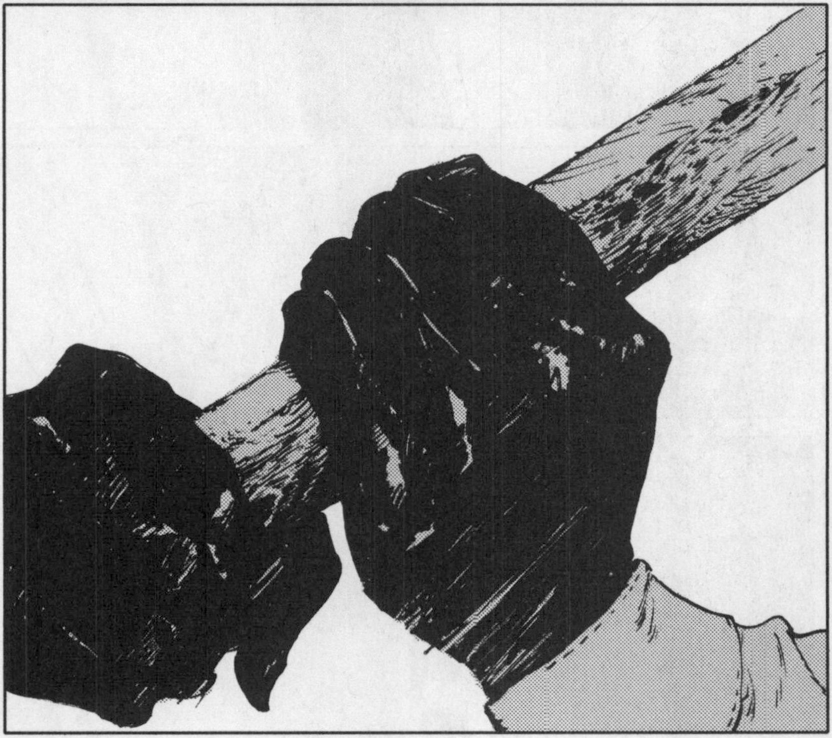

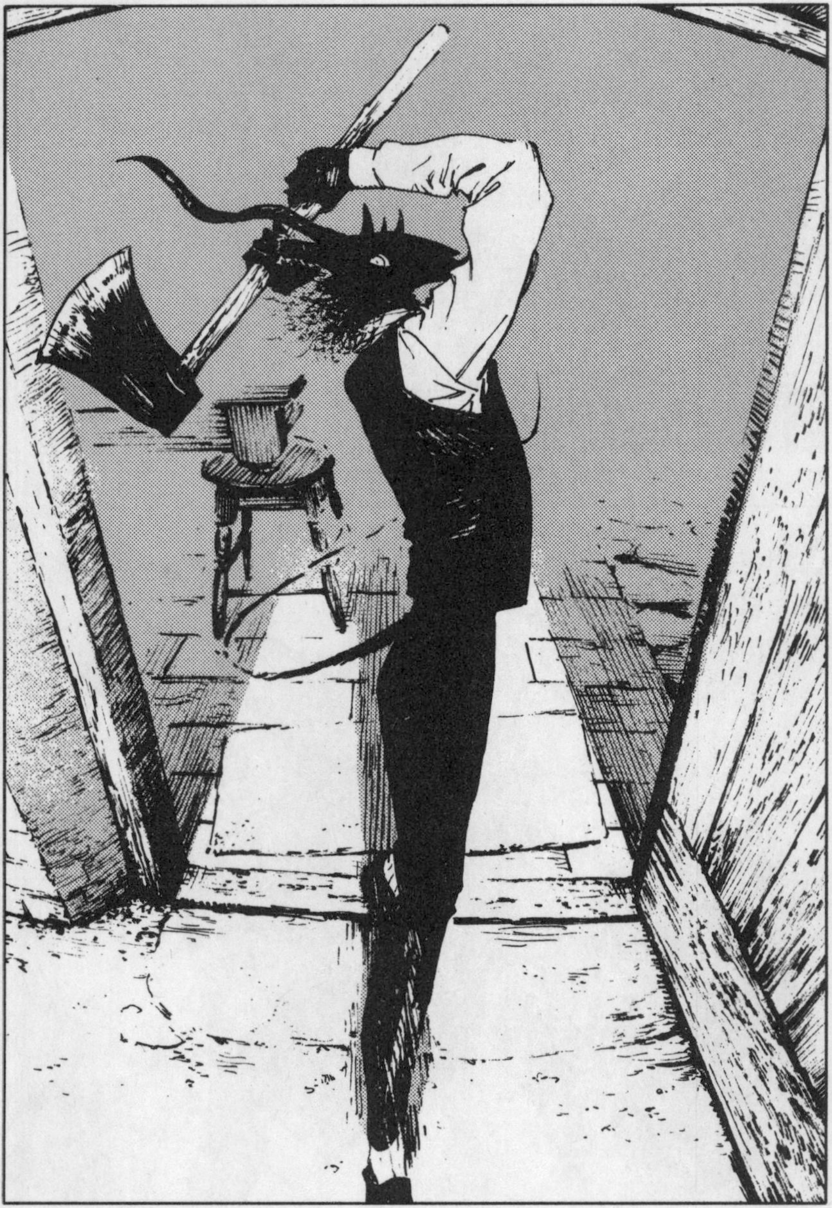

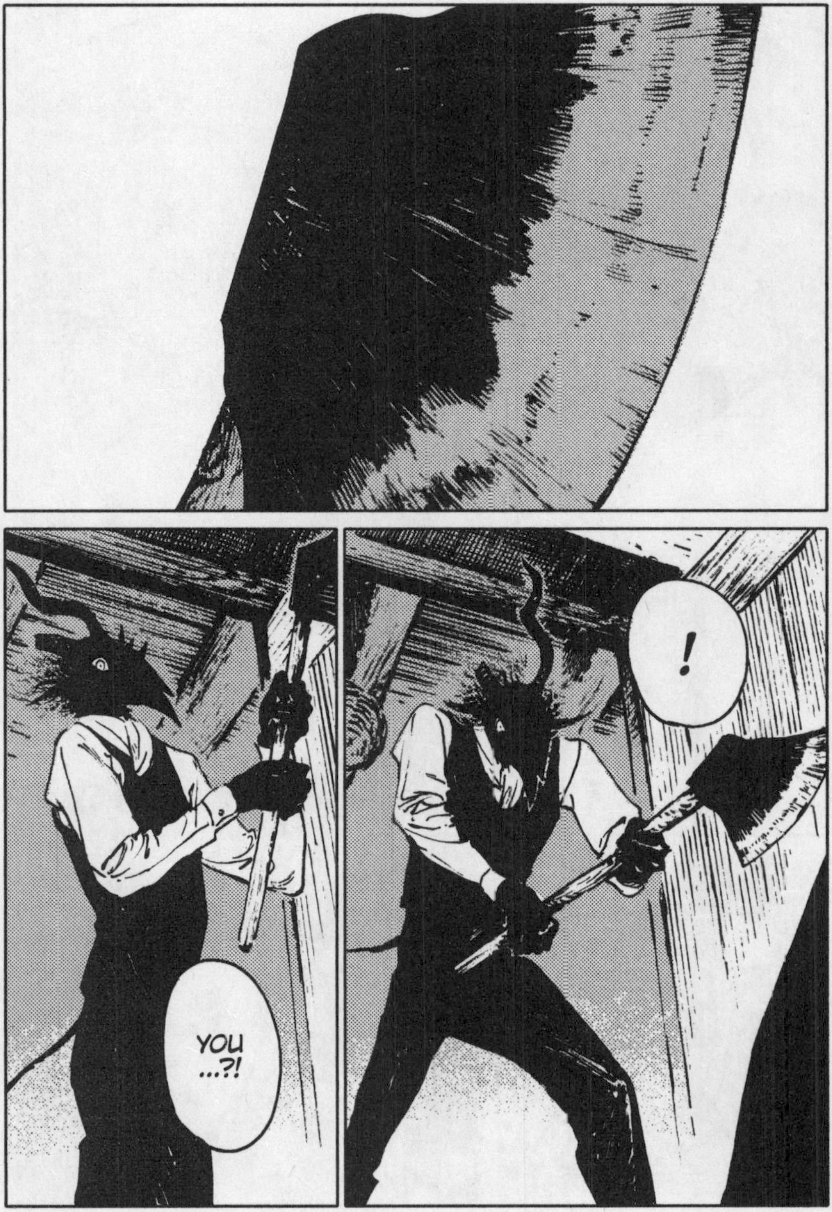
!
YOU ...?!

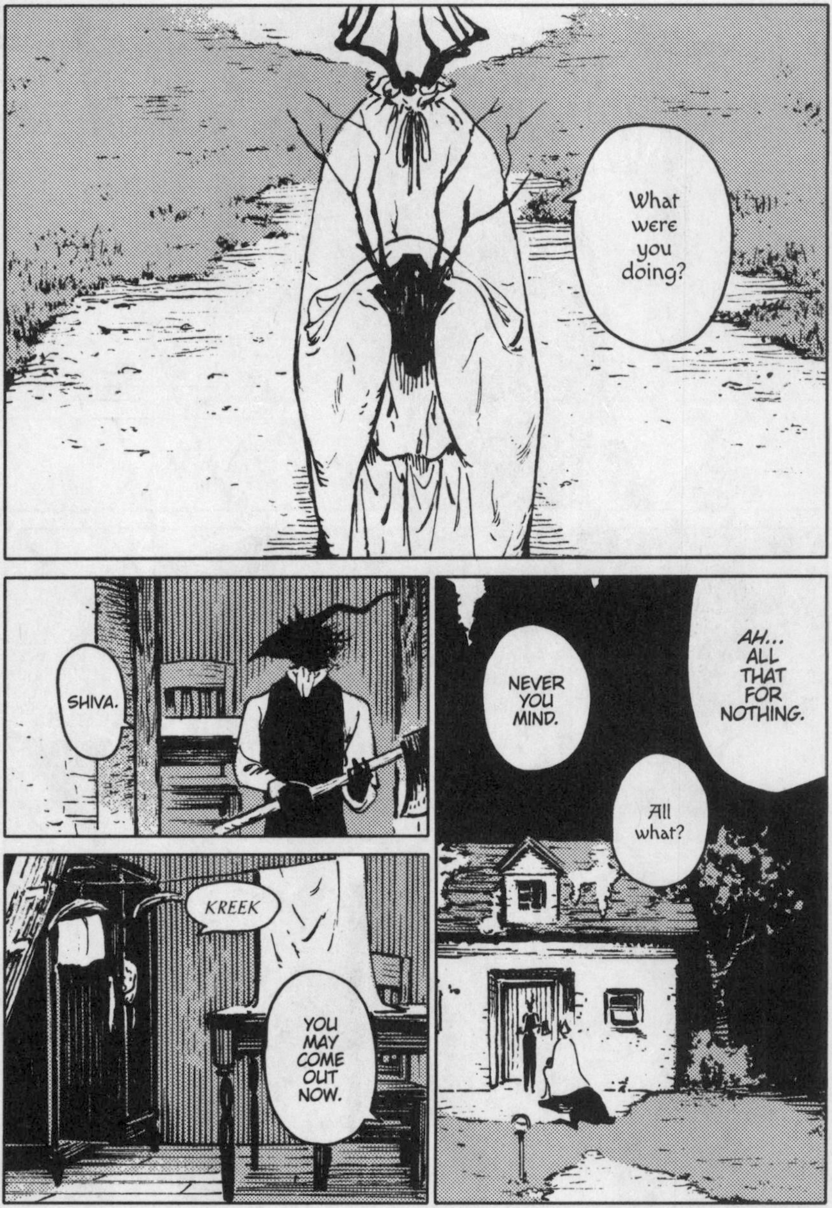
What were you doing?
AH... ALL THAT FOR NOTHING.
NEVER YOU MIND.
All what?
SHIVA.
KREEK
YOU MAY COME OUT NOW.

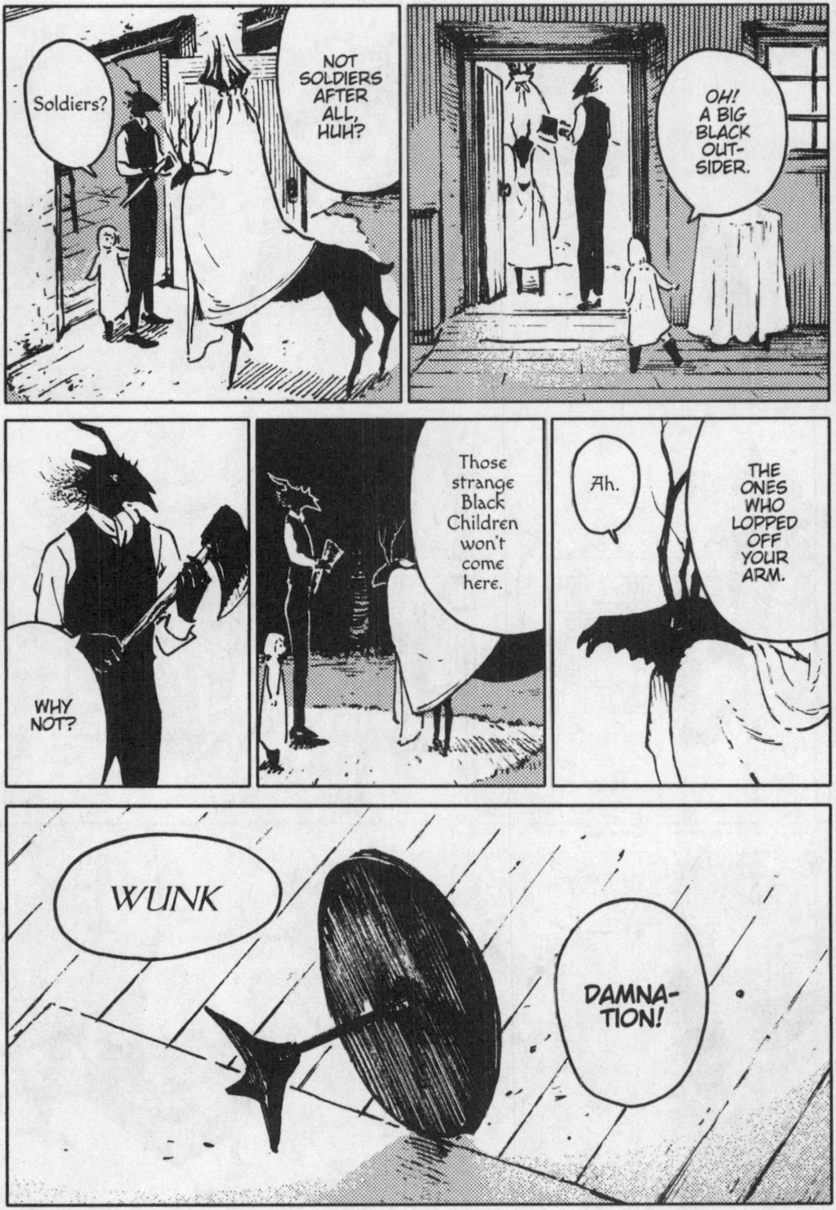
OH! A BIG BLACK OUT-SIDER.
NOT SOLDIERS AFTER ALL, HUH?
Soldiers?
THE ONES WHO LOPPED OFF YOUR ARM.
Ah.
Those strange Black Children won't come here.
WHY NOT?
WUNK
DAMNA-TION!

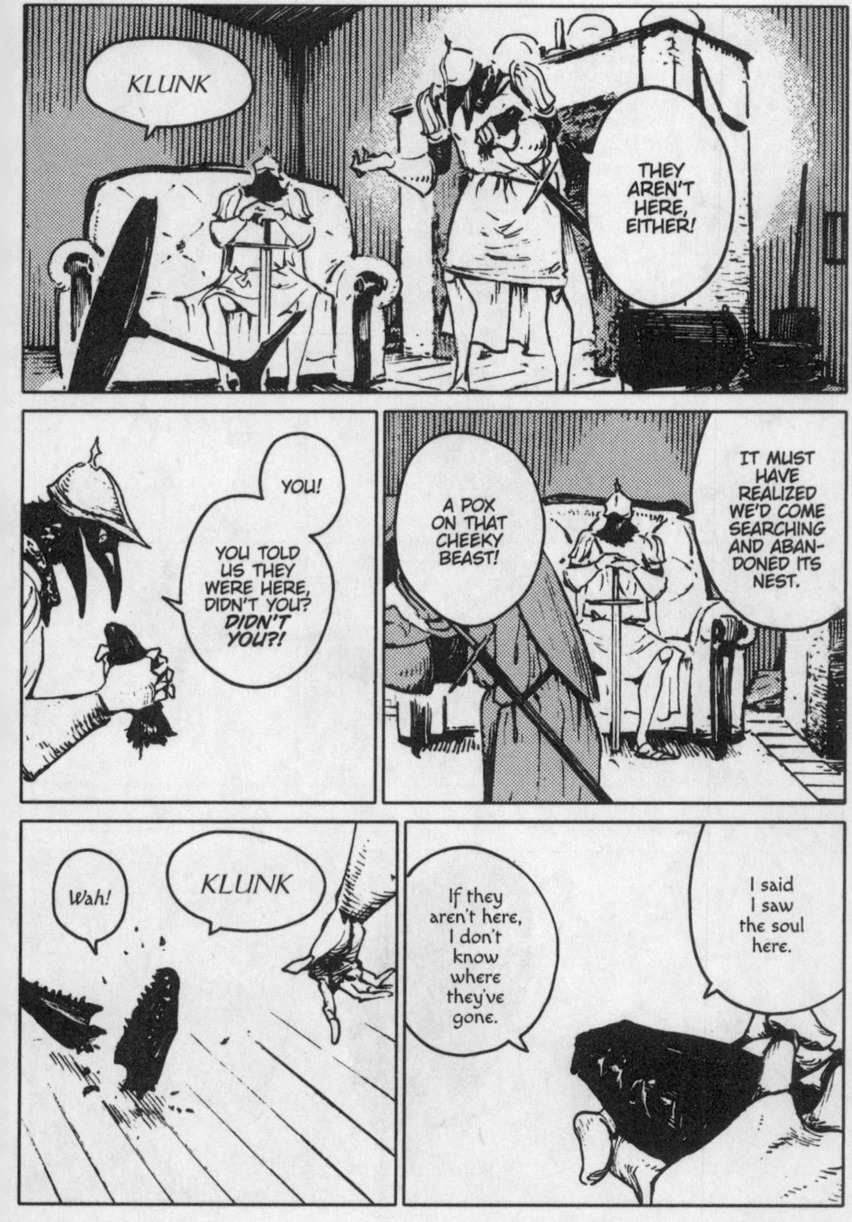
THEY AREN'T HERE, EITHER!
KLUNK
IT MUST HAVE REALIZED WE'D COME SEARCHING AND ABANDONED ITS NEST.
A POX ON THAT CHEEKY BEAST!
YOU!
YOU TOLD US THEY WERE HERE, DIDN'T YOU? *DIDN'T YOU?!*
I said I saw the soul here.
If they aren't here, I don't know where they've gone.
KLUNK
Wah!

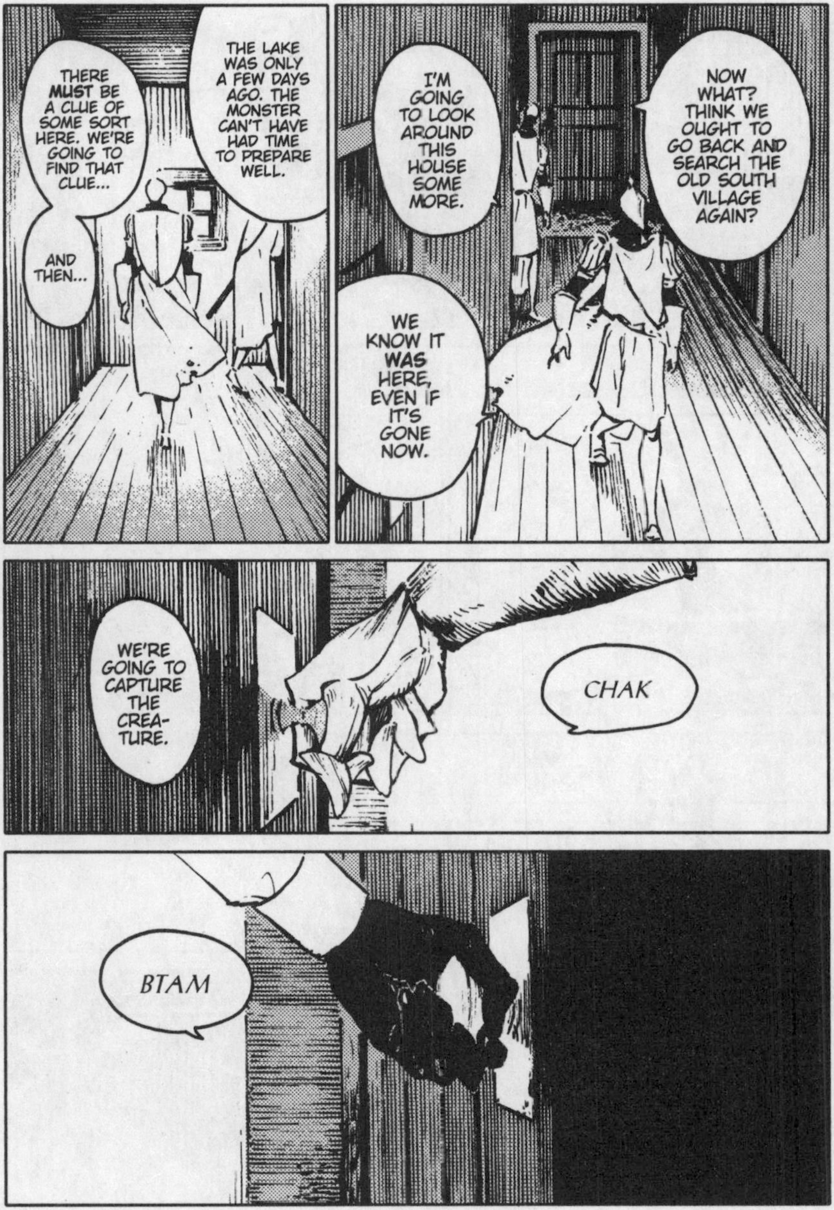
NOW WHAT? THINK WE OUGHT TO GO BACK AND SEARCH THE OLD SOUTH VILLAGE AGAIN?
I'M GOING TO LOOK AROUND THIS HOUSE SOME MORE.
WE KNOW IT WAS HERE, EVEN IF IT'S GONE NOW.
THE LAKE WAS ONLY A FEW DAYS AGO. THE MONSTER CAN'T HAVE HAD TIME TO PREPARE WELL.
THERE MUST BE A CLUE OF SOME SORT HERE. WE'RE GOING TO FIND THAT CLUE...
AND THEN...
CHAK
WE'RE GOING TO CAPTURE THE CREA-TURE.
BTAM

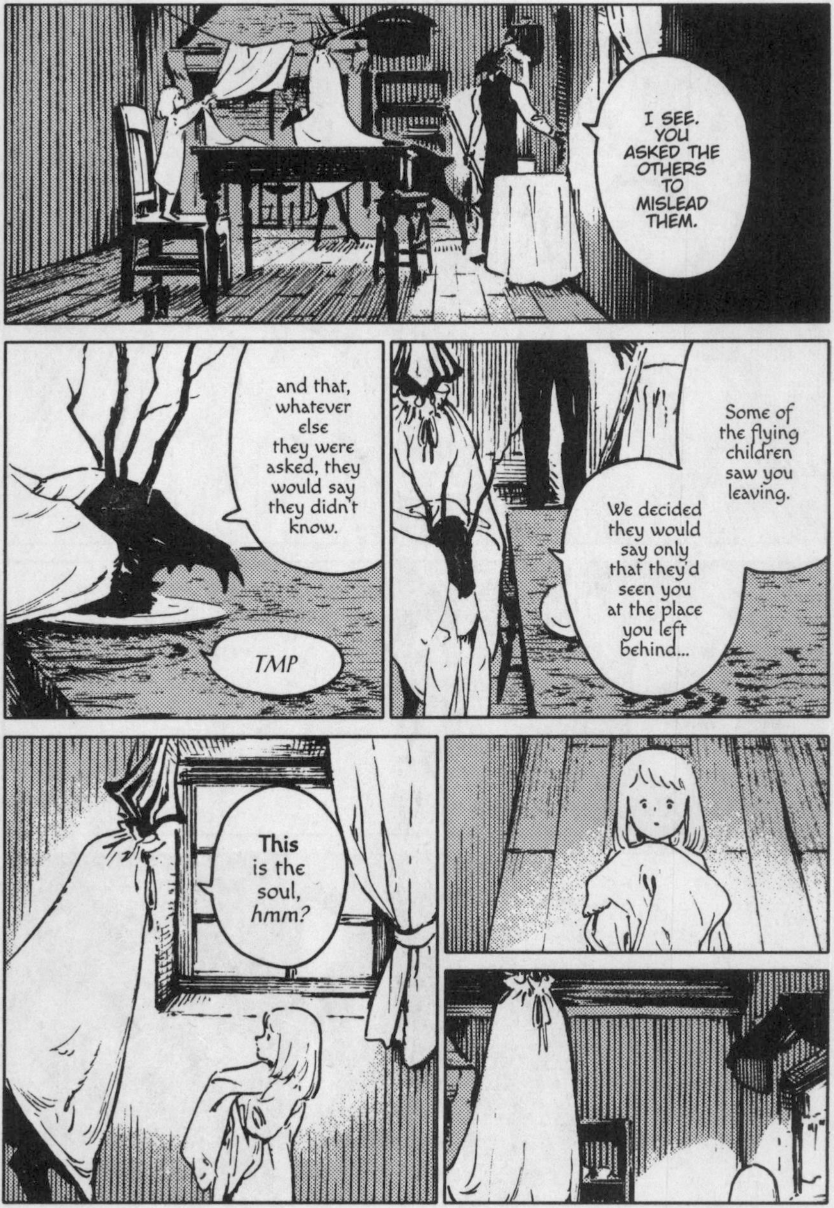
I SEE. YOU ASKED THE OTHERS TO MISLEAD THEM.
Some of the flying children saw you leaving.
We decided they would say only that they'd seen you at the place you left behind...
and that, whatever else they were asked, they would say they didn't know.
TMP
This is the soul, *hmm?*

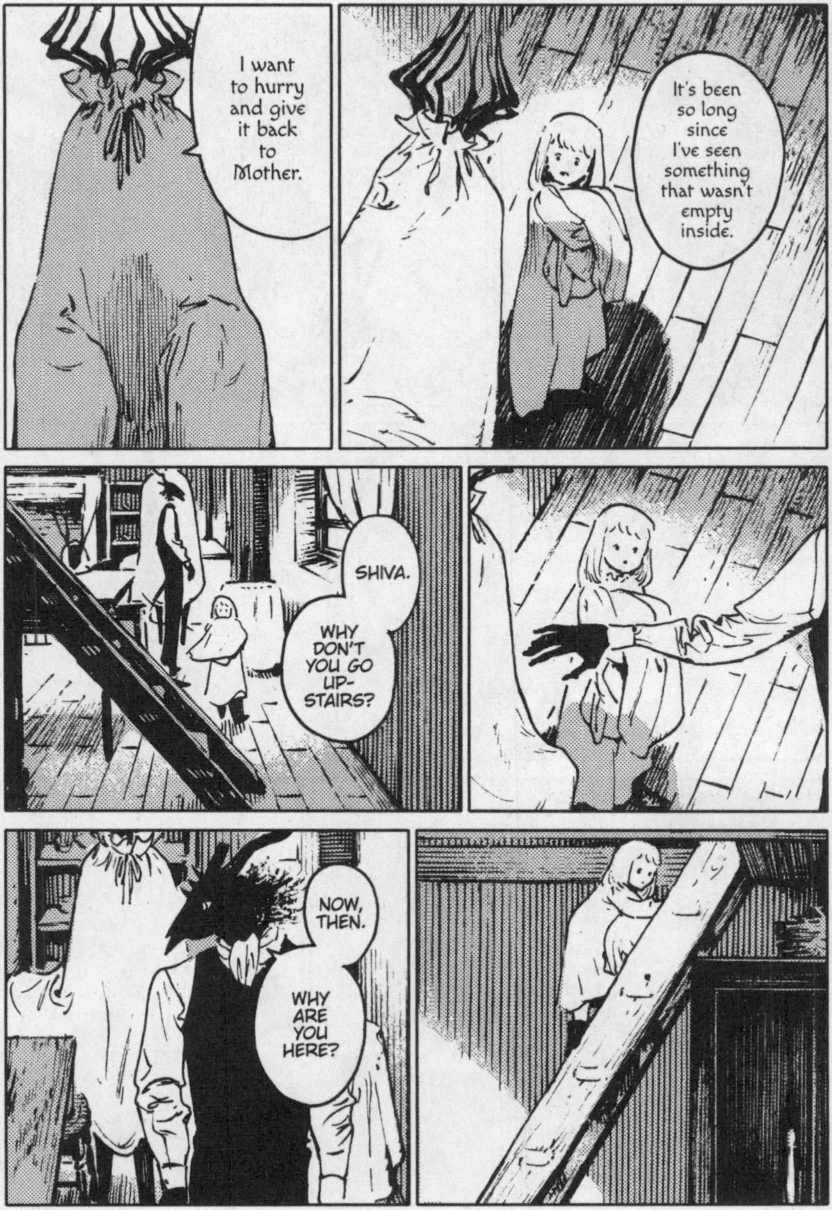
It's been so long since I've seen something that wasn't empty inside.
I want to hurry and give it back to Mother.
SHIVA.
WHY DON'T YOU GO UP-STAIRS?
NOW, THEN.
WHY ARE YOU HERE?

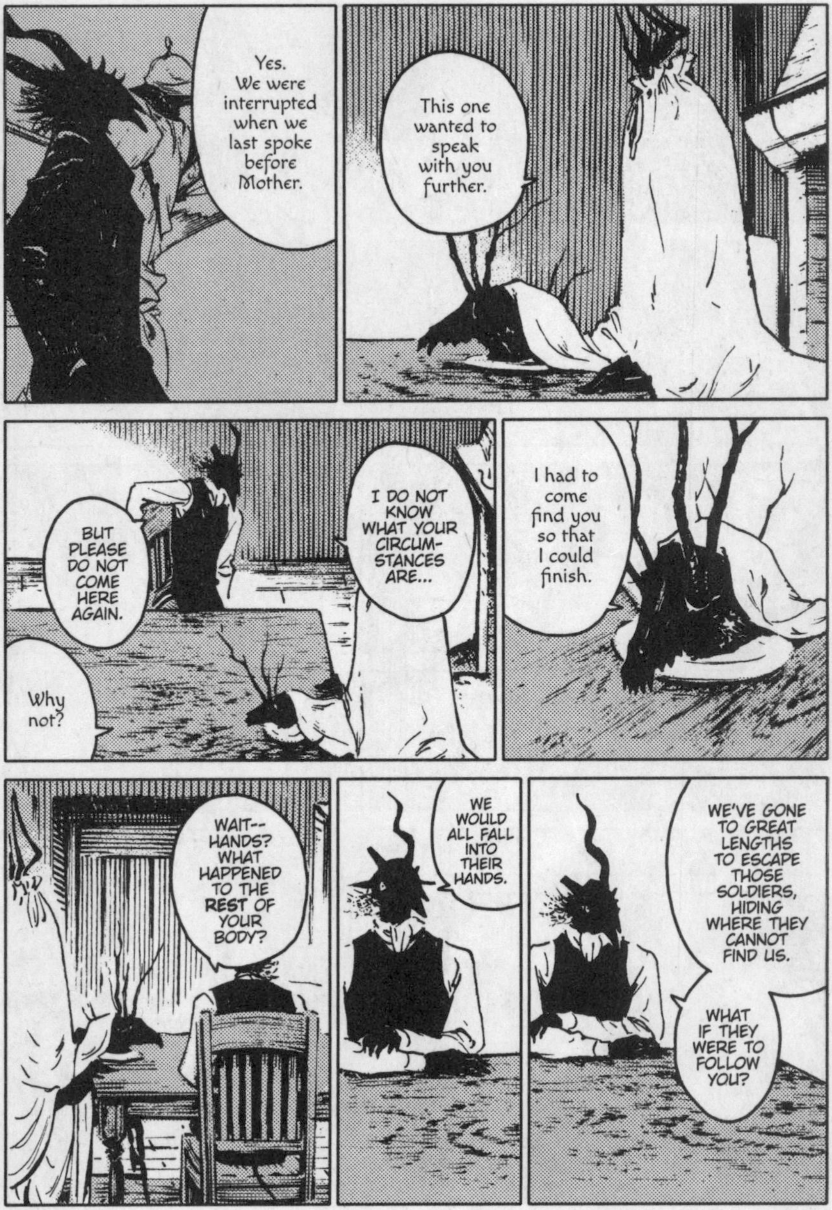
This one wanted to speak with you further.
Yes. We were interrupted when we last spoke before Mother.
I had to come find you so that I could finish.
I DO NOT KNOW WHAT YOUR CIRCUMSTANCES ARE...
BUT PLEASE DO NOT COME HERE AGAIN.
Why not?
WE'VE GONE TO GREAT LENGTHS TO ESCAPE THOSE SOLDIERS, HIDING WHERE THEY CANNOT FIND US.
WHAT IF THEY WERE TO FOLLOW YOU?
WE WOULD ALL FALL INTO THEIR HANDS.
WAIT-- HANDS? WHAT HAPPENED TO THE REST OF YOUR BODY?

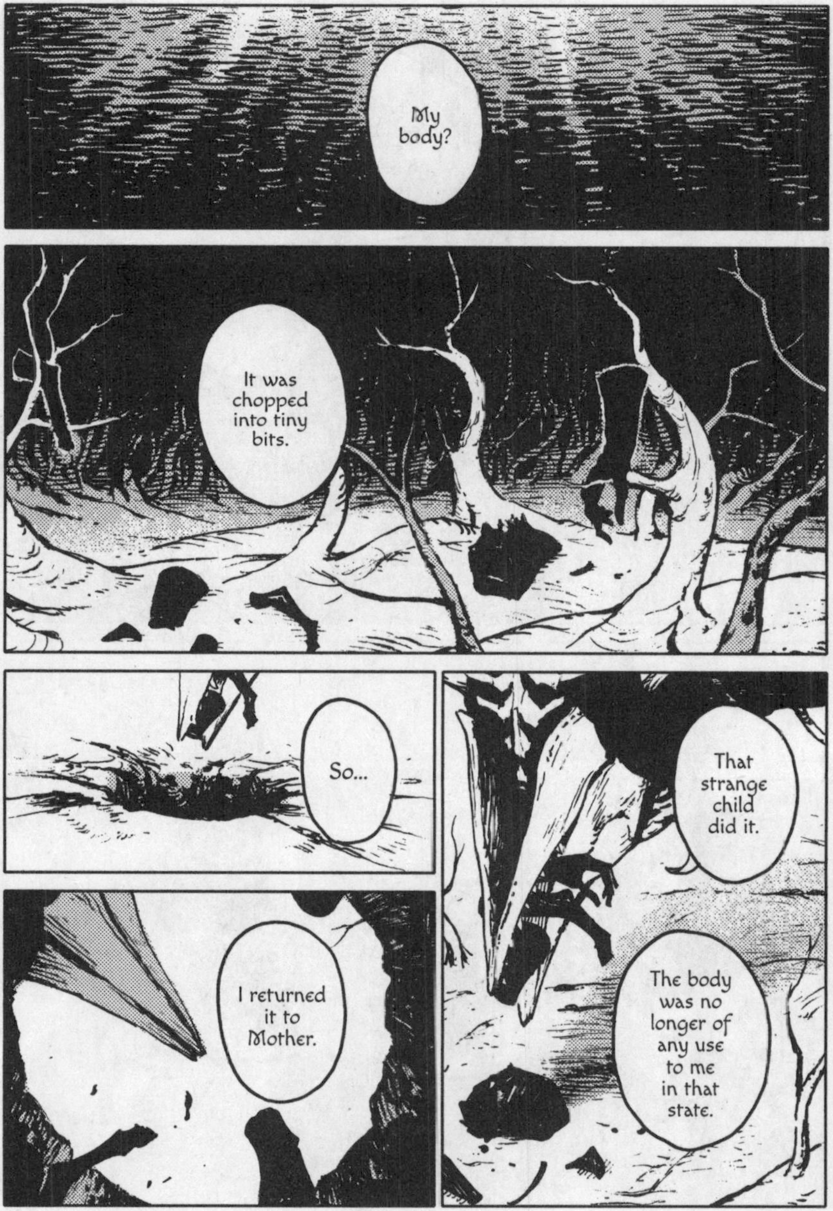
My body?
It was chopped into tiny bits.
That strange child did it.
The body was no longer of any use to me in that state.
So...
I returned it to Mother.

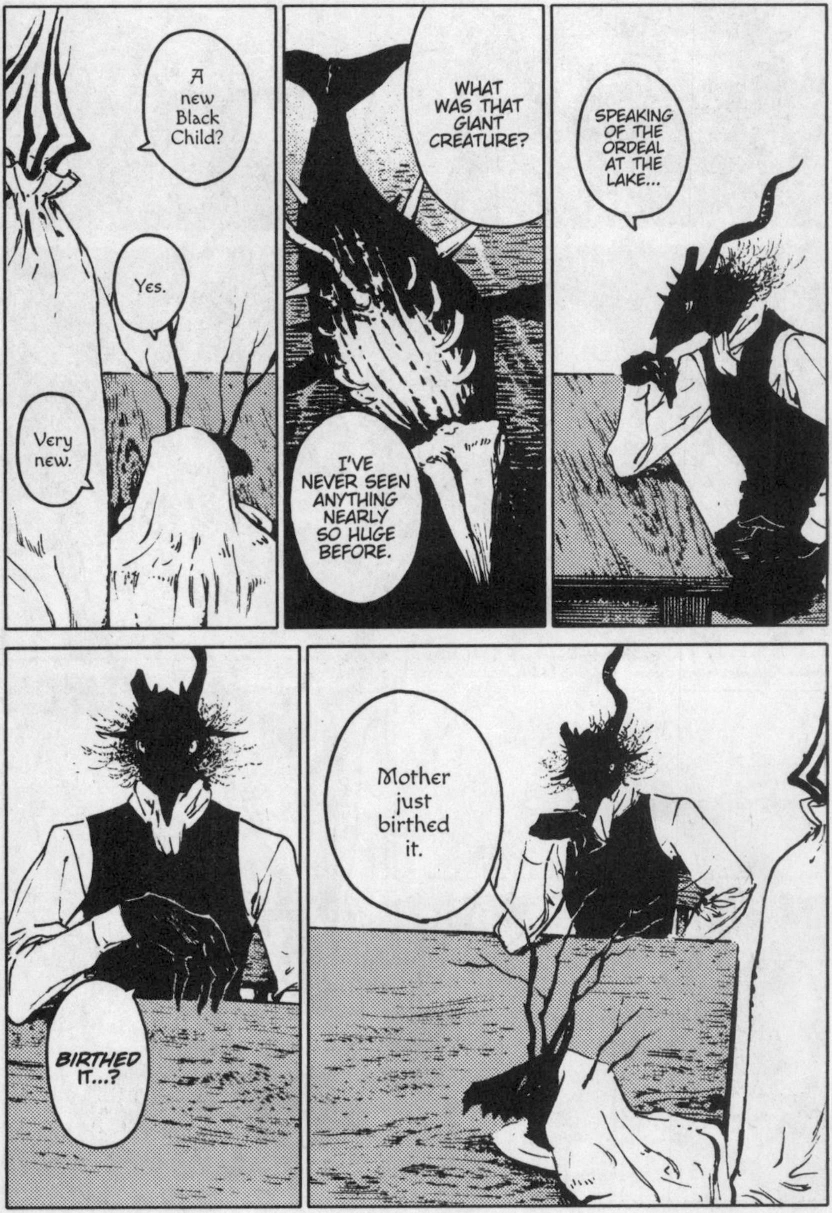
SPEAKING OF THE ORDEAL AT THE LAKE...
WHAT WAS THAT GIANT CREATURE?
I'VE NEVER SEEN ANYTHING NEARLY SO HUGE BEFORE.
A new Black Child?
Yes.
Very new.
Mother just birthed it.
BIRTHED IT...?

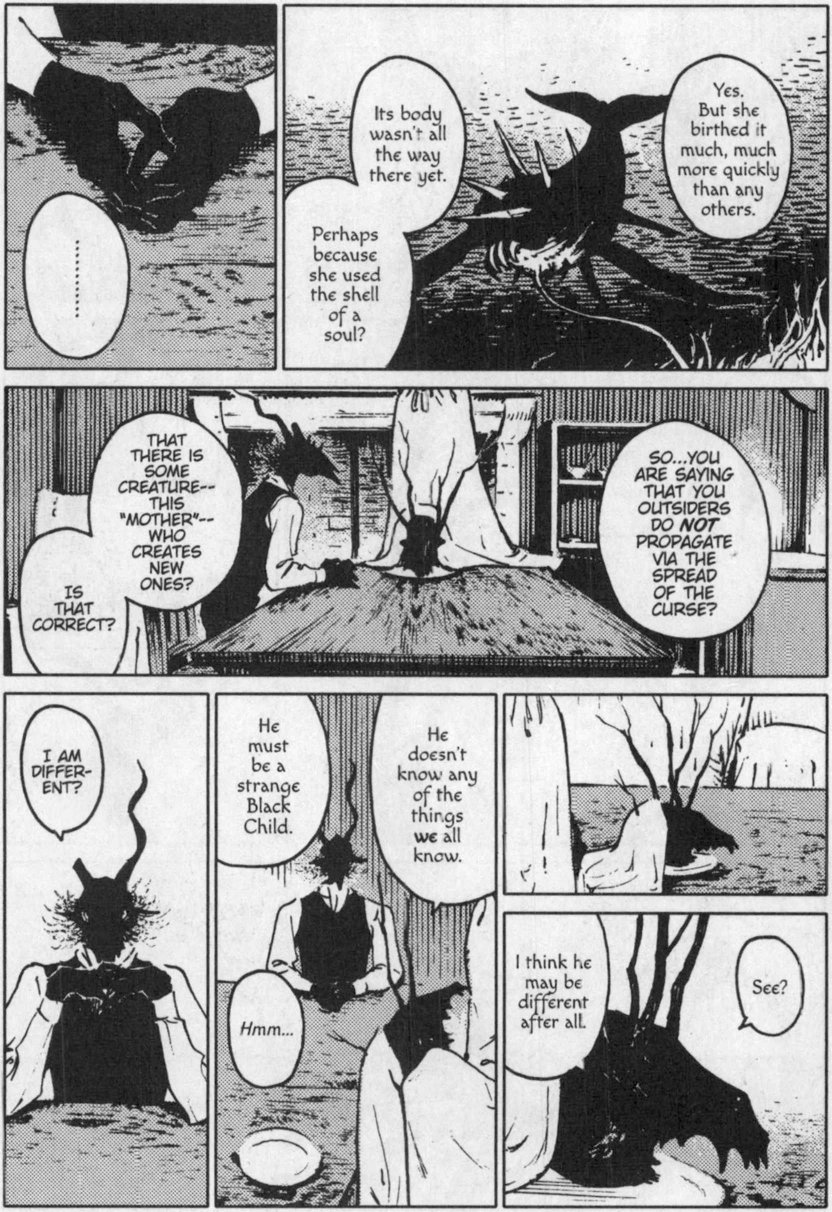
Yes. But she birthed it much, much more quickly than any others.
Its body wasn't all the way there yet.
Perhaps because she used the shell of a soul?
......
SO...YOU ARE SAYING THAT YOU OUTSIDERS DO **NOT** PROPAGATE VIA THE SPREAD OF THE CURSE?
THAT THERE IS SOME CREATURE--THIS "MOTHER"--WHO CREATES NEW ONES?
IS THAT CORRECT?
See?
I think he may be different after all.
He doesn't know any of the things **we** all know.
He must be a strange Black Child.
Hmm...
I AM DIFFER-ENT?

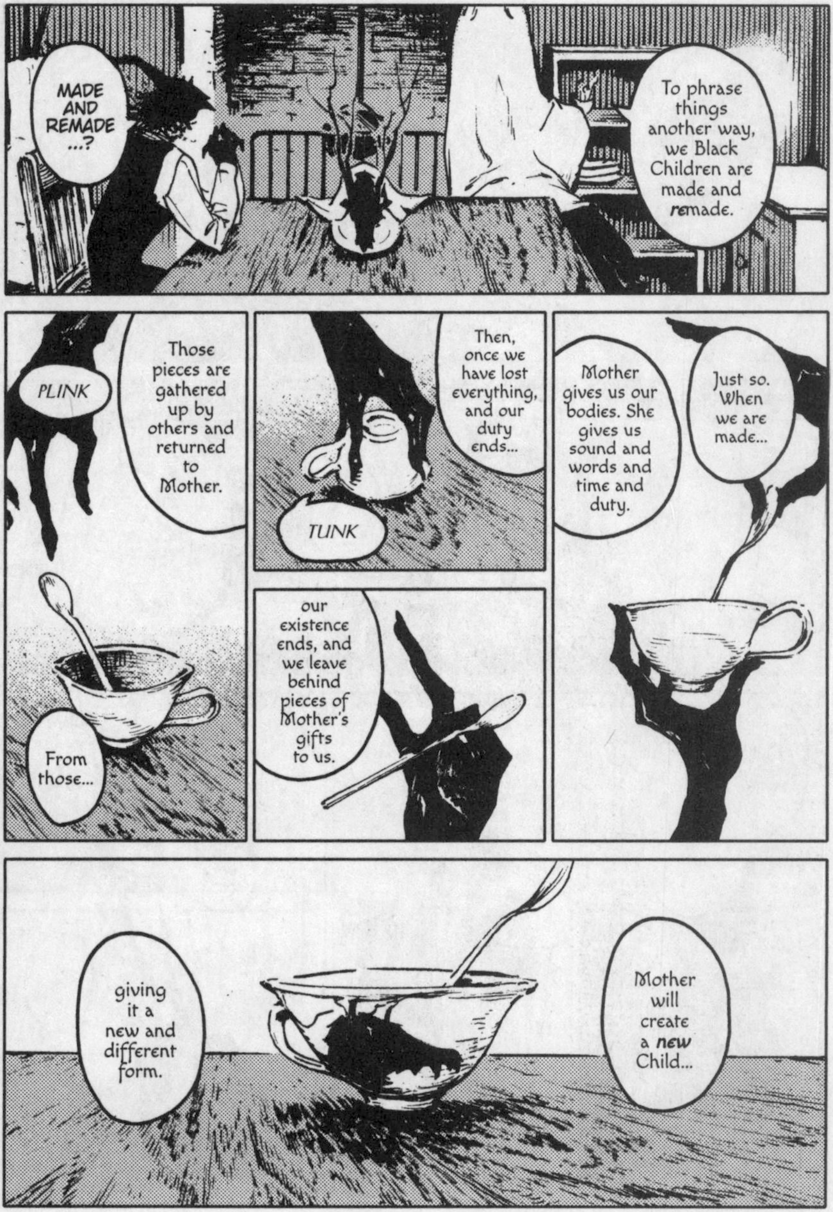
To phrase things another way, we Black Children are made and *re*made.
MADE AND REMADE ...?
Just so. When we are made...
Mother gives us our bodies. She gives us sound and words and time and duty.
Then, once we have lost everything, and our duty ends...
TUNK
our existence ends, and we leave behind pieces of Mother's gifts to us.
Those pieces are gathered up by others and returned to Mother.
PLINK
From those...
Mother will create a ***new*** Child...
giving it a new and different form.

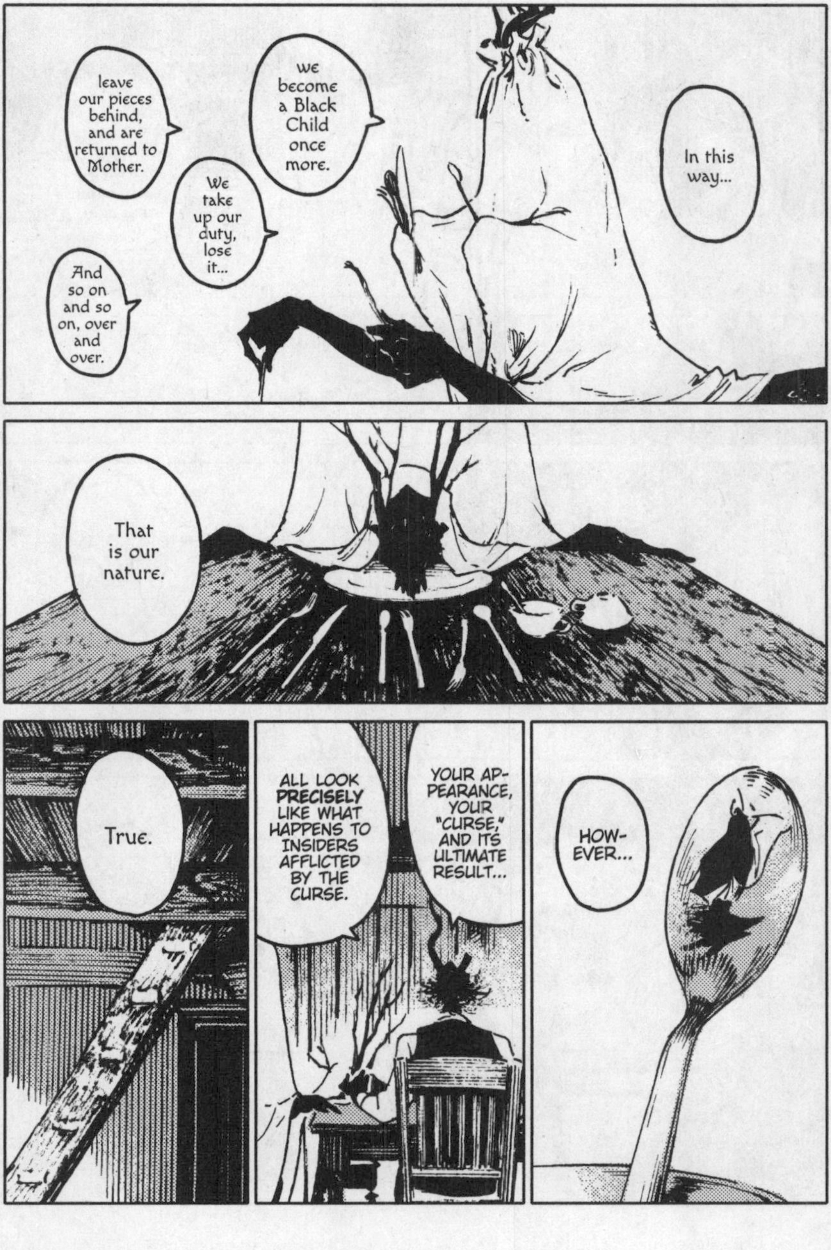
In this way...
we become a Black Child once more.
We take up our duty, lose it...
leave our pieces behind, and are returned to Mother.
And so on and so on, over and over.
That is our nature.
HOW-EVER...
YOUR AP-PEARANCE, YOUR "CURSE," AND ITS ULTIMATE RESULT...
ALL LOOK **PRECISELY** LIKE WHAT HAPPENS TO INSIDERS AFFLICTED BY THE CURSE.
True.

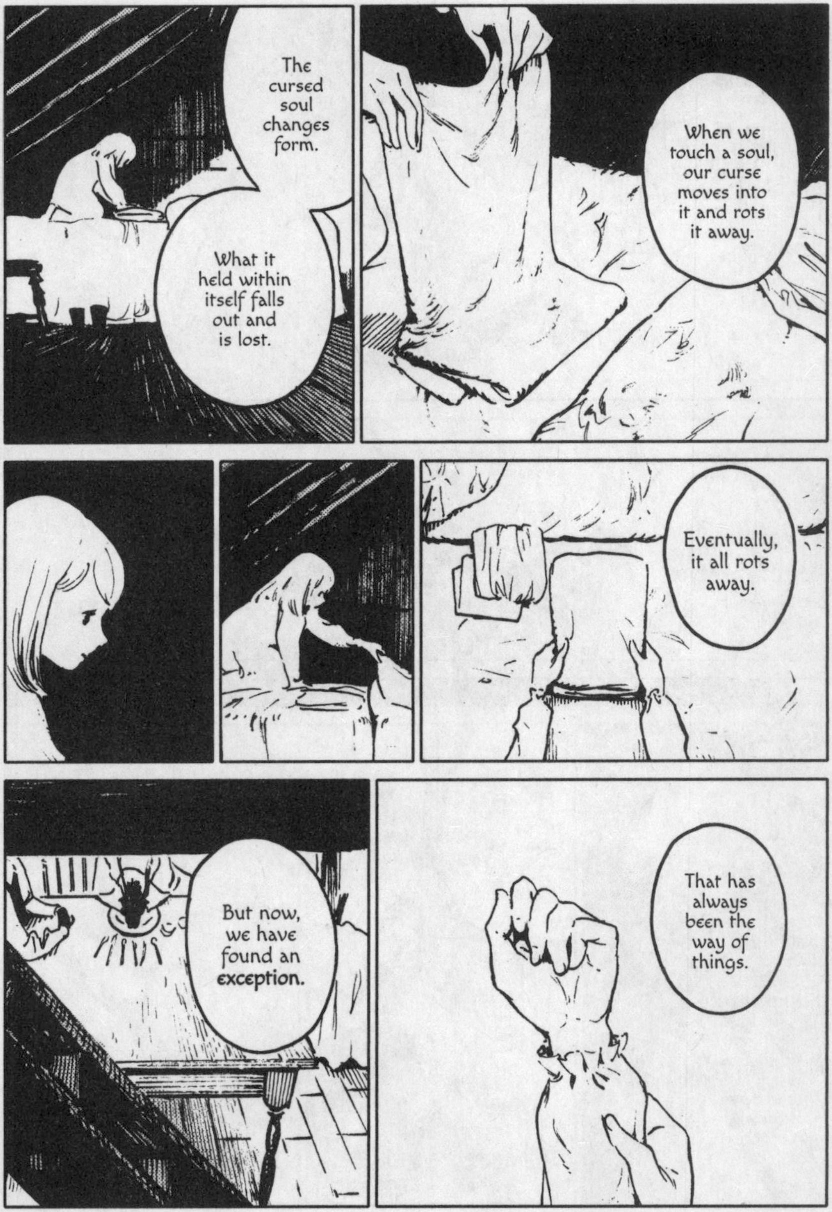
When we touch a soul, our curse moves into it and rots it away.
The cursed soul changes form.
What it held within itself falls out and is lost.
Eventually, it all rots away.
That has always been the way of things.
But now, we have found an **exception.**

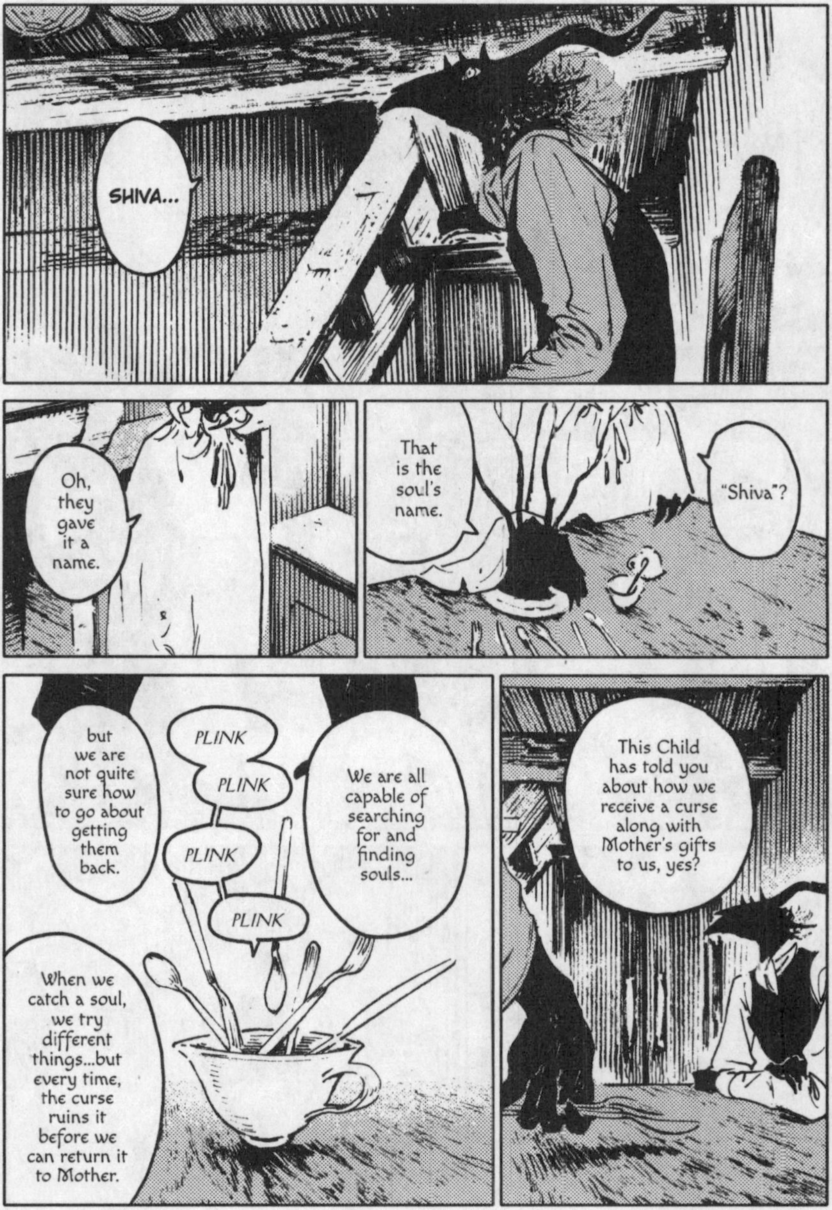
SHIVA...
"Shiva"?
That is the soul's name.
Oh, they gave it a name.
This Child has told you about how we receive a curse along with Mother's gifts to us, yes?
We are all capable of searching for and finding souls...
PLINK
PLINK
PLINK
PLINK
but we are not quite sure how to go about getting them back.
When we catch a soul, we try different things...but every time, the curse ruins it before we can return it to Mother.

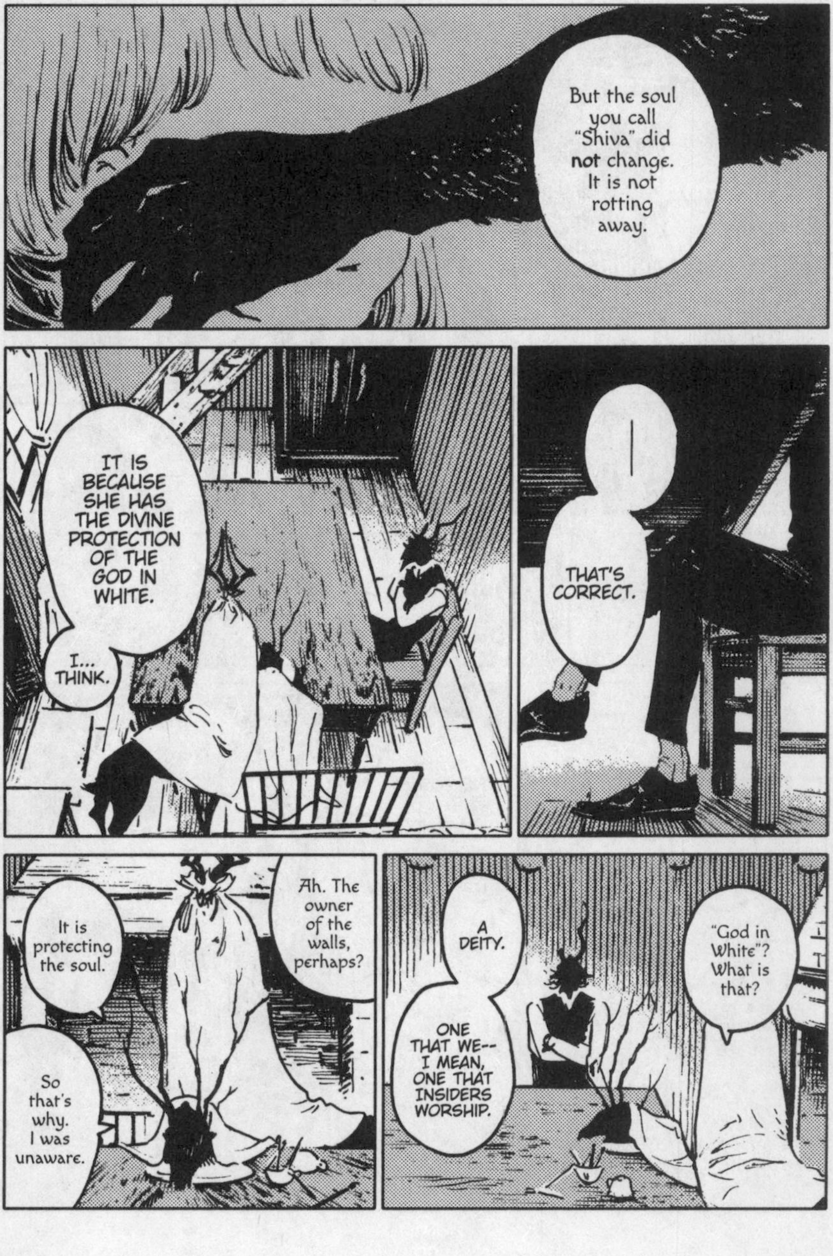
But the soul you call "Shiva" did **not** change. It is not rotting away.
THAT'S CORRECT.
IT IS BECAUSE SHE HAS THE DIVINE PROTECTION OF THE GOD IN WHITE.
I... THINK.
"God in White"? What is that?
A DEITY.
ONE THAT WE-- I MEAN, ONE THAT INSIDERS WORSHIP.
Ah. The owner of the walls, perhaps?
It is protecting the soul.
So that's why. I was unaware.

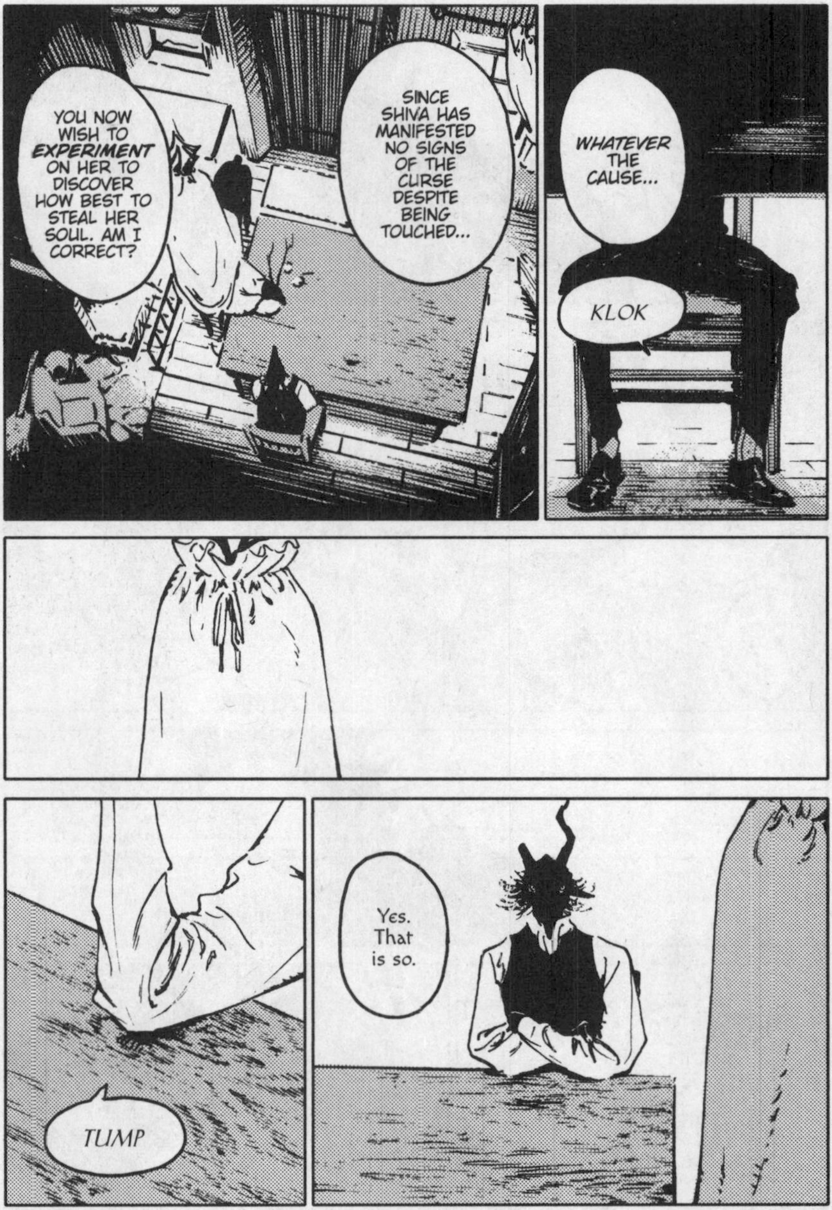
WHATEVER THE CAUSE...
KLOK
SINCE SHIVA HAS MANIFESTED NO SIGNS OF THE CURSE DESPITE BEING TOUCHED...
YOU NOW WISH TO **EXPERIMENT** ON HER TO DISCOVER HOW BEST TO STEAL HER SOUL. AM I CORRECT?
Yes. That is so.
TUMP

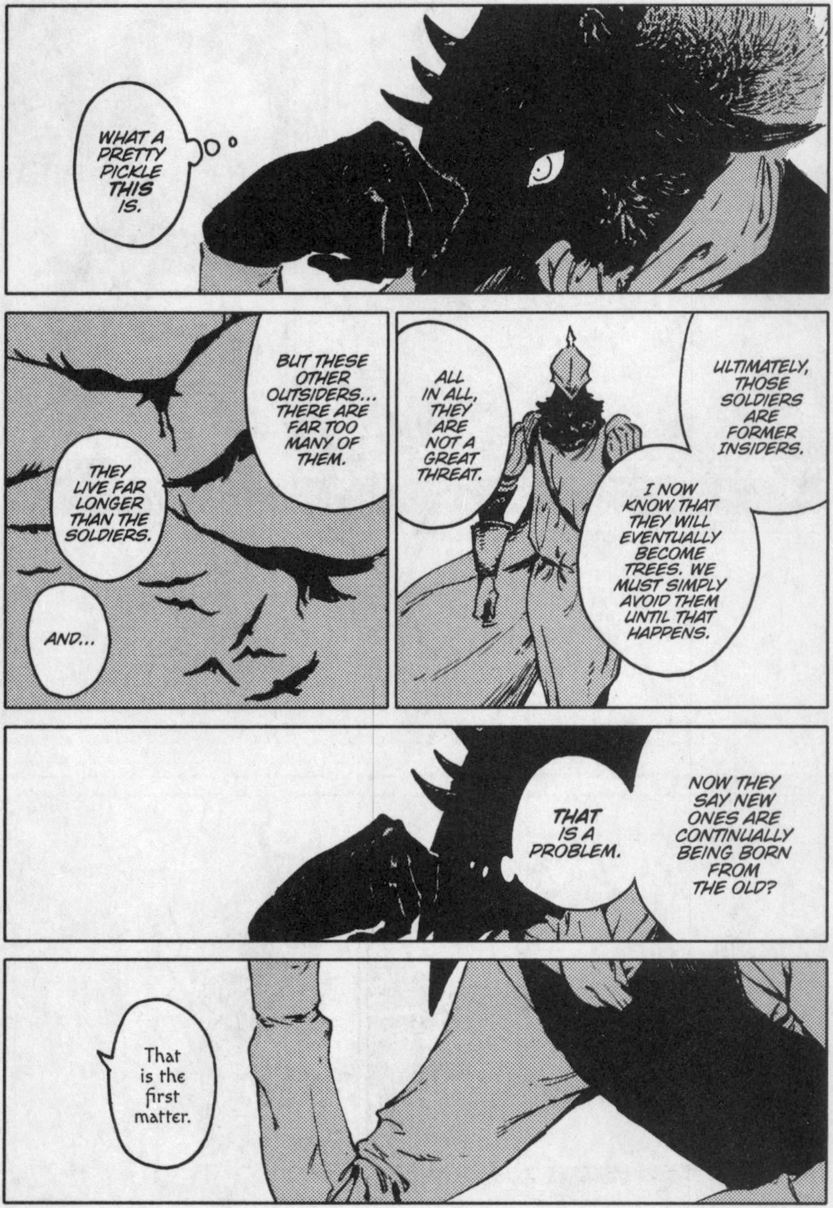
WHAT A PRETTY PICKLE THIS IS.
ULTIMATELY, THOSE SOLDIERS ARE FORMER INSIDERS.
I NOW KNOW THAT THEY WILL EVENTUALLY BECOME TREES. WE MUST SIMPLY AVOID THEM UNTIL THAT HAPPENS.
ALL IN ALL, THEY ARE NOT A GREAT THREAT.
BUT THESE OTHER OUTSIDERS... THERE ARE FAR TOO MANY OF THEM.
THEY LIVE FAR LONGER THAN THE SOLDIERS.
AND...
NOW THEY SAY NEW ONES ARE CONTINUALLY BEING BORN FROM THE OLD?
THAT IS A PROBLEM.
That is the first matter.

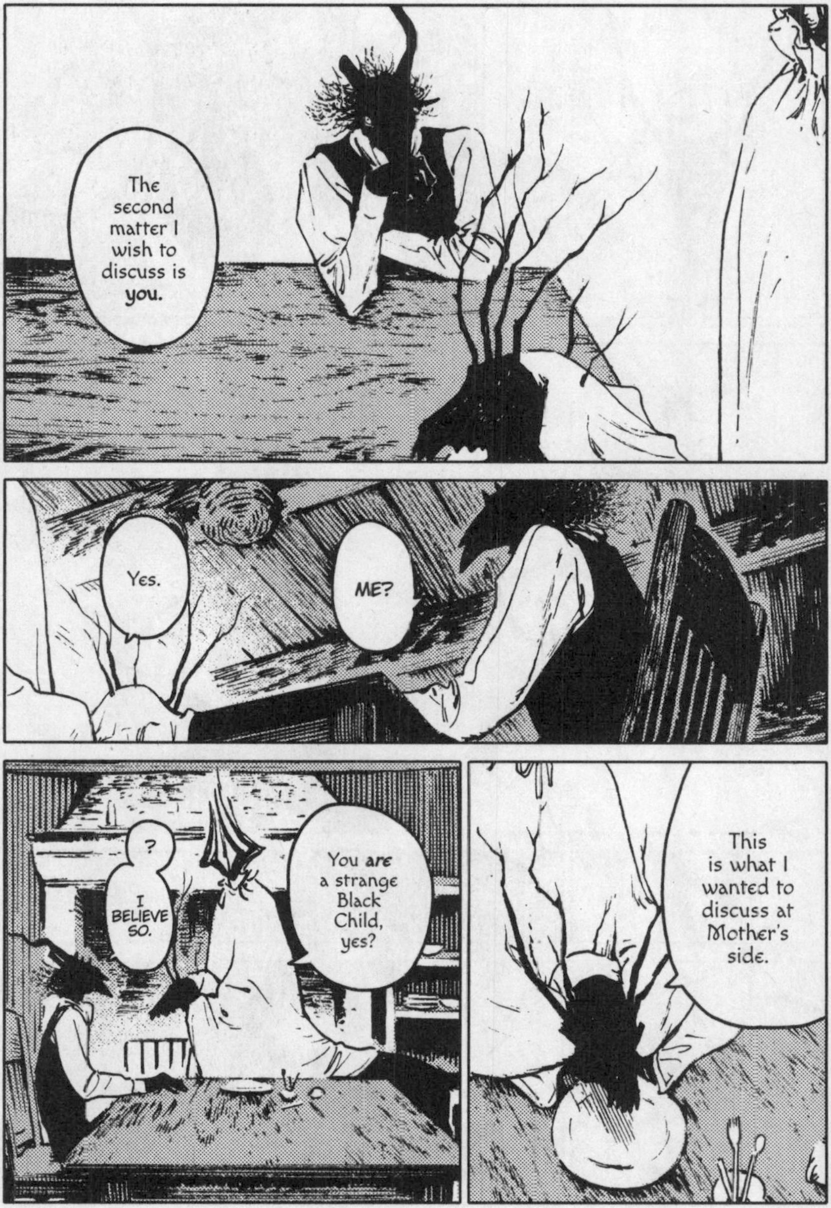
The second matter I wish to discuss is **you.**
ME?
Yes.
This is what I wanted to discuss at Mother's side.
You **are** a strange Black Child, yes?
?
I BELIEVE SO.

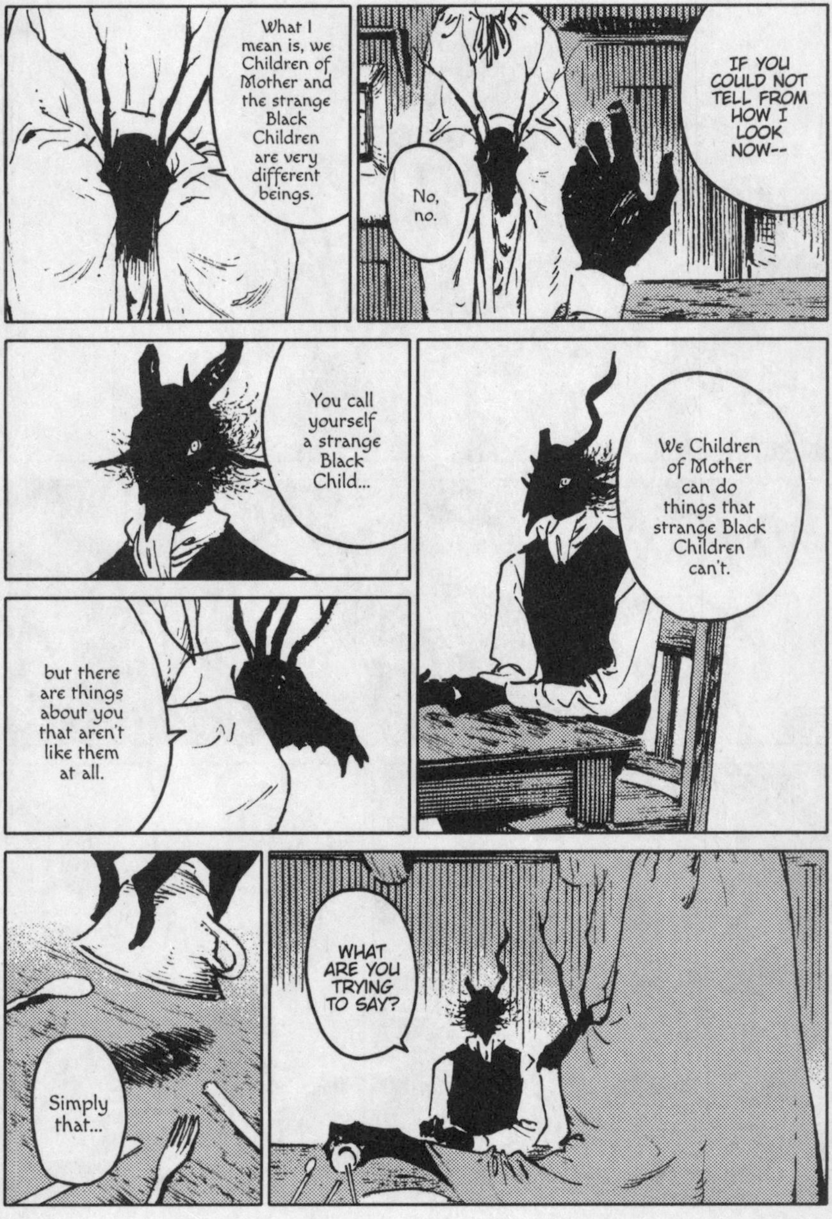
IF YOU COULD NOT TELL FROM HOW I LOOK NOW--
No, no.
What I mean is, we Children of Mother and the strange Black Children are very different beings.
We Children of Mother can do things that strange Black Children can't.
You call yourself a strange Black Child...
but there are things about you that aren't like them at all.
WHAT ARE YOU TRYING TO SAY?
Simply that...

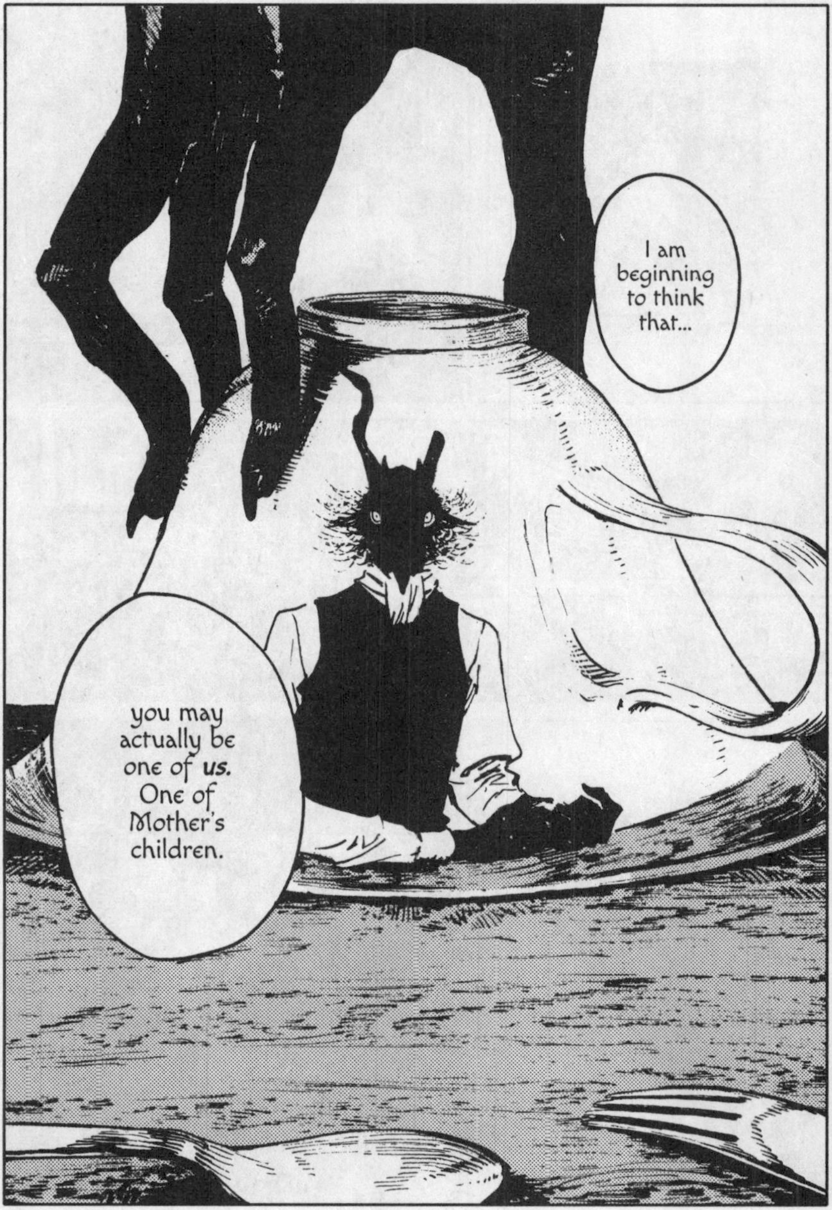
I am beginning to think that...
you may actually be one of us. One of Mother's children.

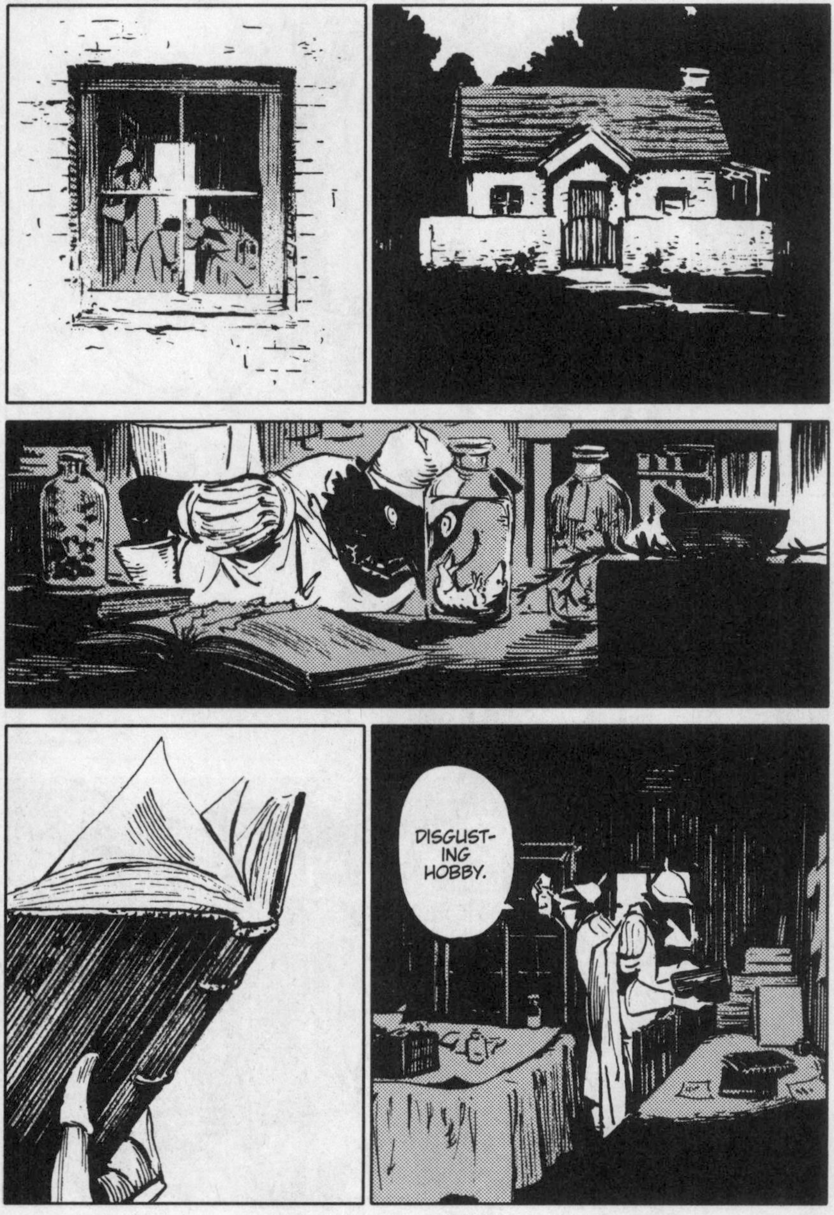
DISGUSTING HOBBY.

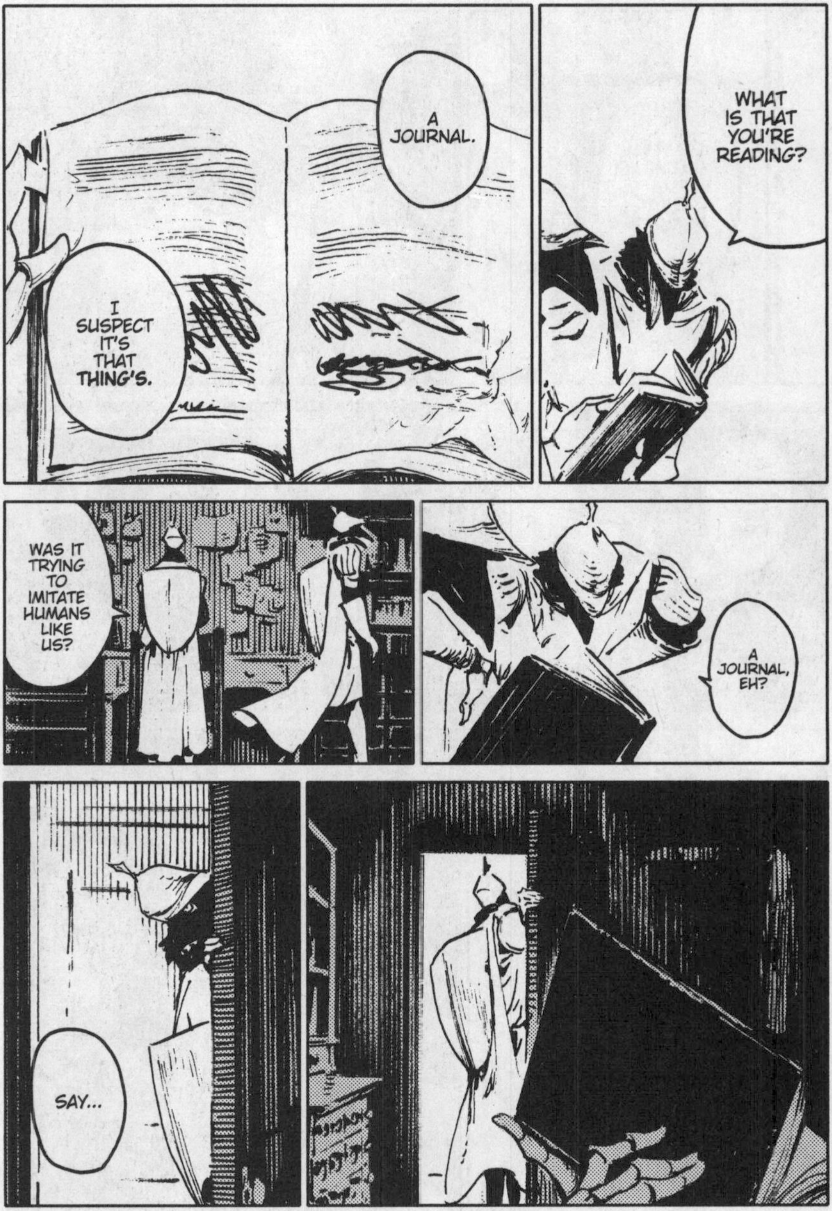
WHAT IS THAT YOU'RE READING?
A JOURNAL.
I SUSPECT IT'S THAT THING'S.
A JOURNAL, EH?
WAS IT TRYING TO IMITATE HUMANS LIKE US?
SAY...

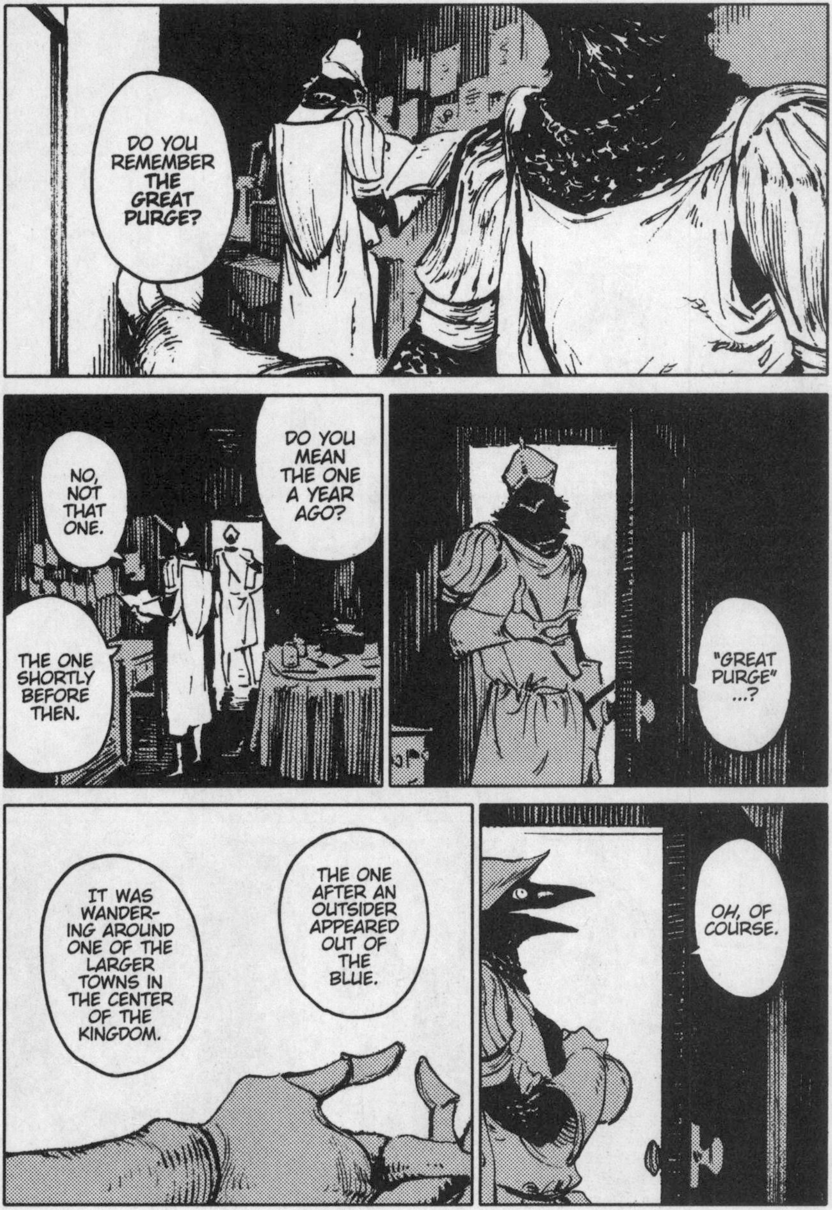
DO YOU REMEMBER THE GREAT PURGE?
"GREAT PURGE" ...?
DO YOU MEAN THE ONE A YEAR AGO?
NO, NOT THAT ONE.
THE ONE SHORTLY BEFORE THEN.
OH, OF COURSE.
THE ONE AFTER AN OUTSIDER APPEARED OUT OF THE BLUE.
IT WAS WANDER-ING AROUND ONE OF THE LARGER TOWNS IN THE CENTER OF THE KINGDOM.

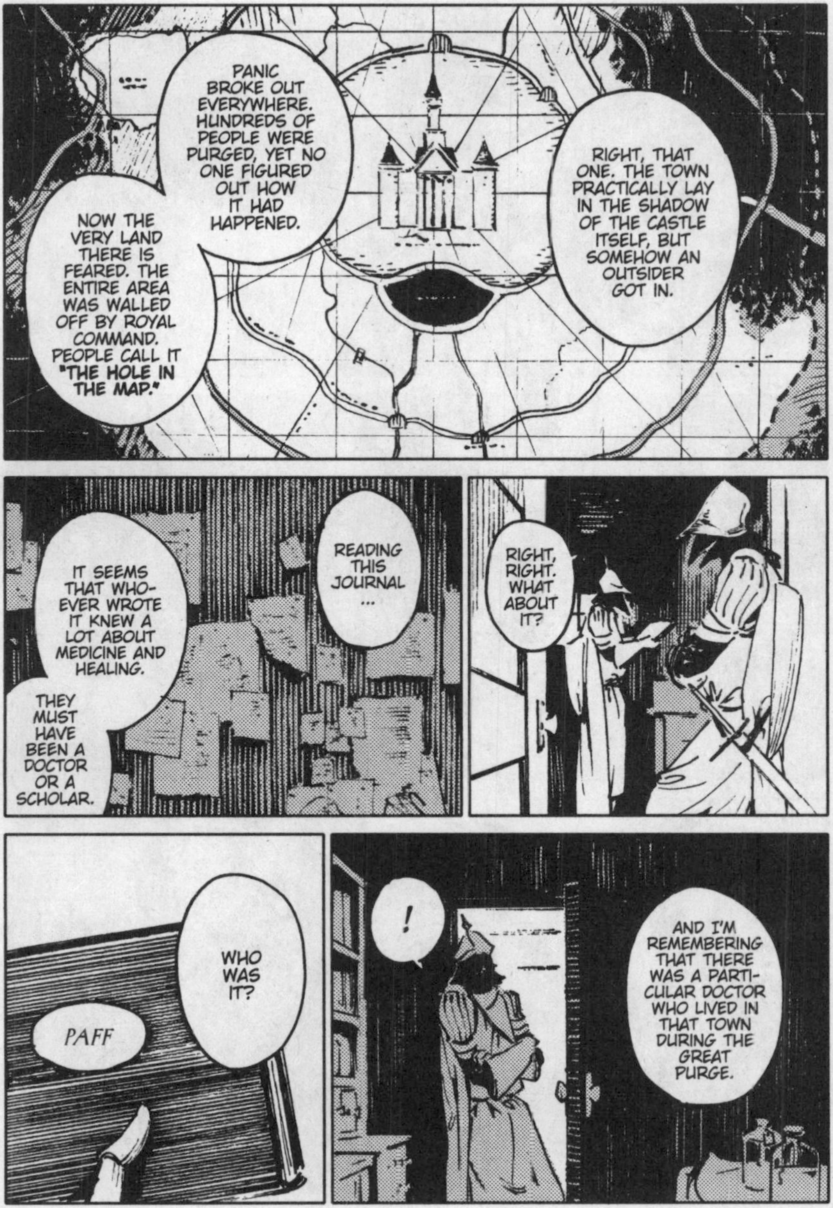
RIGHT, THAT ONE. THE TOWN PRACTICALLY LAY IN THE SHADOW OF THE CASTLE ITSELF, BUT SOMEHOW AN OUTSIDER GOT IN.
PANIC BROKE OUT EVERYWHERE. HUNDREDS OF PEOPLE WERE PURGED, YET NO ONE FIGURED OUT HOW IT HAD HAPPENED.
NOW THE VERY LAND THERE IS FEARED. THE ENTIRE AREA WAS WALLED OFF BY ROYAL COMMAND. PEOPLE CALL IT **"THE HOLE IN THE MAP."**
RIGHT, RIGHT. WHAT ABOUT IT?
READING THIS JOURNAL ...
IT SEEMS THAT WHO-EVER WROTE IT KNEW A LOT ABOUT MEDICINE AND HEALING.
THEY MUST HAVE BEEN A DOCTOR OR A SCHOLAR.
AND I'M REMEMBERING THAT THERE WAS A PARTI-CULAR DOCTOR WHO LIVED IN THAT TOWN DURING THE GREAT PURGE.
!
WHO WAS IT?
PAFF

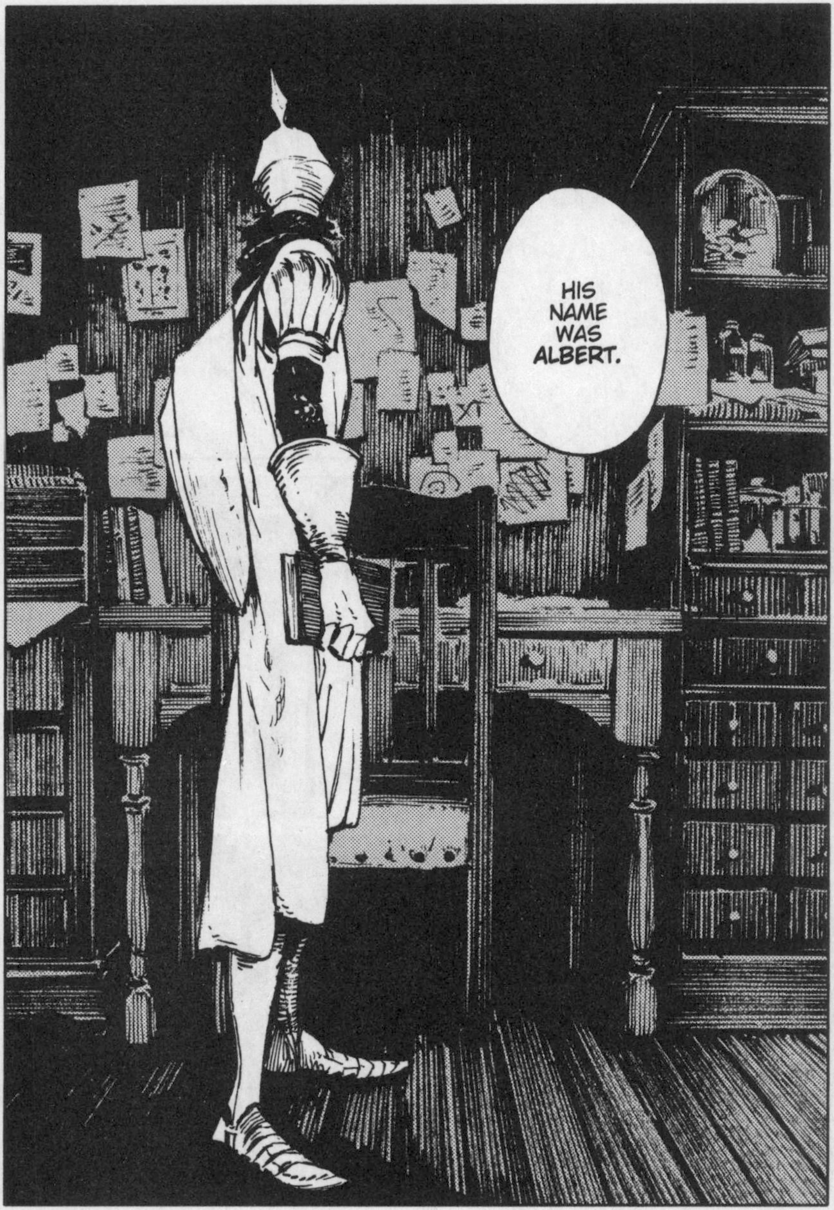
HIS NAME WAS ALBERT.

Chapter 29

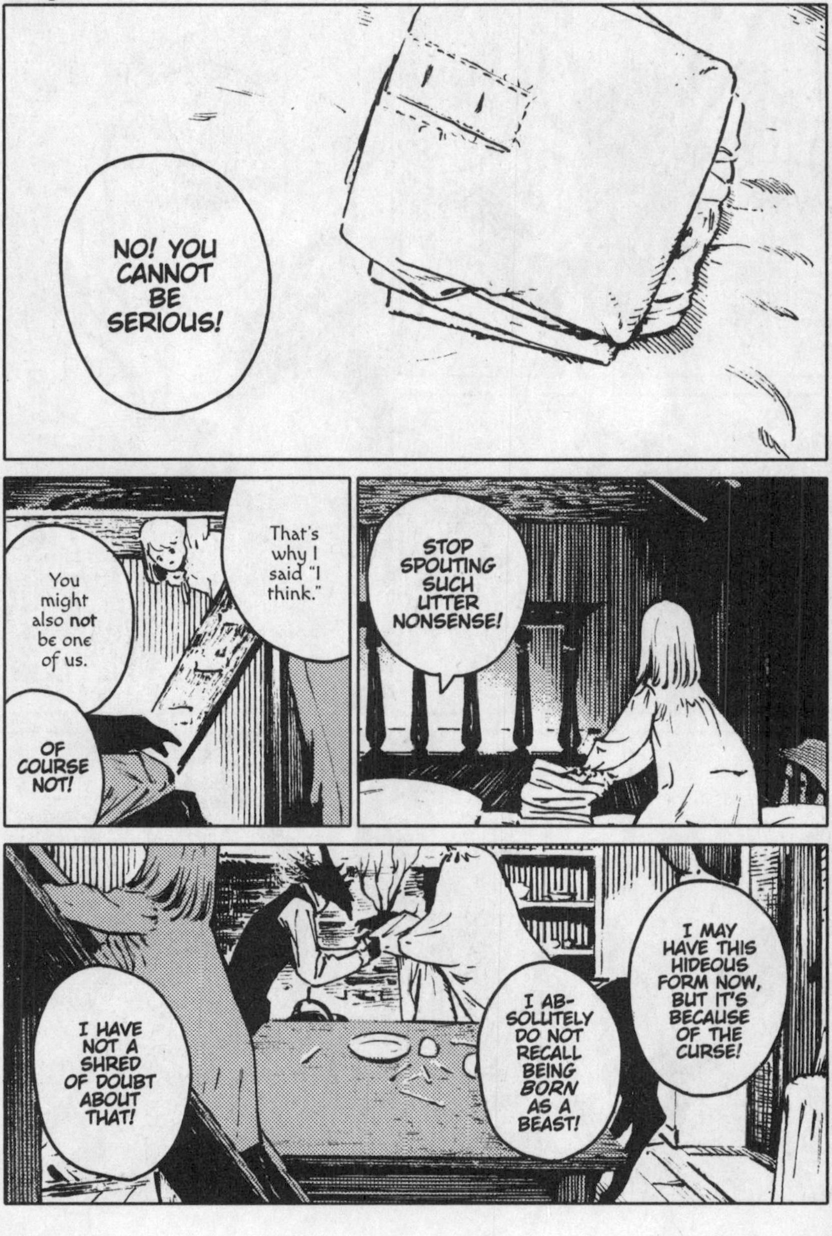
NO! YOU CANNOT BE SERIOUS!
STOP SPOUTING SUCH UTTER NONSENSE!
That's why I said "I think."
You might also not be one of us.
OF COURSE NOT!
I MAY HAVE THIS HIDEOUS FORM NOW, BUT IT'S BECAUSE OF THE CURSE!
I ABSOLUTELY DO NOT RECALL BEING BORN AS A BEAST!
I HAVE NOT A SHRED OF DOUBT ABOUT THAT!

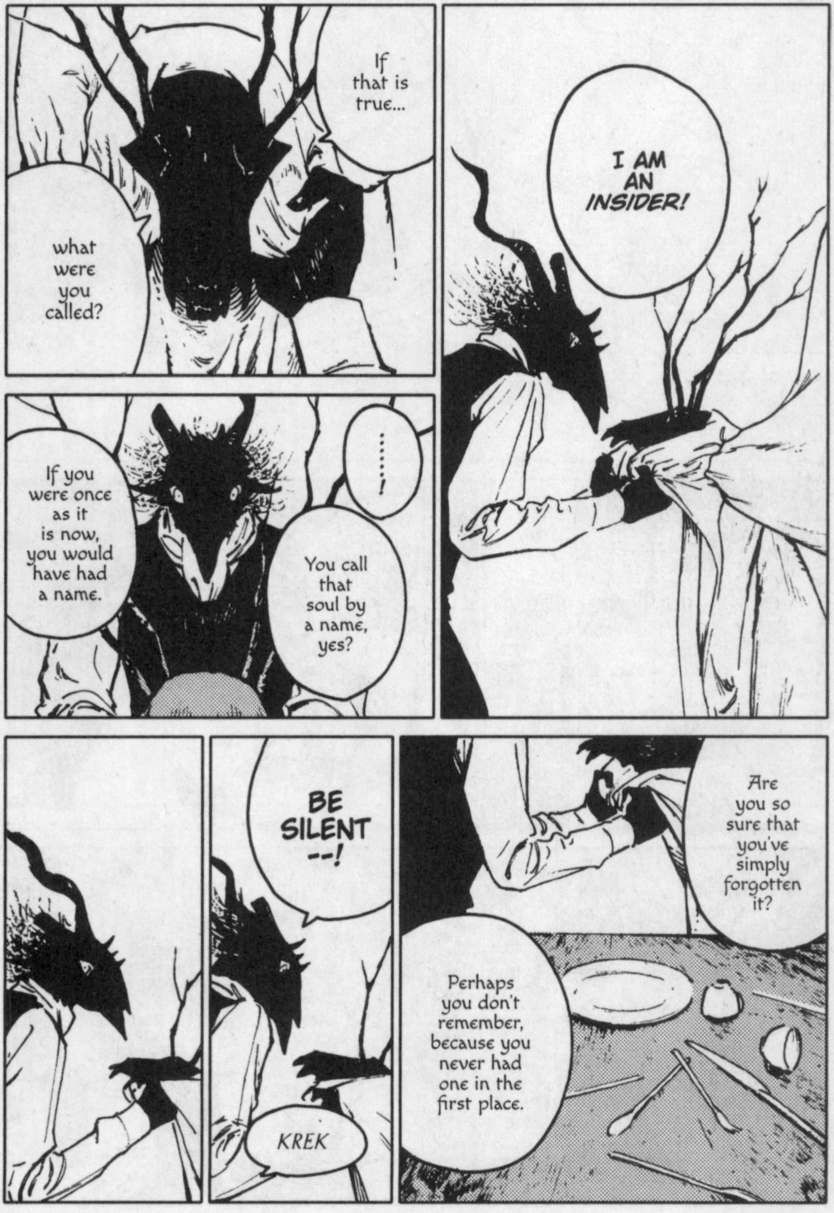
I AM AN INSIDER!
If that is true...
what were you called?
......!
If you were once as it is now, you would have had a name.
You call that soul by a name, yes?
Are you so sure that you've simply forgotten it?
Perhaps you don't remember, because you never had one in the first place.
BE SILENT--!
KREK

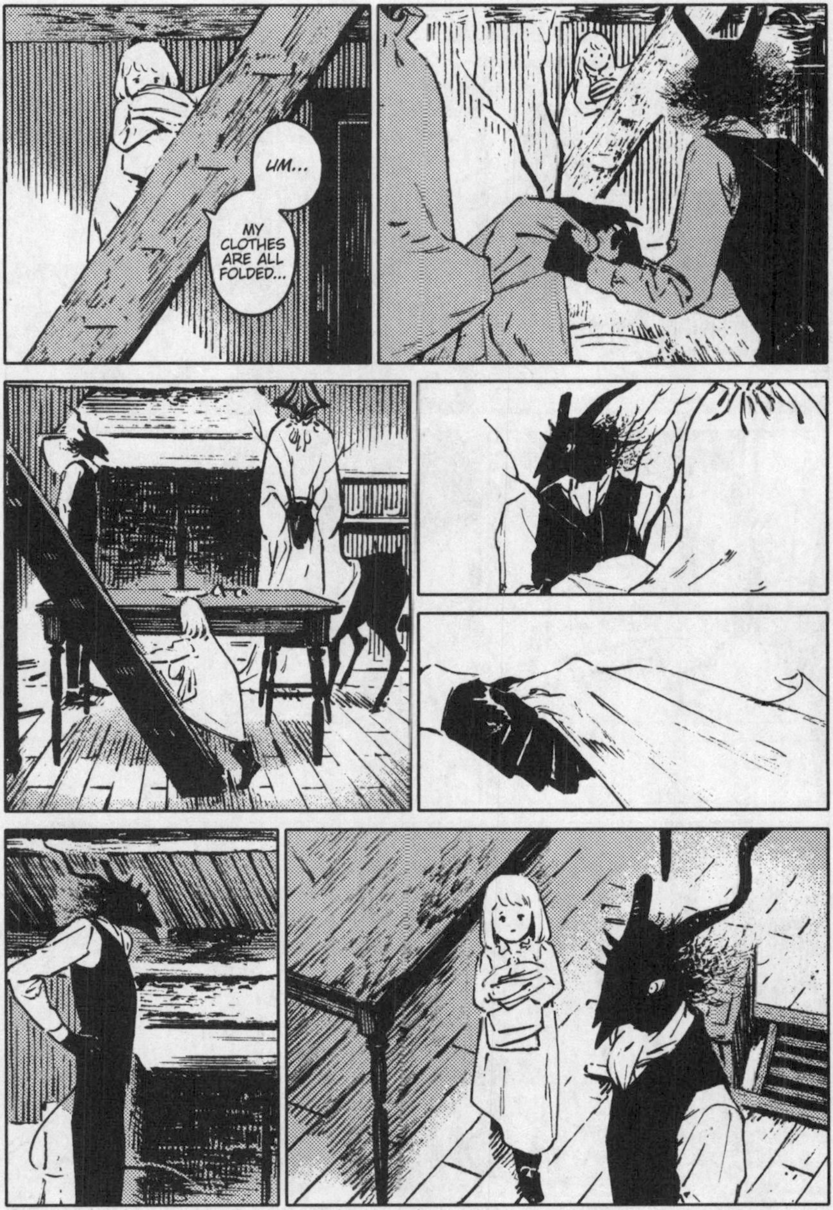
UM...
MY CLOTHES ARE ALL FOLDED...

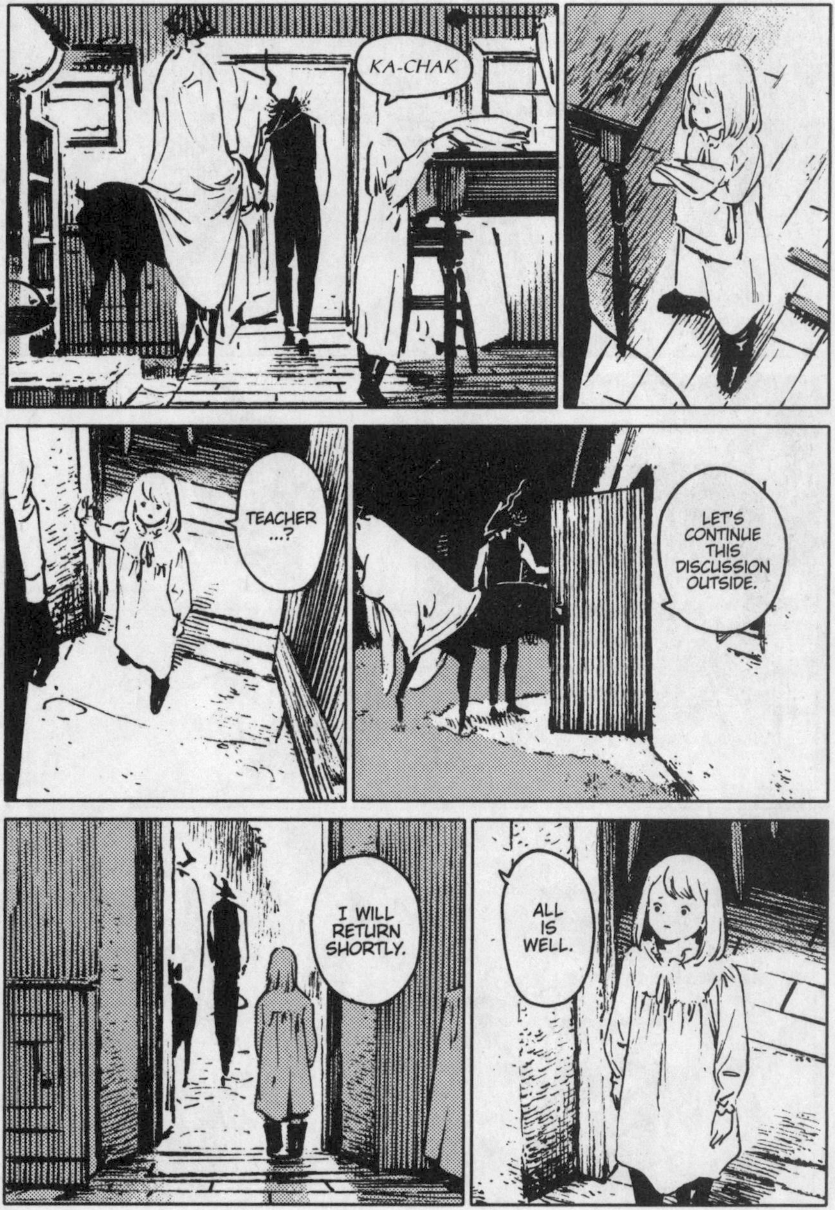
KA-CHAK
LET'S CONTINUE THIS DISCUSSION OUTSIDE.
TEACHER ...?
ALL IS WELL.
I WILL RETURN SHORTLY.

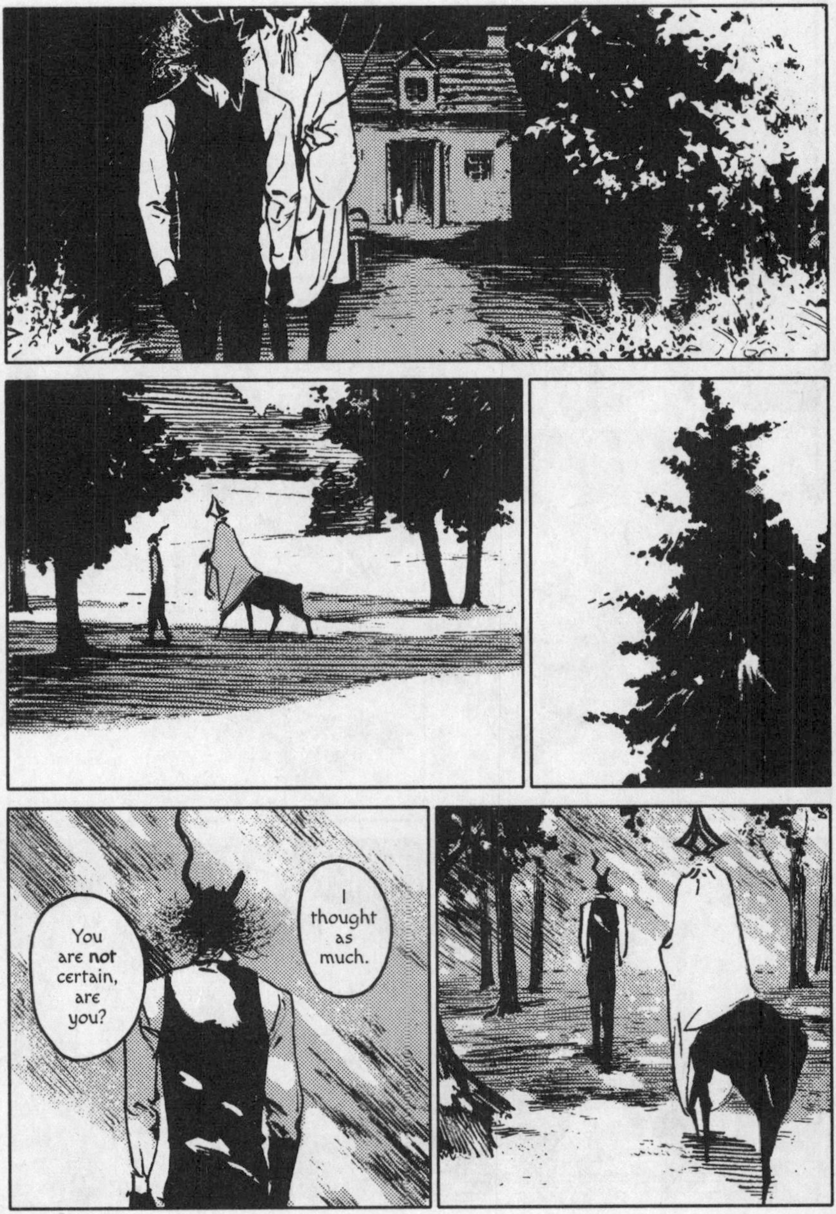
I thought as much.
You are **not** certain, are you?

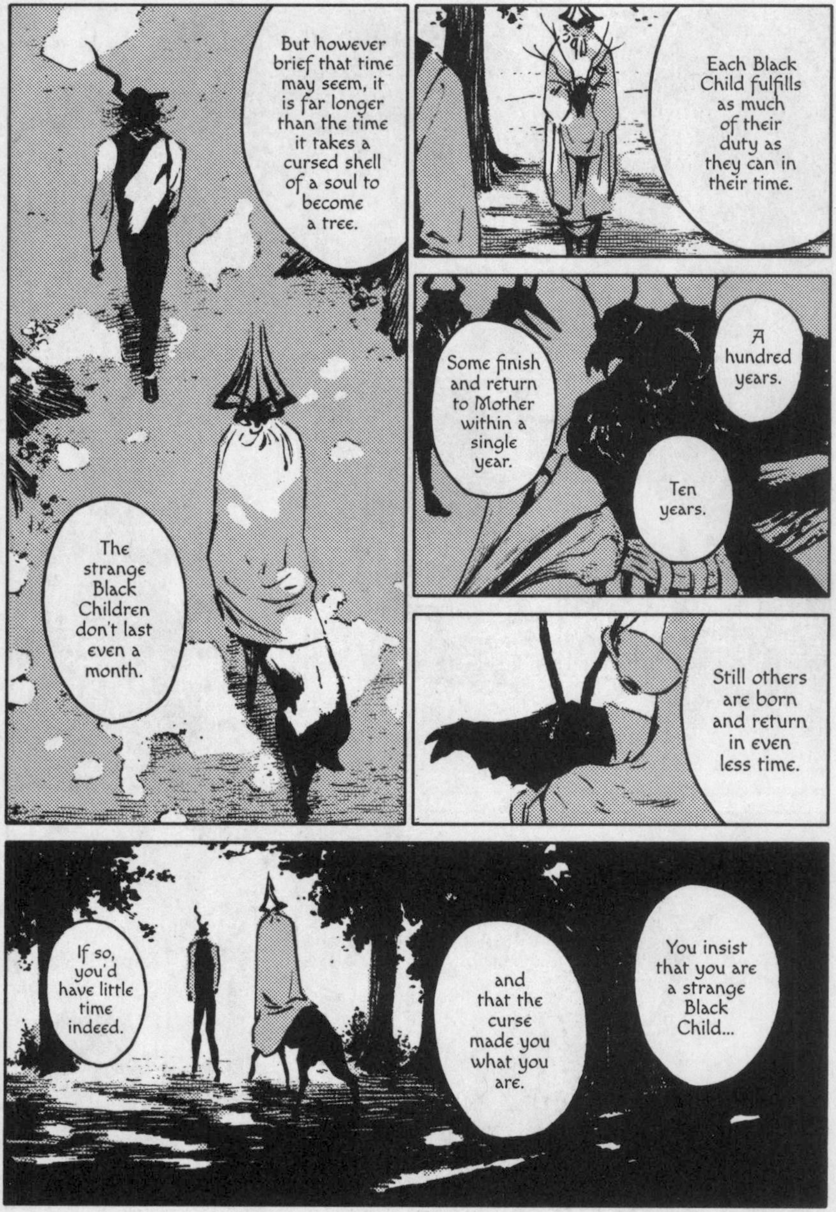
Each Black Child fulfills as much of their duty as they can in their time.
A hundred years.
Some finish and return to Mother within a single year.
Ten years.
Still others are born and return in even less time.
But however brief that time may seem, it is far longer than the time it takes a cursed shell of a soul to become a tree.
The strange Black Children don't last even a month.
You insist that you are a strange Black Child...
and that the curse made you what you are.
If so, you'd have little time indeed.

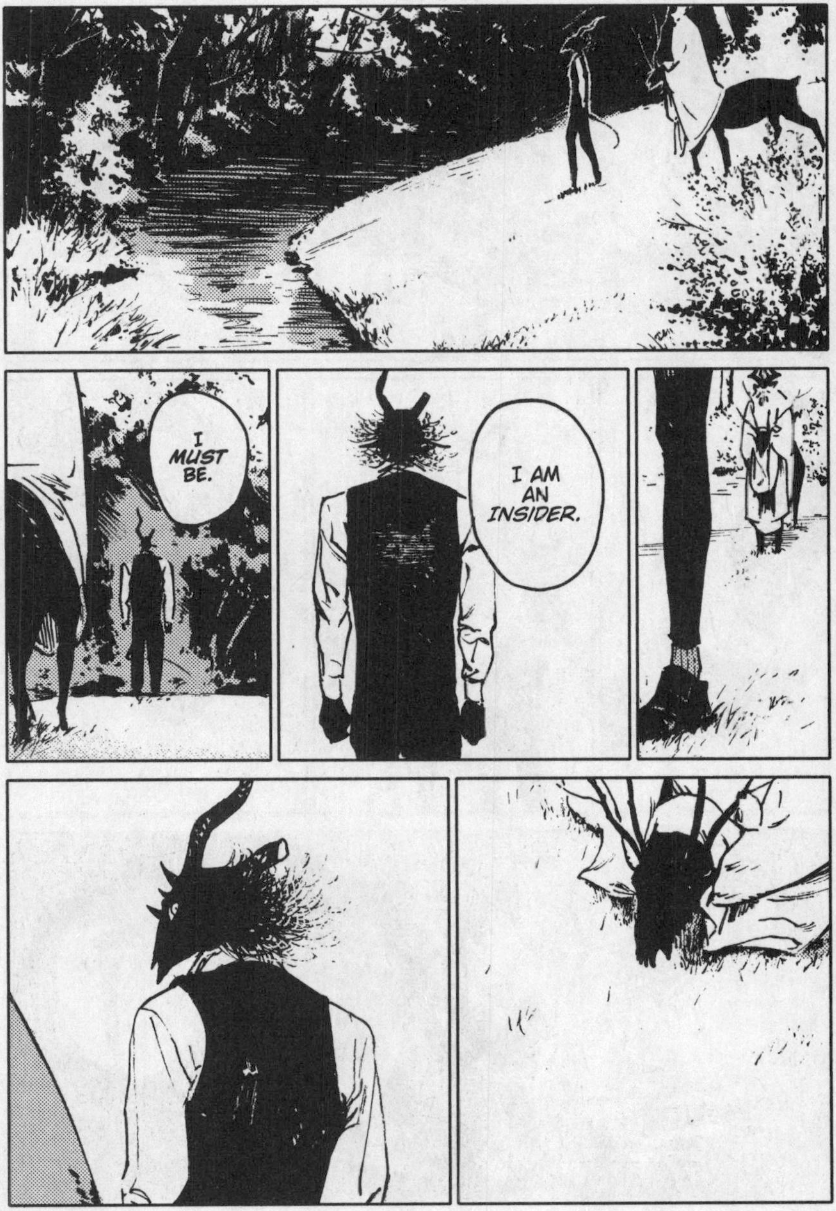
I AM AN INSIDER.
I MUST BE.

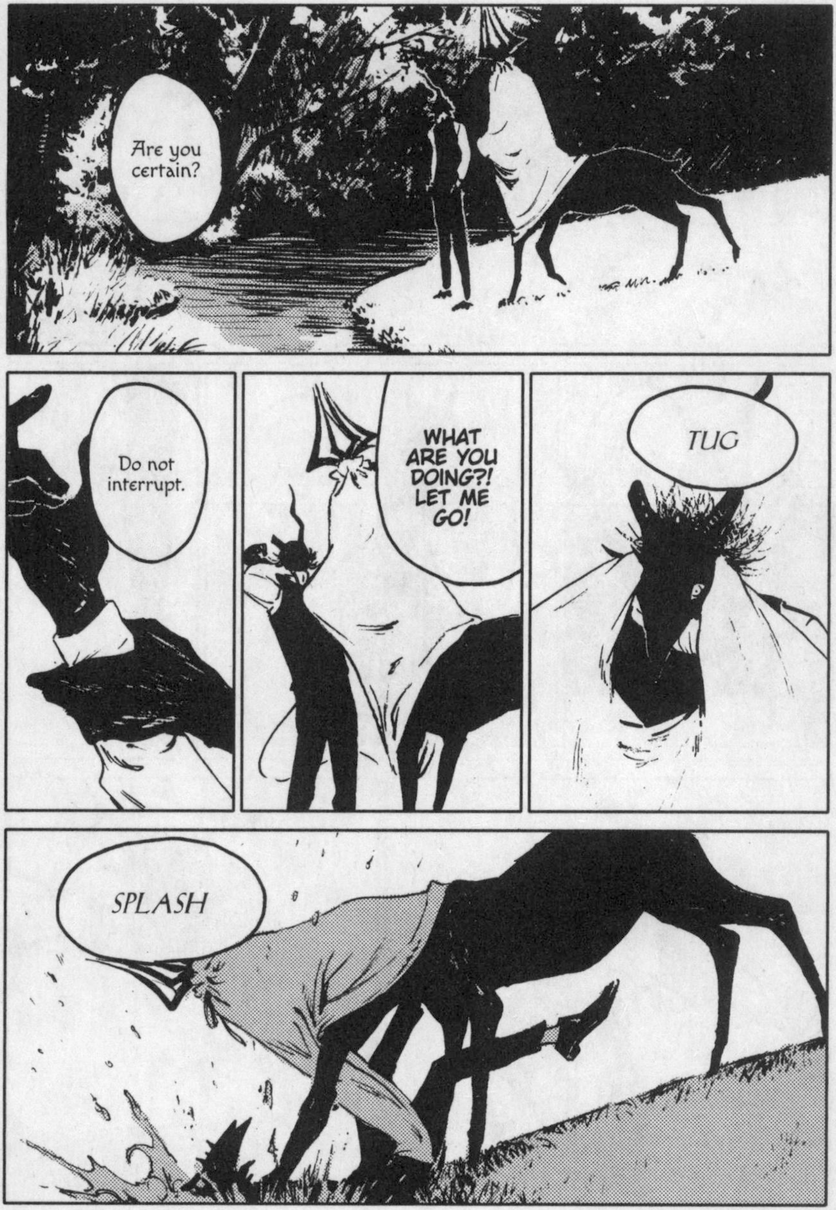
Are you certain?
TUG
WHAT ARE YOU DOING?! LET ME GO!
Do not interrupt.
SPLASH

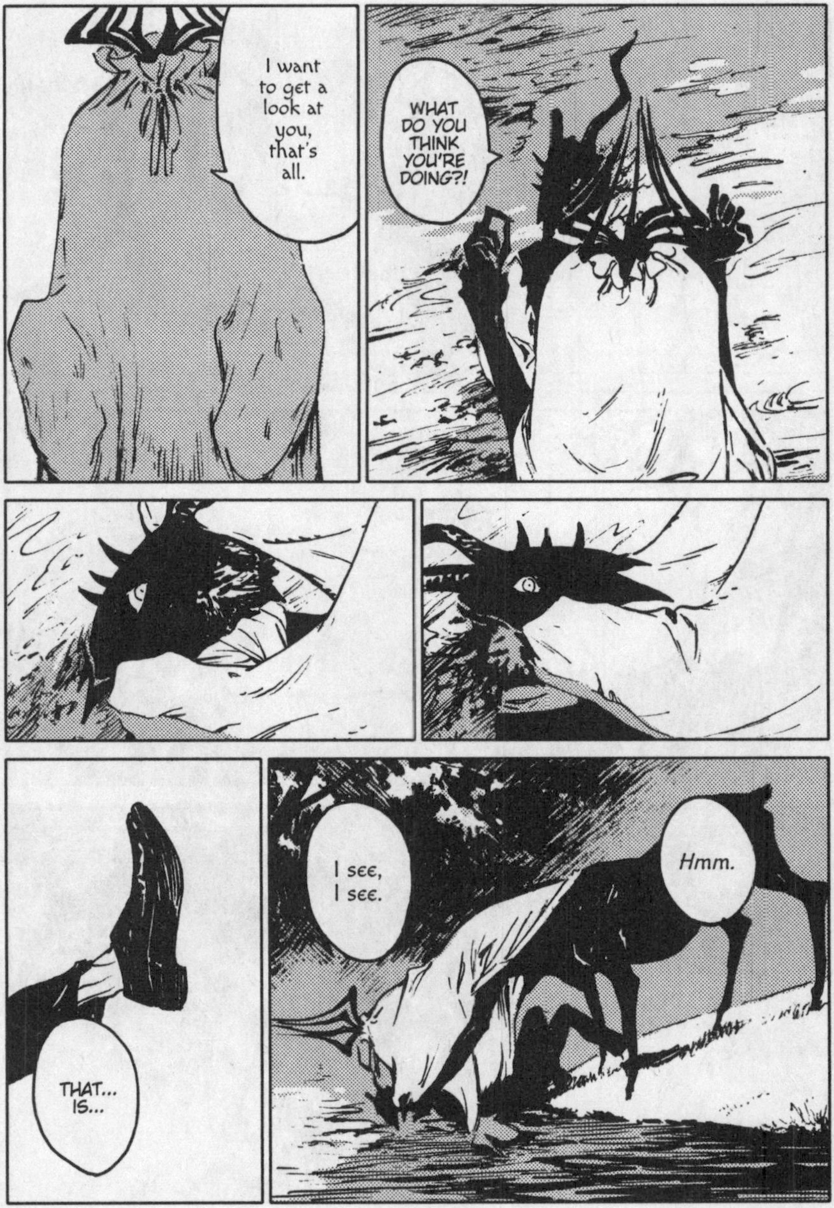
WHAT DO YOU THINK YOU'RE DOING?!
I want to get a look at you, that's all.
Hmm.
I see, I see.
THAT... IS...

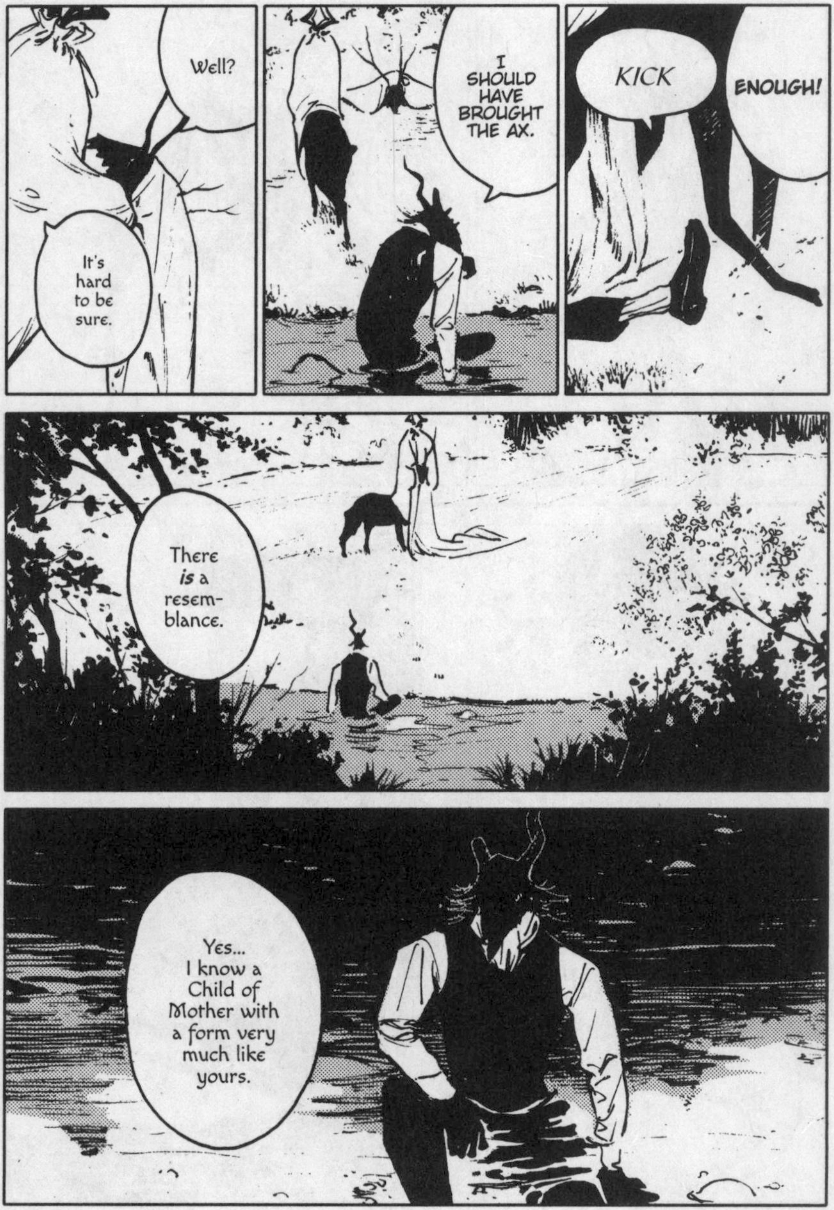
ENOUGH!
KICK
I SHOULD HAVE BROUGHT THE AX.
Well?
It's hard to be sure.
There *is* a resemblance.
Yes... I know a Child of Mother with a form very much like yours.

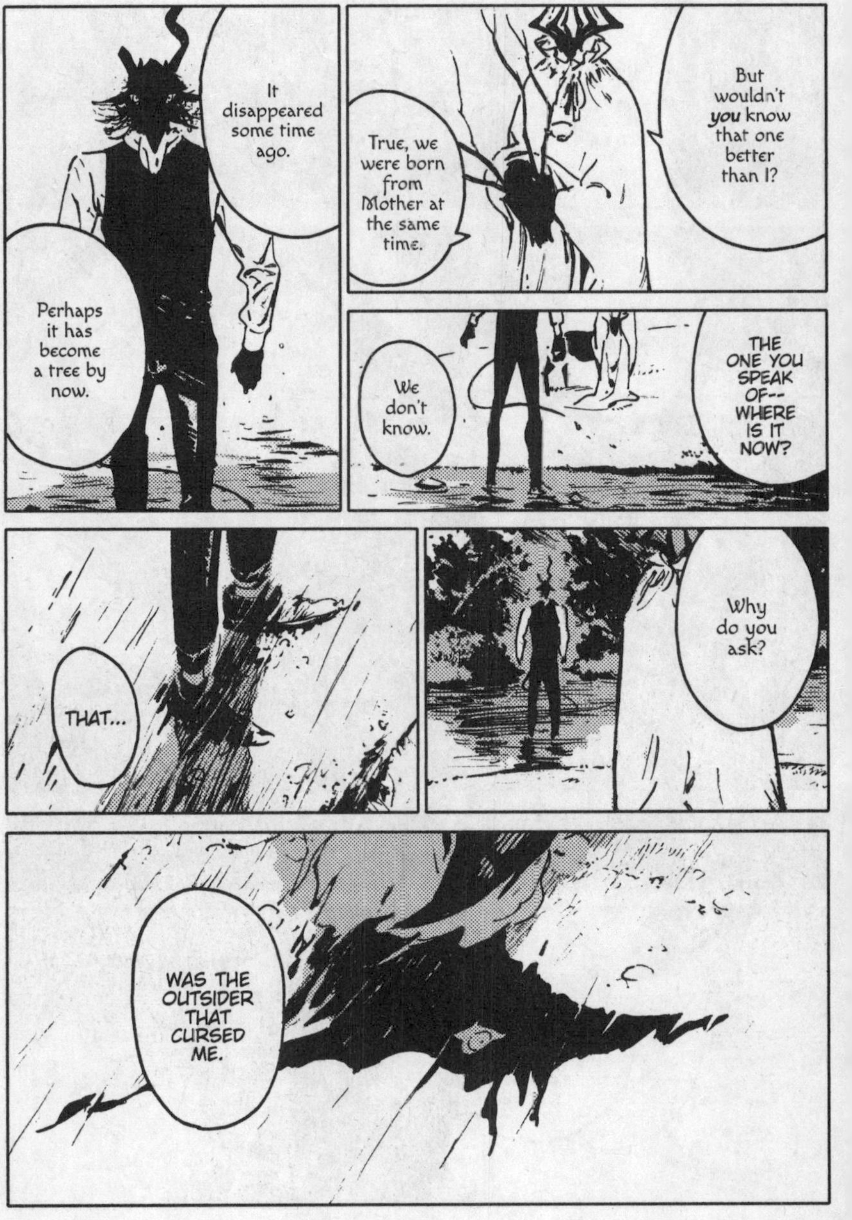
But wouldn't *you* know that one better than I?
True, we were born from Mother at the same time.
THE ONE YOU SPEAK OF-- WHERE IS IT NOW?
We don't know.
It disappeared some time ago.
Perhaps it has become a tree by now.
Why do you ask?
THAT...
WAS THE OUTSIDER THAT CURSED ME.

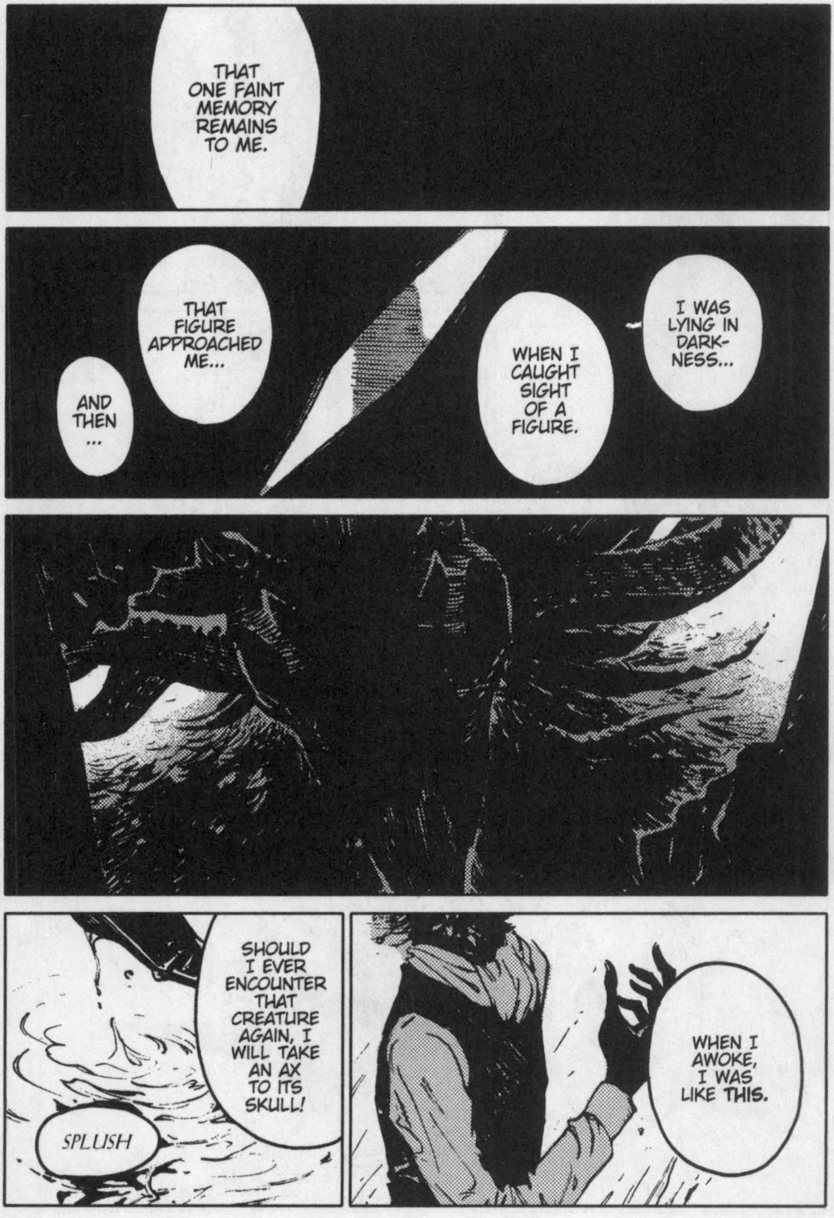
THAT ONE FAINT MEMORY REMAINS TO ME.
I WAS LYING IN DARK-NESS...
WHEN I CAUGHT SIGHT OF A FIGURE.
THAT FIGURE APPROACHED ME...
AND THEN ...
WHEN I AWOKE, I WAS LIKE THIS.
SHOULD I EVER ENCOUNTER THAT CREATURE AGAIN, I WILL TAKE AN AX TO ITS SKULL!
SPLUSH

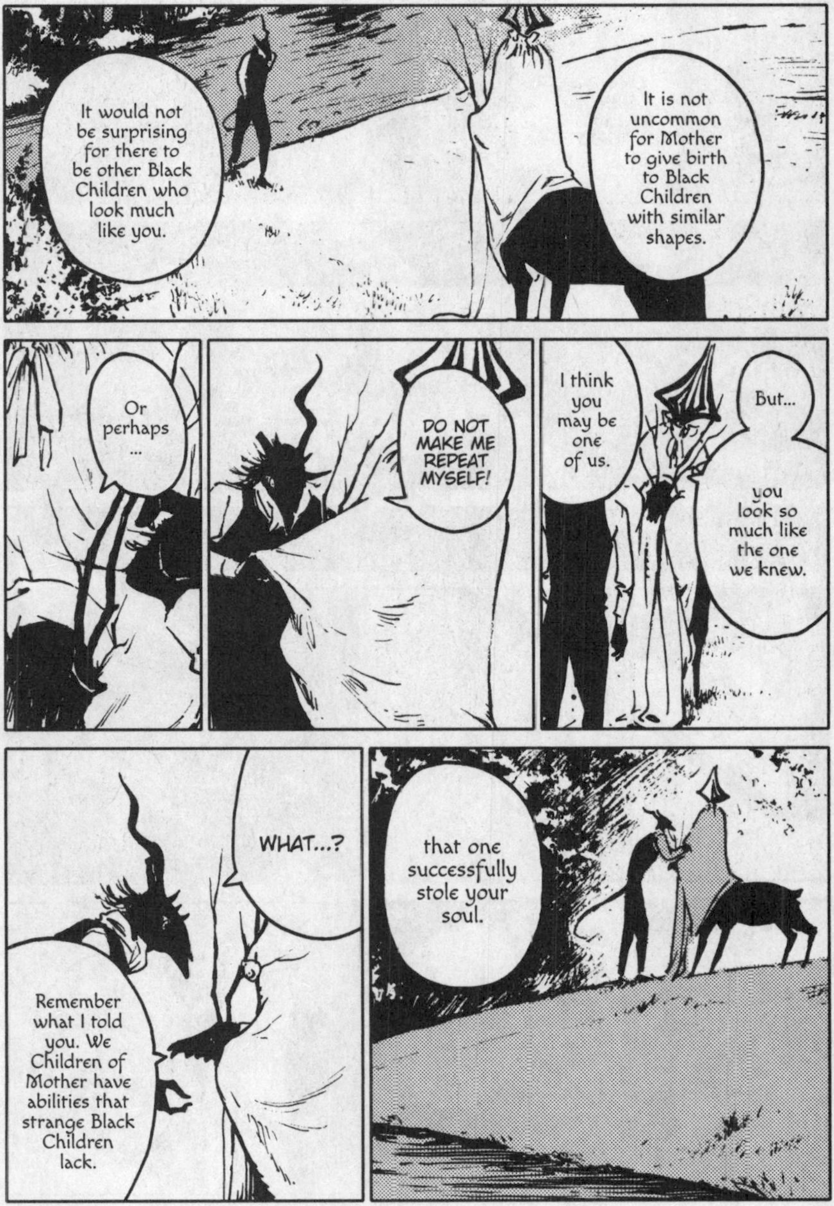
It is not uncommon for Mother to give birth to Black Children with similar shapes.
It would not be surprising for there to be other Black Children who look much like you.
But...
you look so much like the one we knew.
I think you may be one of us.
DO NOT MAKE ME REPEAT MYSELF!
Or perhaps ...
that one successfully stole your soul.
WHAT...?
Remember what I told you. We Children of Mother have abilities that strange Black Children lack.

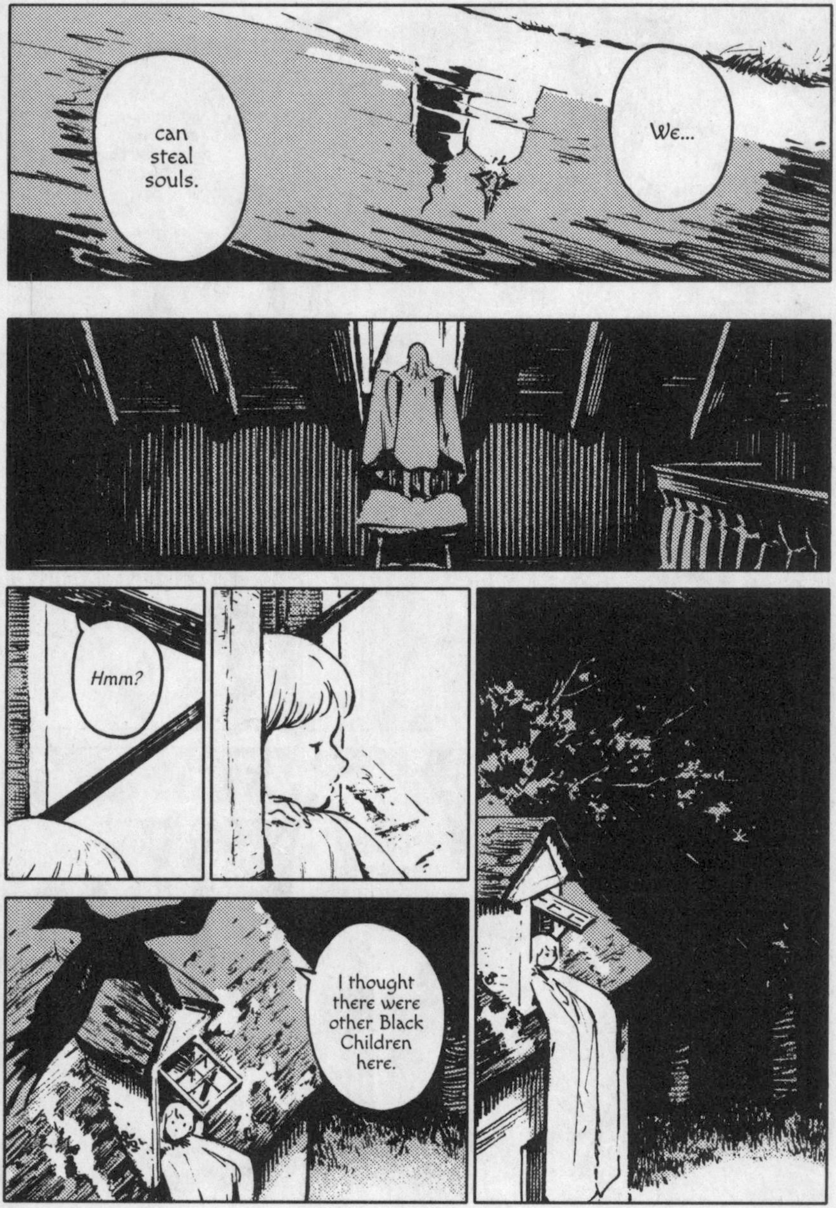
We...
can steal souls.
Hmm?
I thought there were other Black Children here.

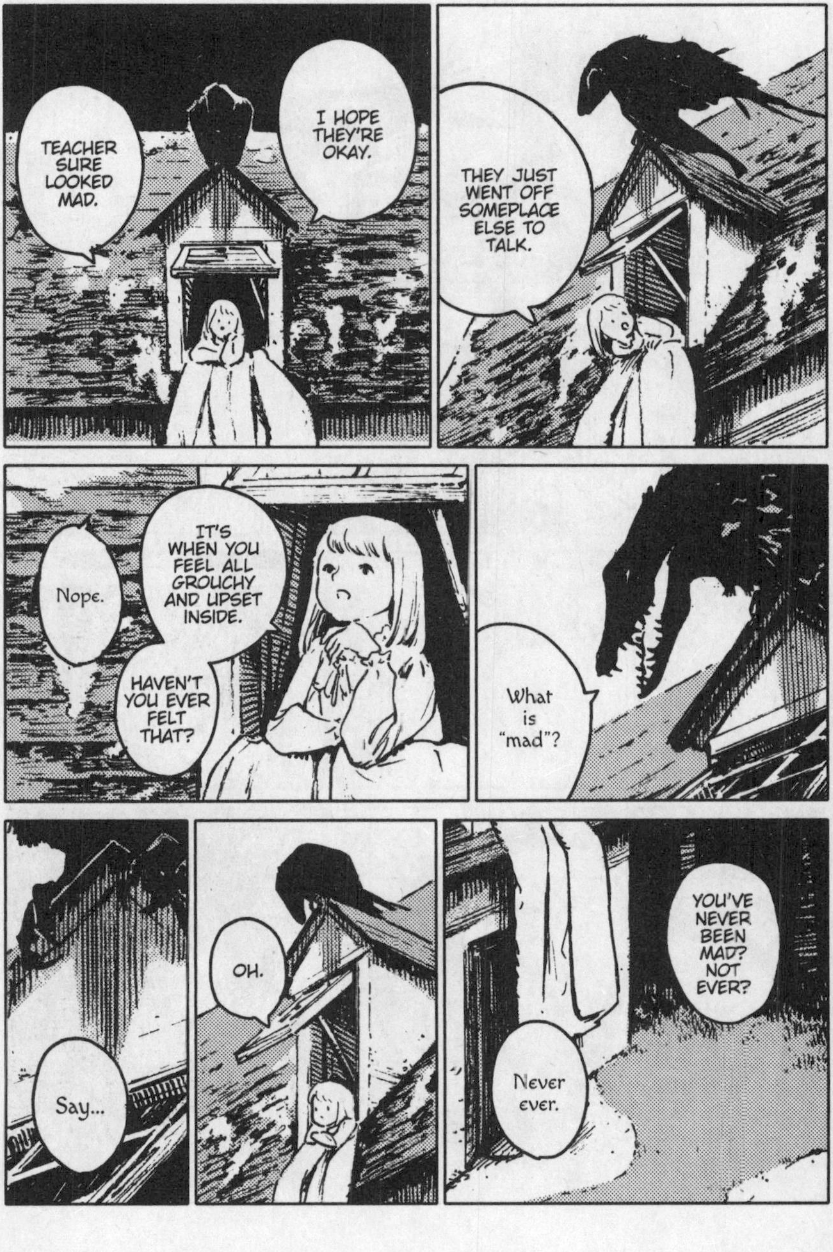
THEY JUST WENT OFF SOMEPLACE ELSE TO TALK.
I HOPE THEY'RE OKAY.
TEACHER SURE LOOKED MAD.
What is "mad"?
IT'S WHEN YOU FEEL ALL GROUCHY AND UPSET INSIDE.
HAVEN'T YOU EVER FELT THAT?
Nope.
YOU'VE NEVER BEEN MAD? NOT EVER?
Never ever.
OH.
Say...

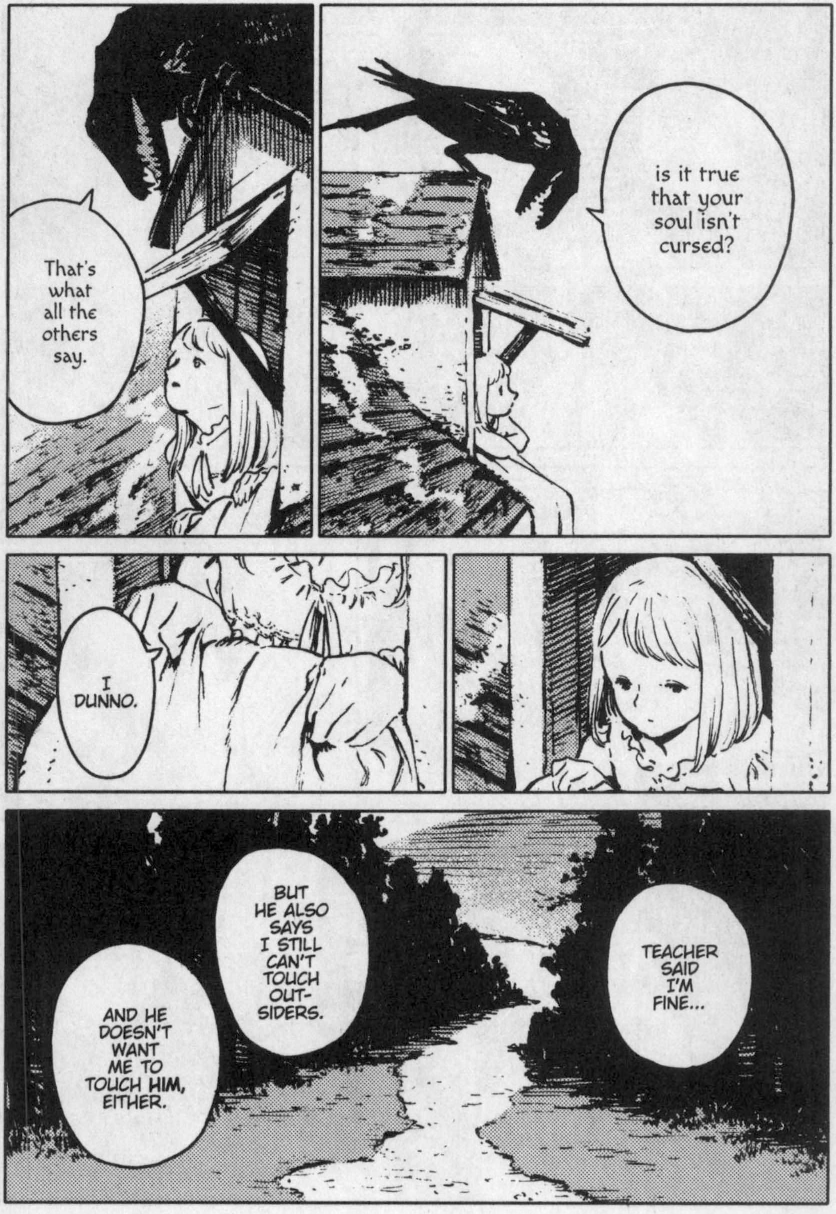
is it true that your soul isn't cursed?
That's what all the others say.
I DUNNO.
TEACHER SAID I'M FINE...
BUT HE ALSO SAYS I STILL CAN'T TOUCH OUT-SIDERS.
AND HE DOESN'T WANT ME TO TOUCH HIM, EITHER.

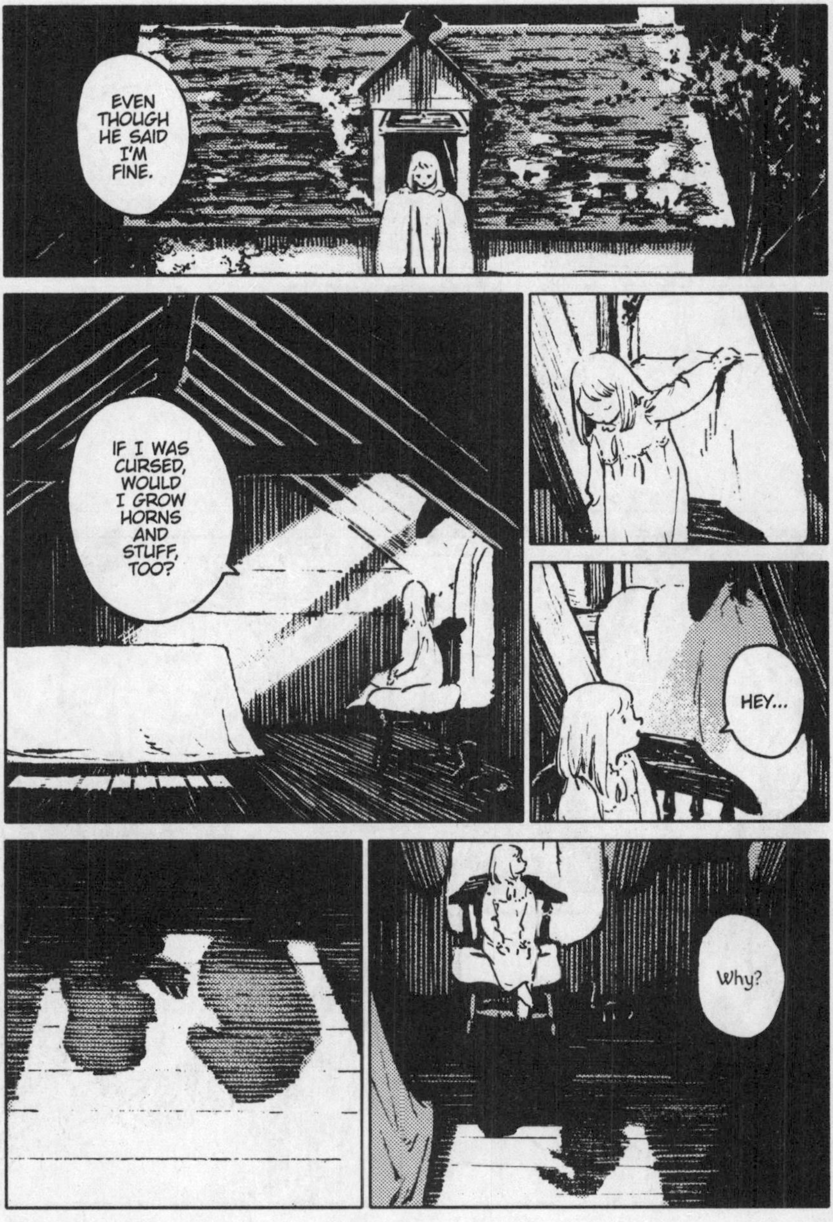
EVEN THOUGH HE SAID I'M FINE.
HEY...
IF I WAS CURSED, WOULD I GROW HORNS AND STUFF, TOO?
Why?

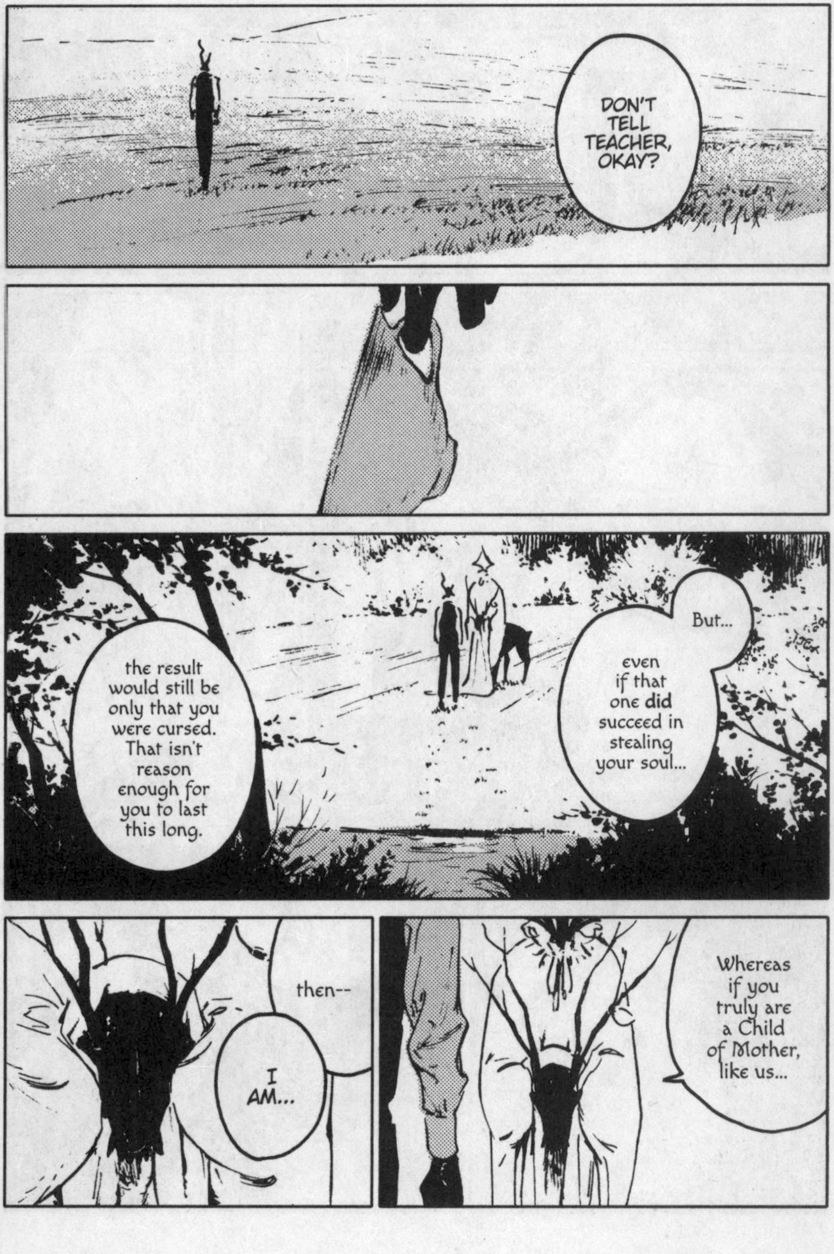
DON'T TELL TEACHER, OKAY?
But...
even if that one **did** succeed in stealing your soul...
the result would still be only that you were cursed. That isn't reason enough for you to last this long.
Whereas if you truly are a Child of Mother, like us...
then--
I AM...

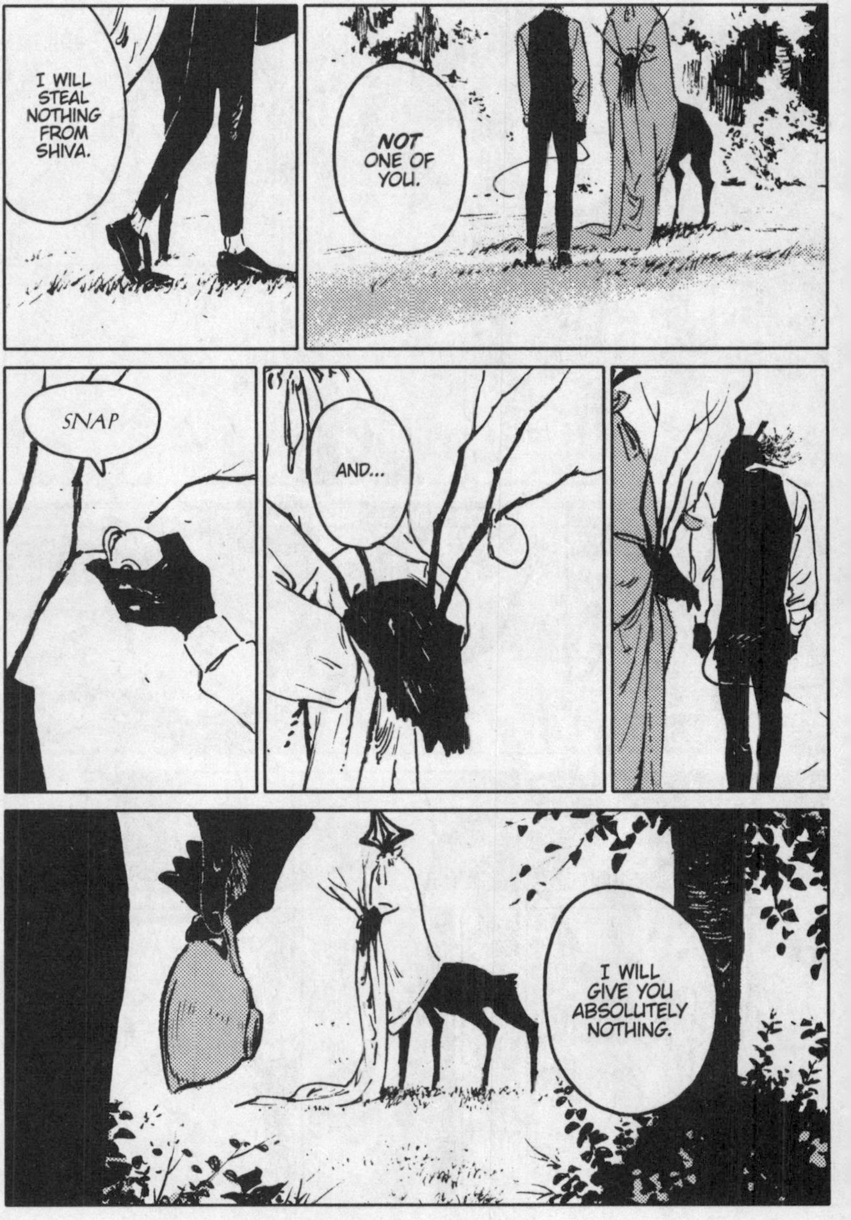
NOT ONE OF YOU.
I WILL STEAL NOTHING FROM SHIVA.
AND...
SNAP
I WILL GIVE YOU ABSOLUTELY NOTHING.

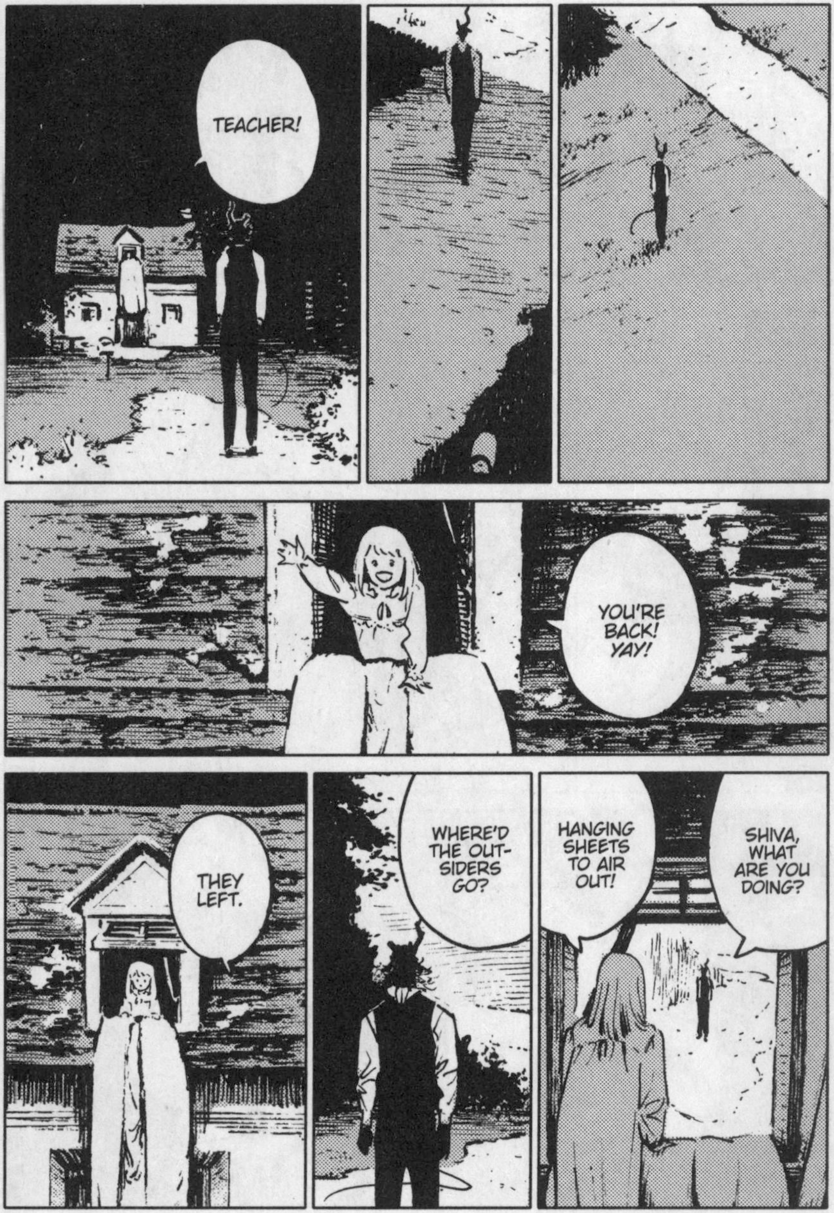
TEACHER!
YOU'RE BACK! YAY!
SHIVA, WHAT ARE YOU DOING?
HANGING SHEETS TO AIR OUT!
WHERE'D THE OUT-SIDERS GO?
THEY LEFT.

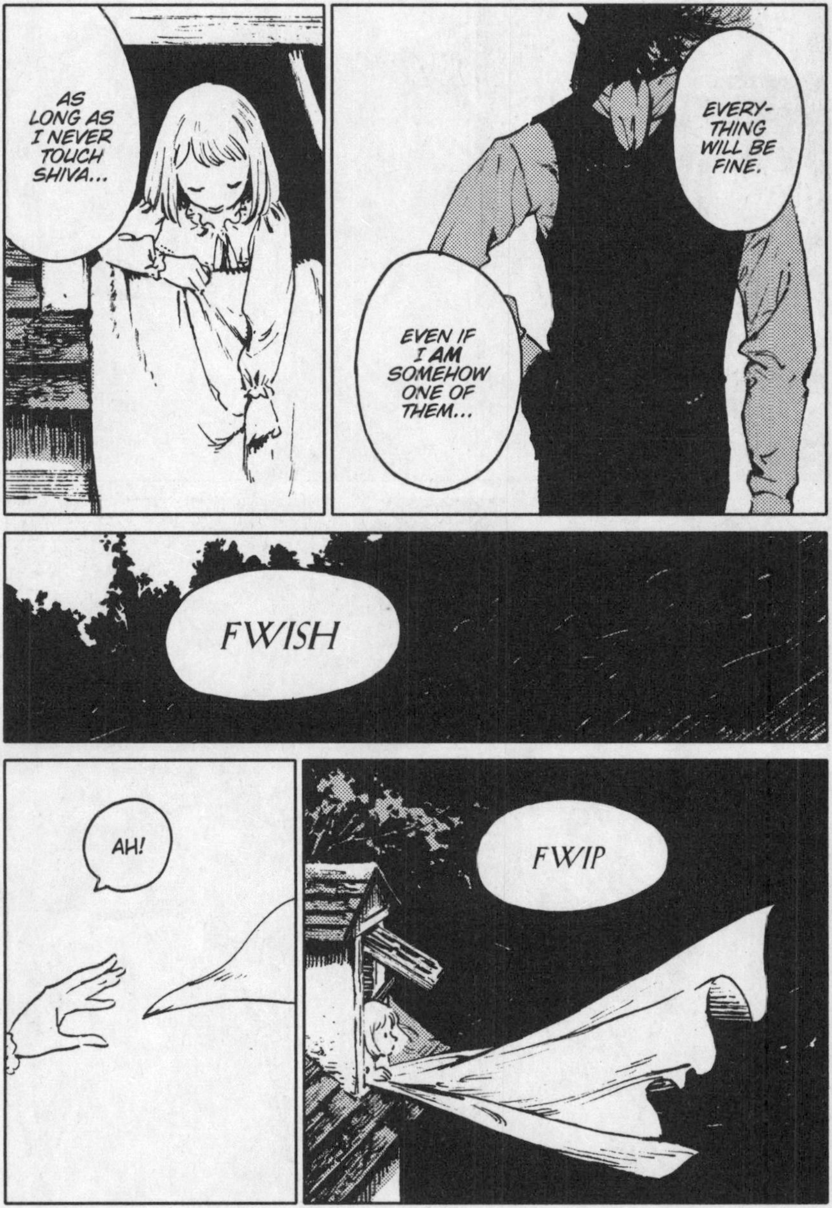
EVERY-THING WILL BE FINE.
EVEN IF I AM SOMEHOW ONE OF THEM...
AS LONG AS I NEVER TOUCH SHIVA...
FWISH
FWIP
AH!

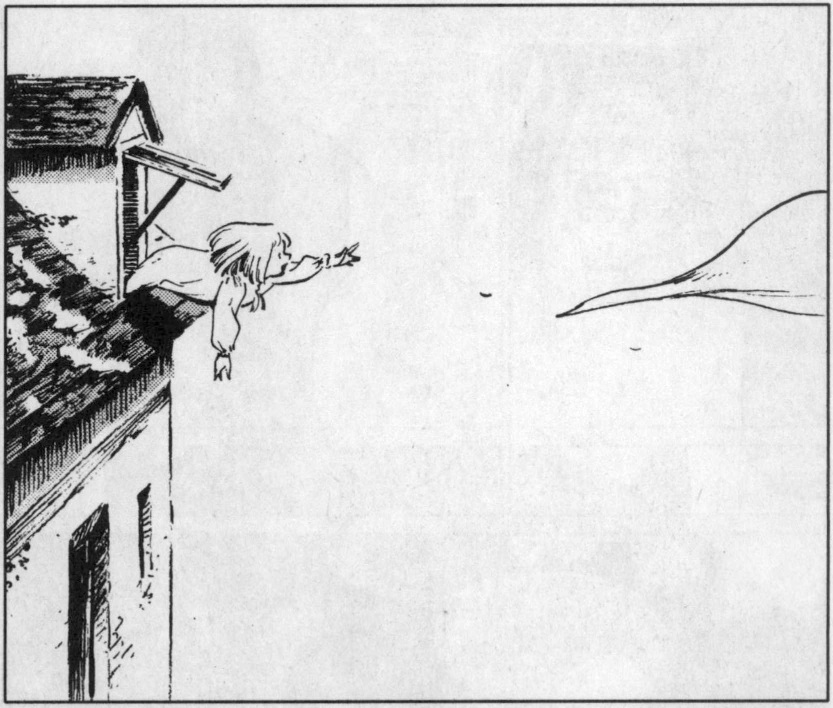
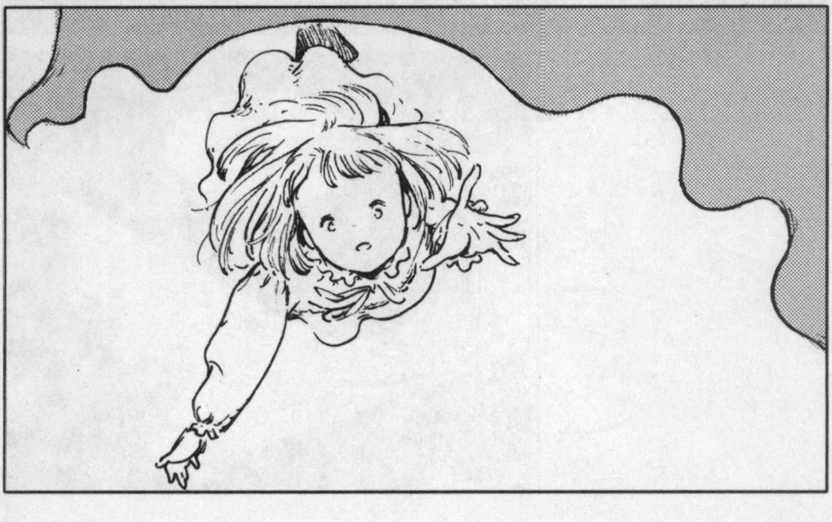

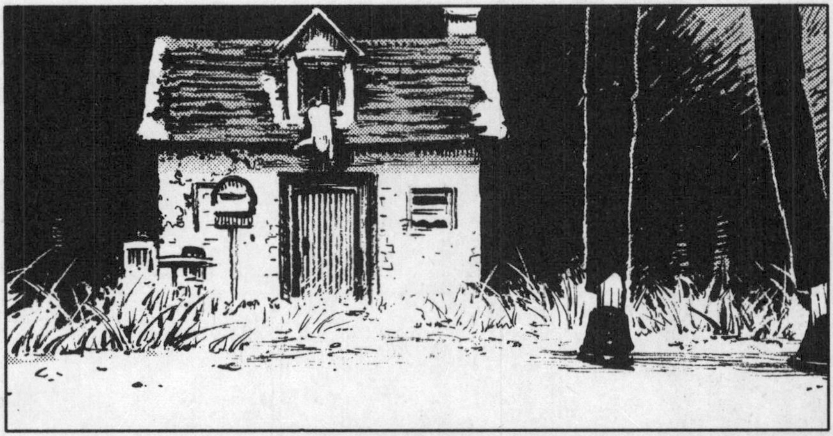

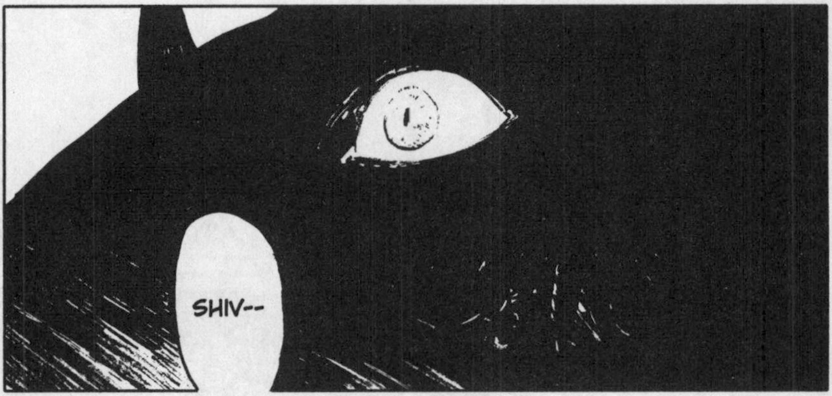
SHIV--

WUMP

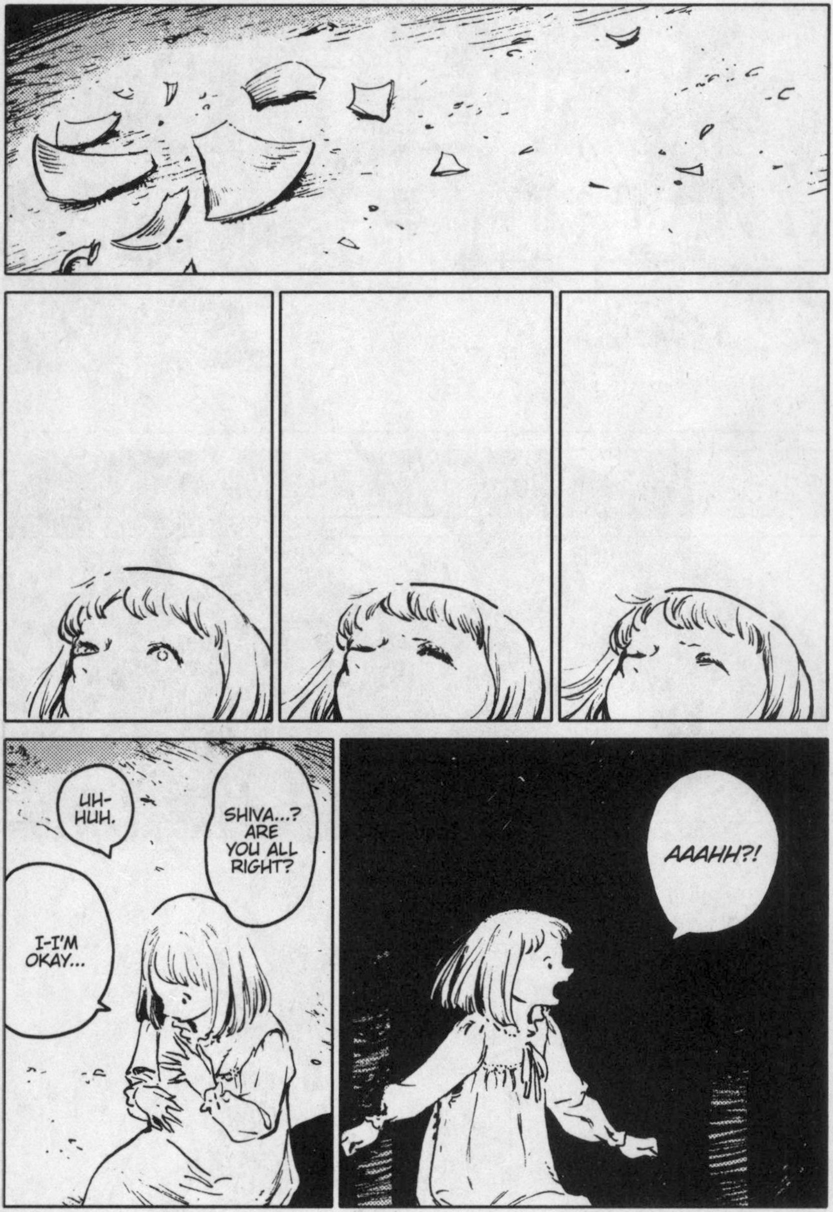
AAAHH?!
SHIVA...? ARE YOU ALL RIGHT?
UH-HUH.
I-I'M OKAY...

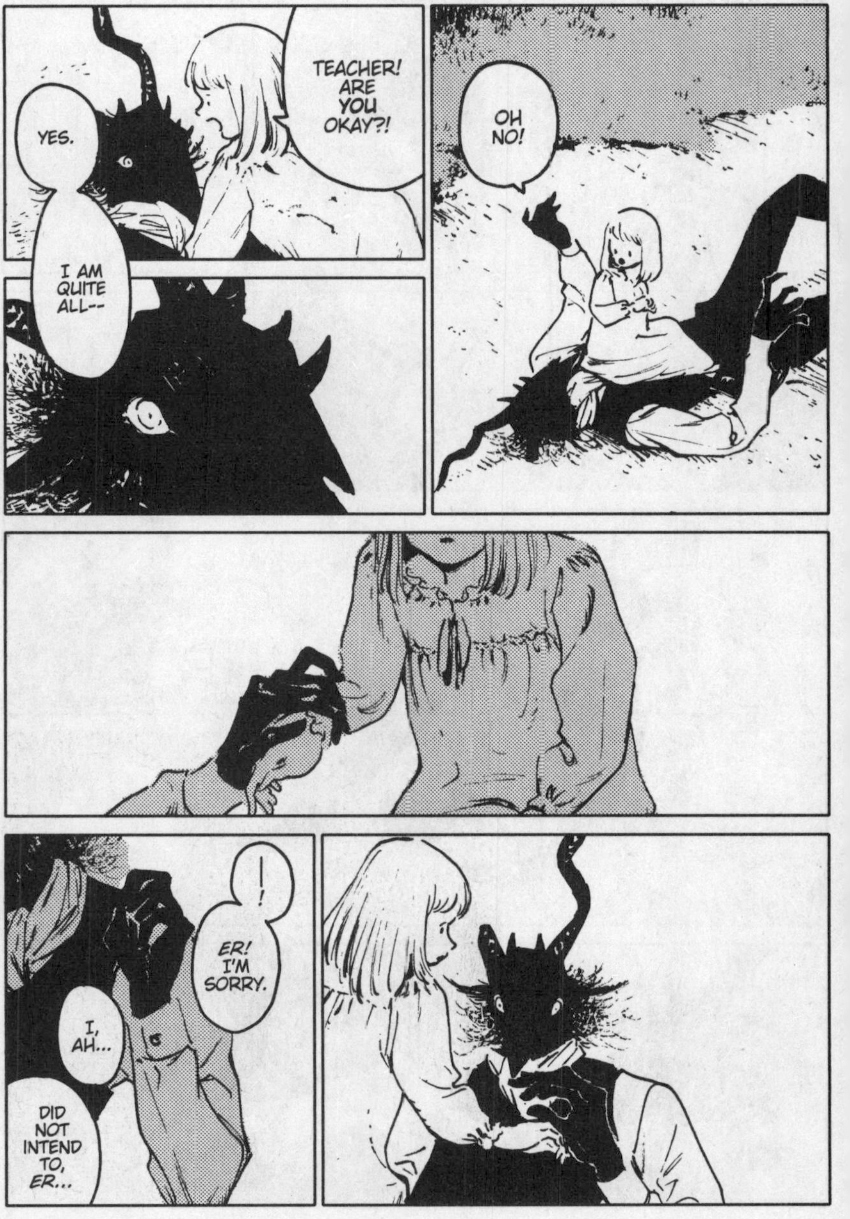
OH NO!
TEACHER! ARE YOU OKAY?!
YES.
I AM QUITE ALL--
!
ER! I'M SORRY.
I, AH...
DID NOT INTEND TO, ER...

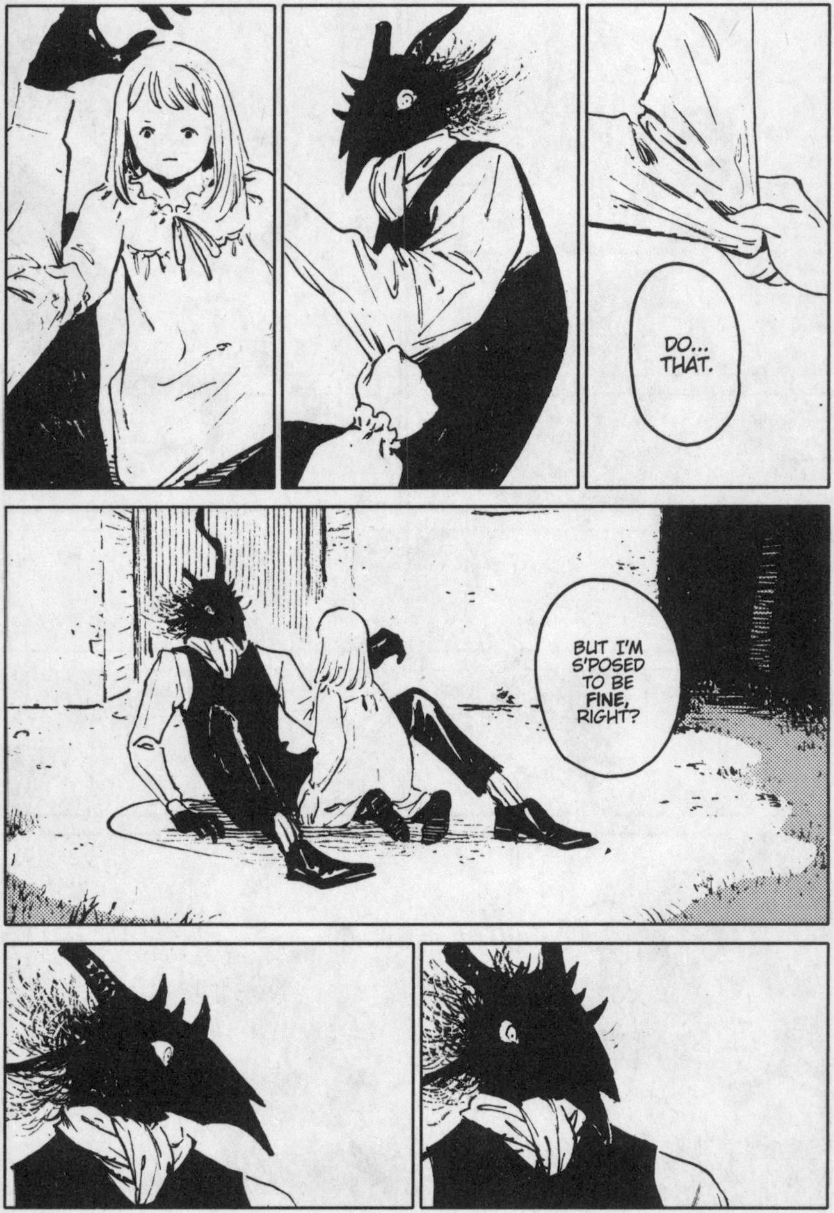
DO... THAT.
BUT I'M S'POSED TO BE FINE, RIGHT?

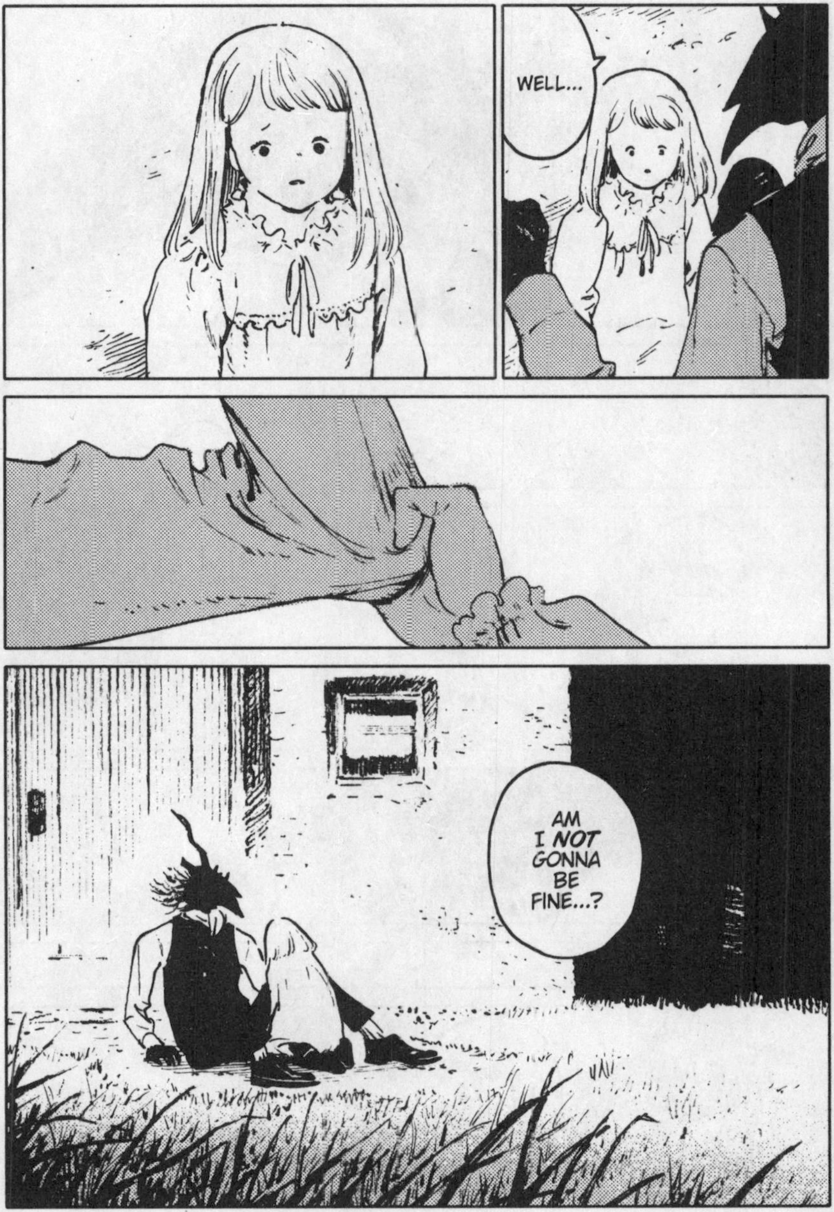
WELL...
AM I *NOT* GONNA BE FINE...?

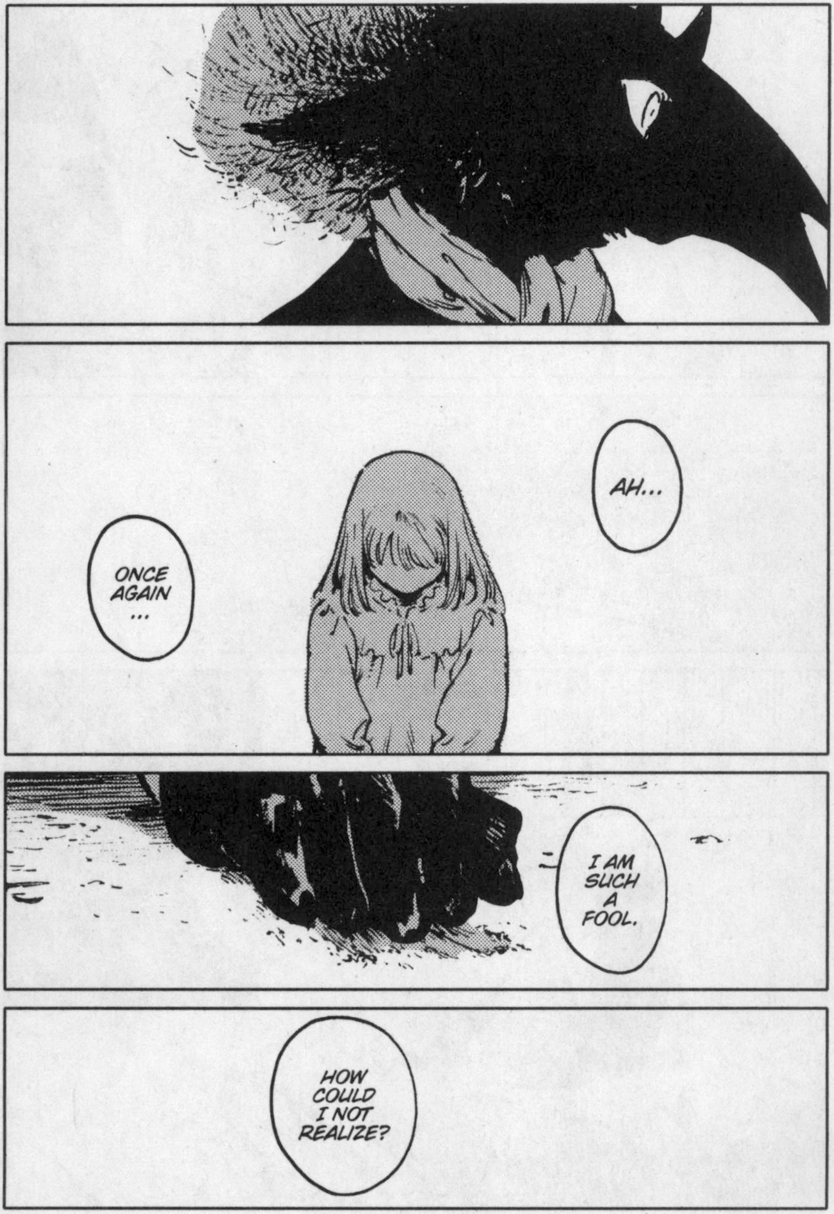
AH...
ONCE AGAIN ...
I AM SUCH A FOOL.
HOW COULD I NOT REALIZE?

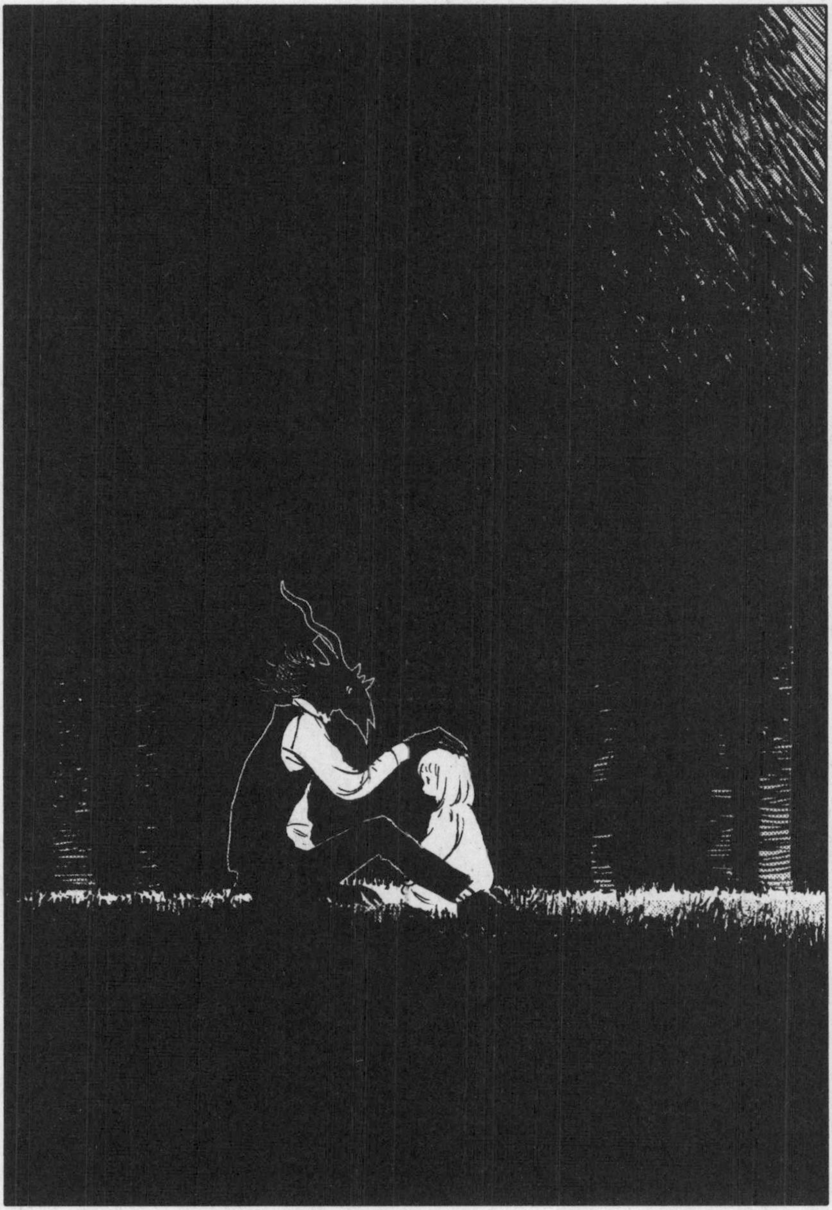

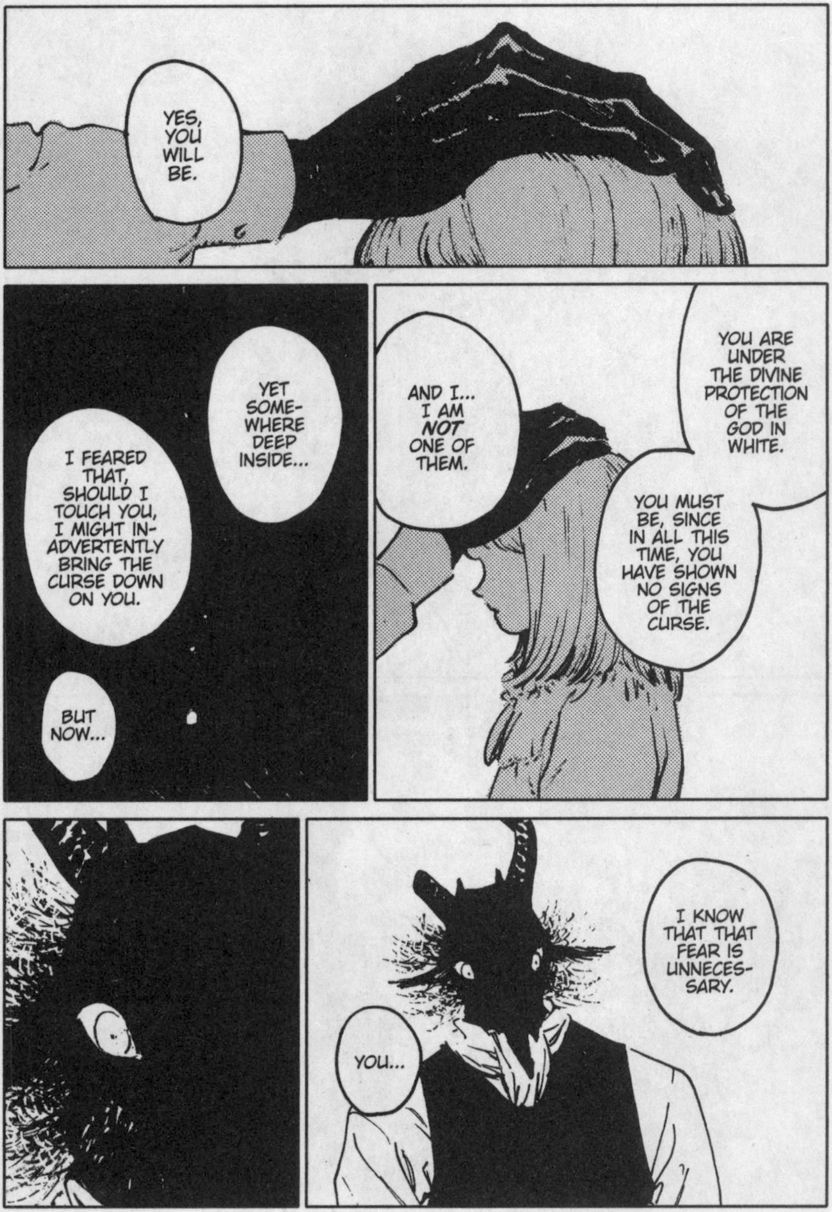
YES, YOU WILL BE.
YOU ARE UNDER THE DIVINE PROTECTION OF THE GOD IN WHITE.
YOU MUST BE, SINCE IN ALL THIS TIME, YOU HAVE SHOWN NO SIGNS OF THE CURSE.
AND I... I AM *NOT* ONE OF THEM.
YET SOMEWHERE DEEP INSIDE...
I FEARED THAT, SHOULD I TOUCH YOU, I MIGHT INADVERTENTLY BRING THE CURSE DOWN ON YOU.
BUT NOW...
I KNOW THAT THAT FEAR IS UNNECESSARY.
YOU...

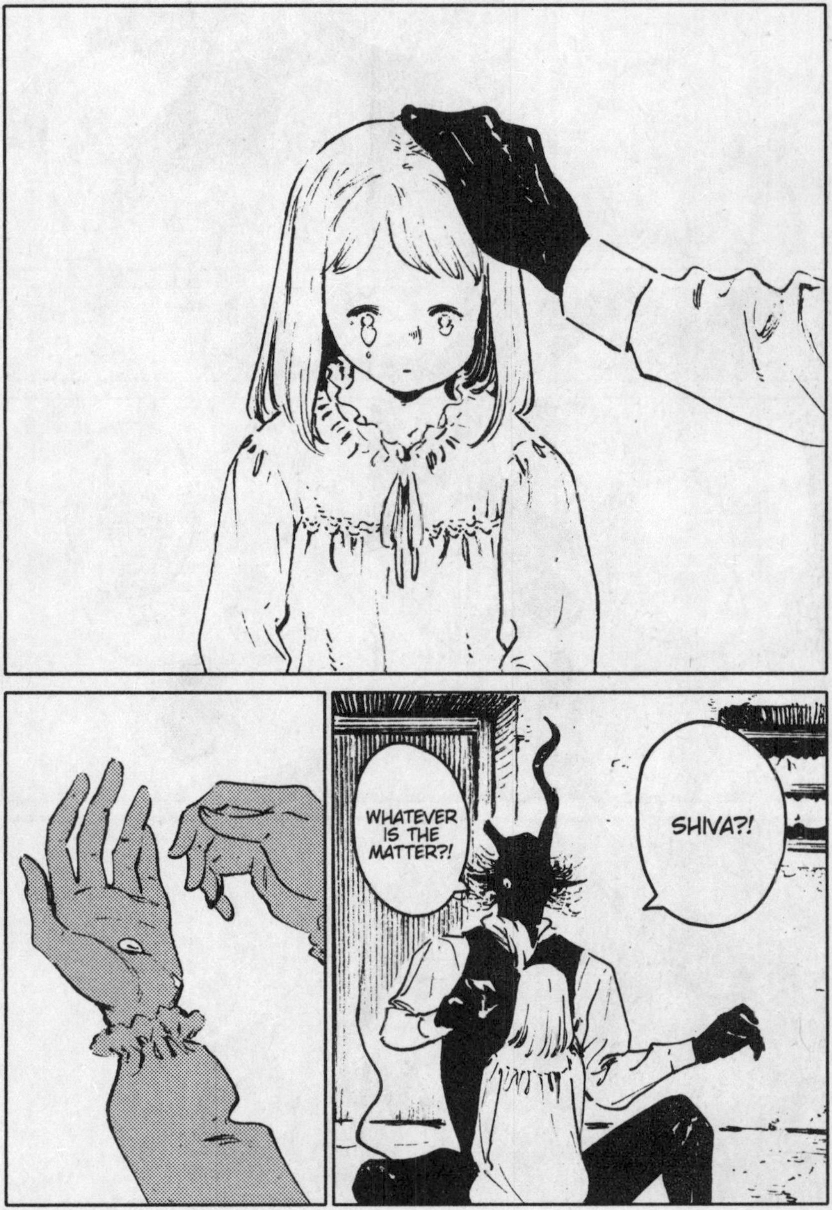
SHIVA?!
WHATEVER IS THE MATTER?!

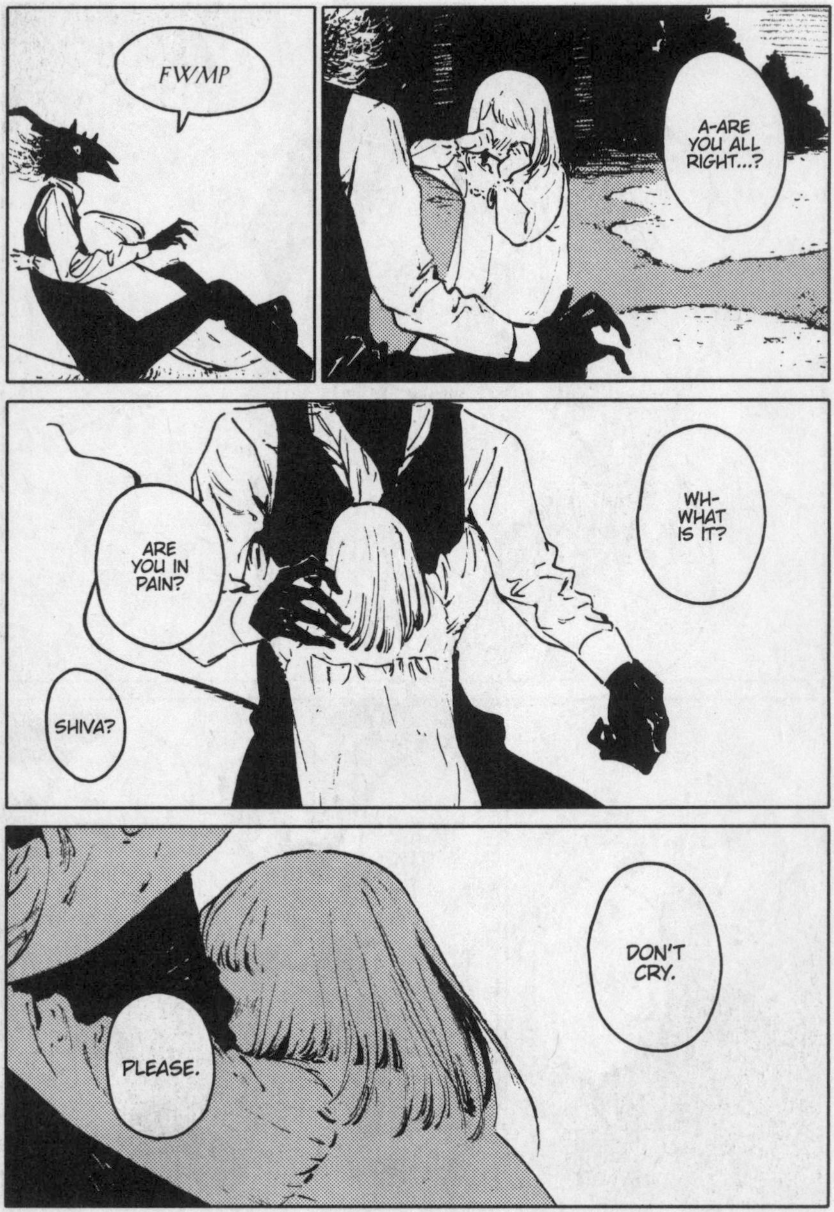
A-ARE YOU ALL RIGHT...?
FWMP
WH- WHAT IS IT?
ARE YOU IN PAIN?
SHIVA?
DON'T CRY.
PLEASE.

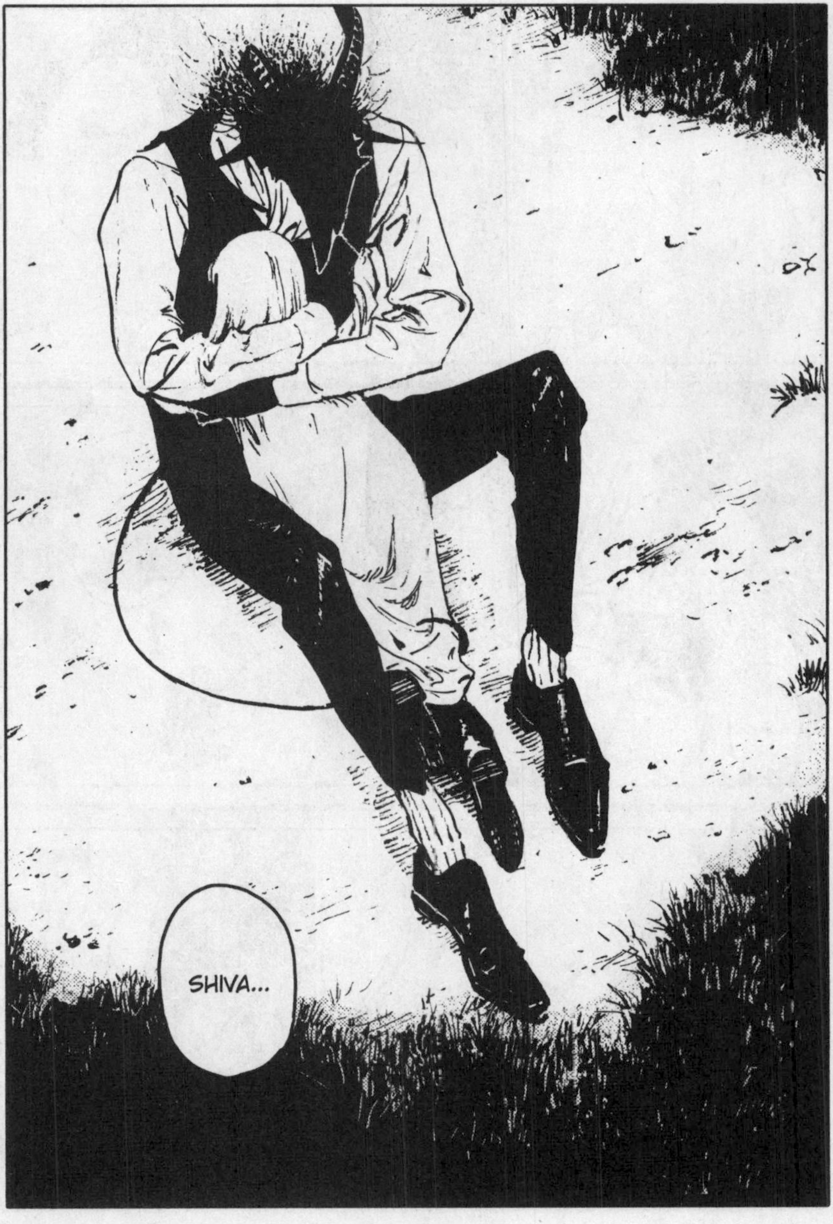
SHIVA...

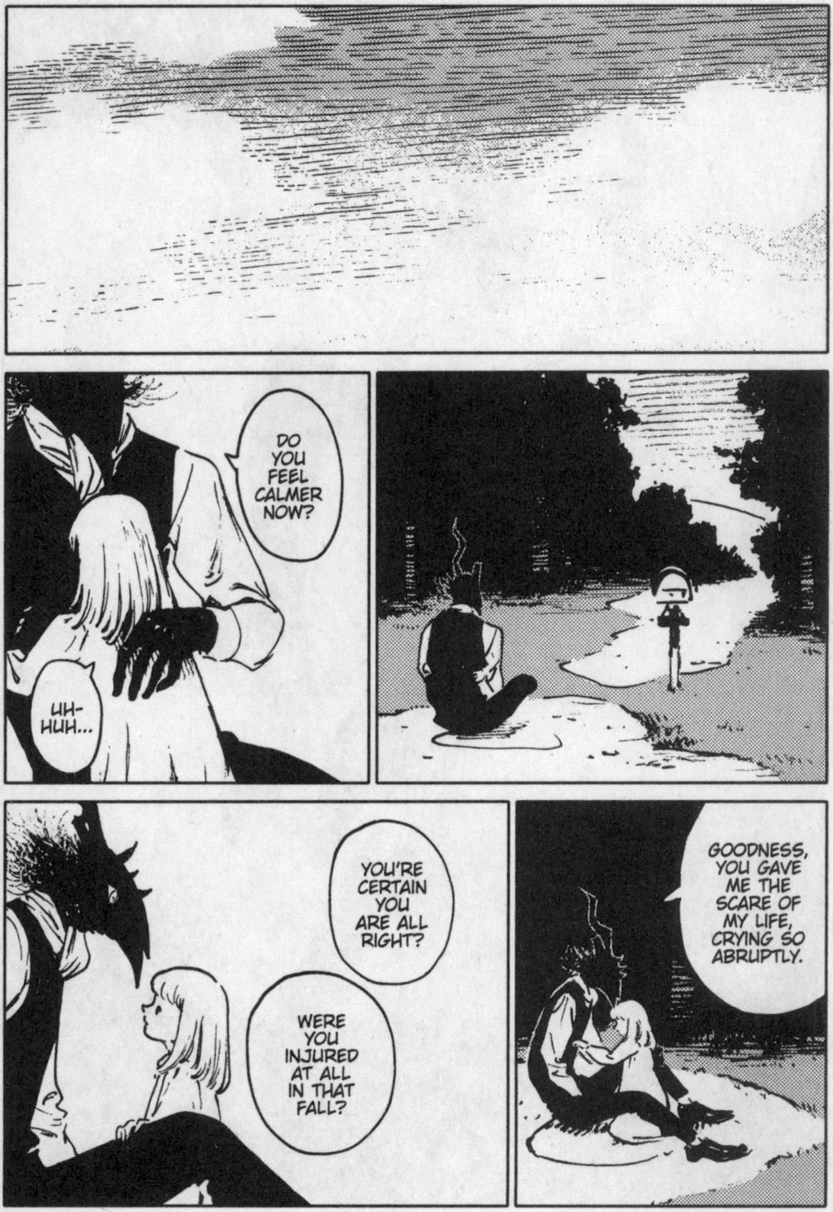
DO YOU FEEL CALMER NOW?
UH-HUH...
GOODNESS, YOU GAVE ME THE SCARE OF MY LIFE, CRYING SO ABRUPTLY.
YOU'RE CERTAIN YOU ARE ALL RIGHT?
WERE YOU INJURED AT ALL IN THAT FALL?

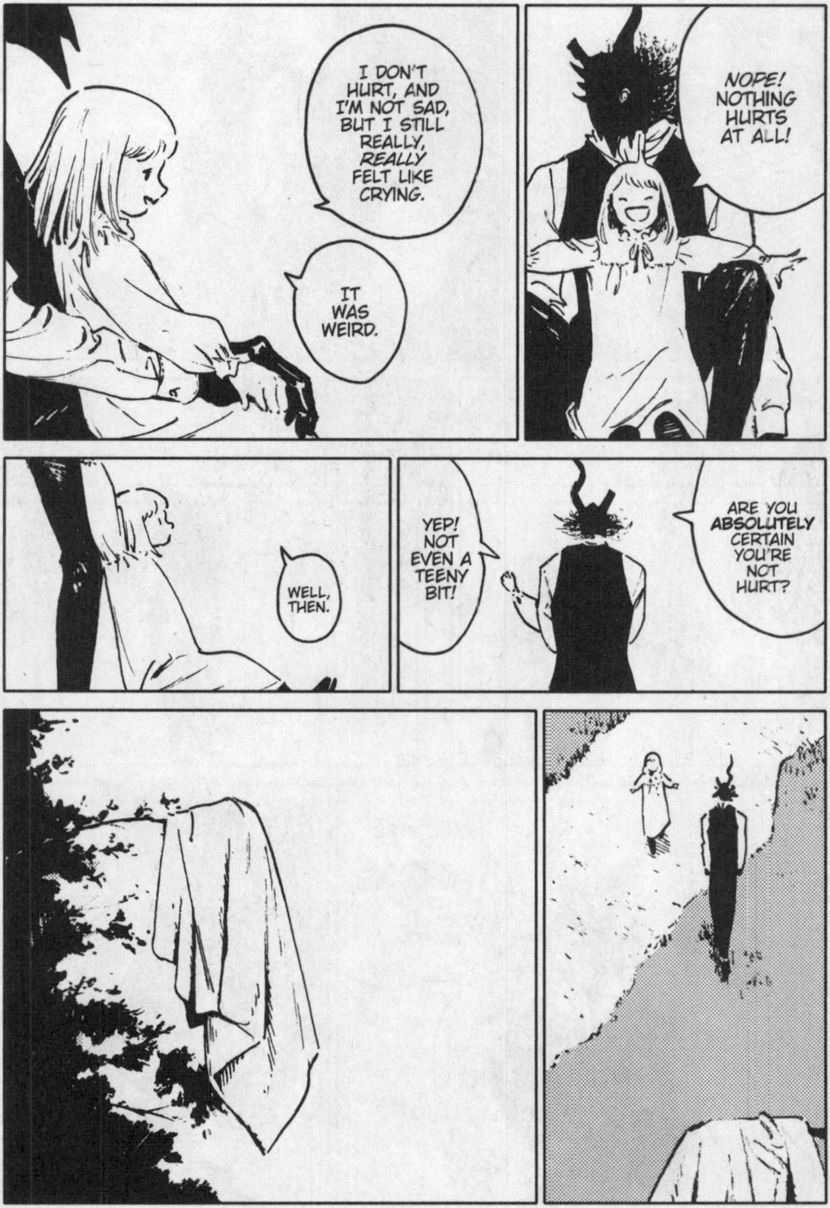
NOPE! NOTHING HURTS AT ALL!
I DON'T HURT, AND I'M NOT SAD, BUT I STILL REALLY, REALLY FELT LIKE CRYING.
IT WAS WEIRD.
ARE YOU ABSOLUTELY CERTAIN YOU'RE NOT HURT?
YEP! NOT EVEN A TEENY BIT!
WELL, THEN.

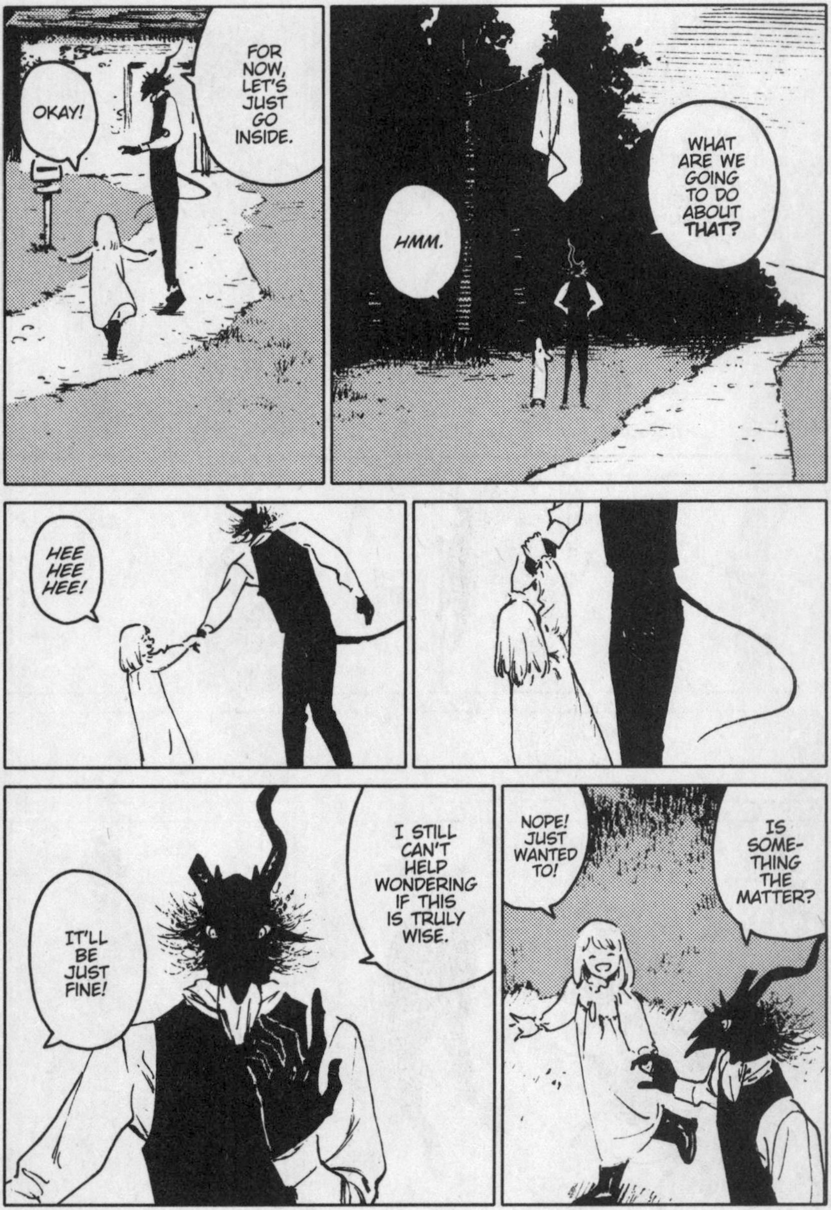
WHAT ARE WE GOING TO DO ABOUT THAT?
HMM.
FOR NOW, LET'S JUST GO INSIDE.
OKAY!
HEE HEE HEE!
IS SOME-THING THE MATTER?
NOPE! JUST WANTED TO!
I STILL CAN'T HELP WONDERING IF THIS IS TRULY WISE.
IT'LL BE JUST FINE!

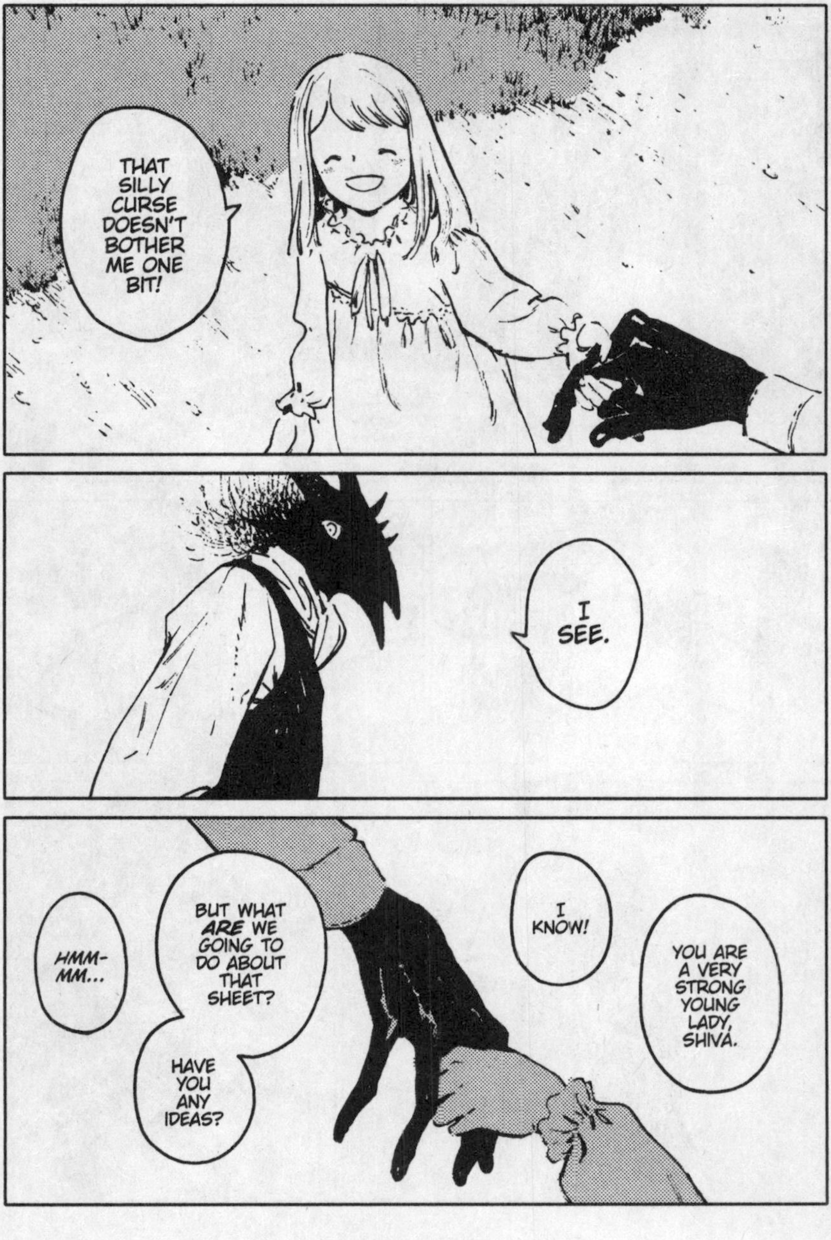
THAT SILLY CURSE DOESN'T BOTHER ME ONE BIT!
I SEE.
YOU ARE A VERY STRONG YOUNG LADY, SHIVA.
I KNOW!
BUT WHAT *ARE* WE GOING TO DO ABOUT THAT SHEET?
HAVE YOU ANY IDEAS?
HMM-MM...

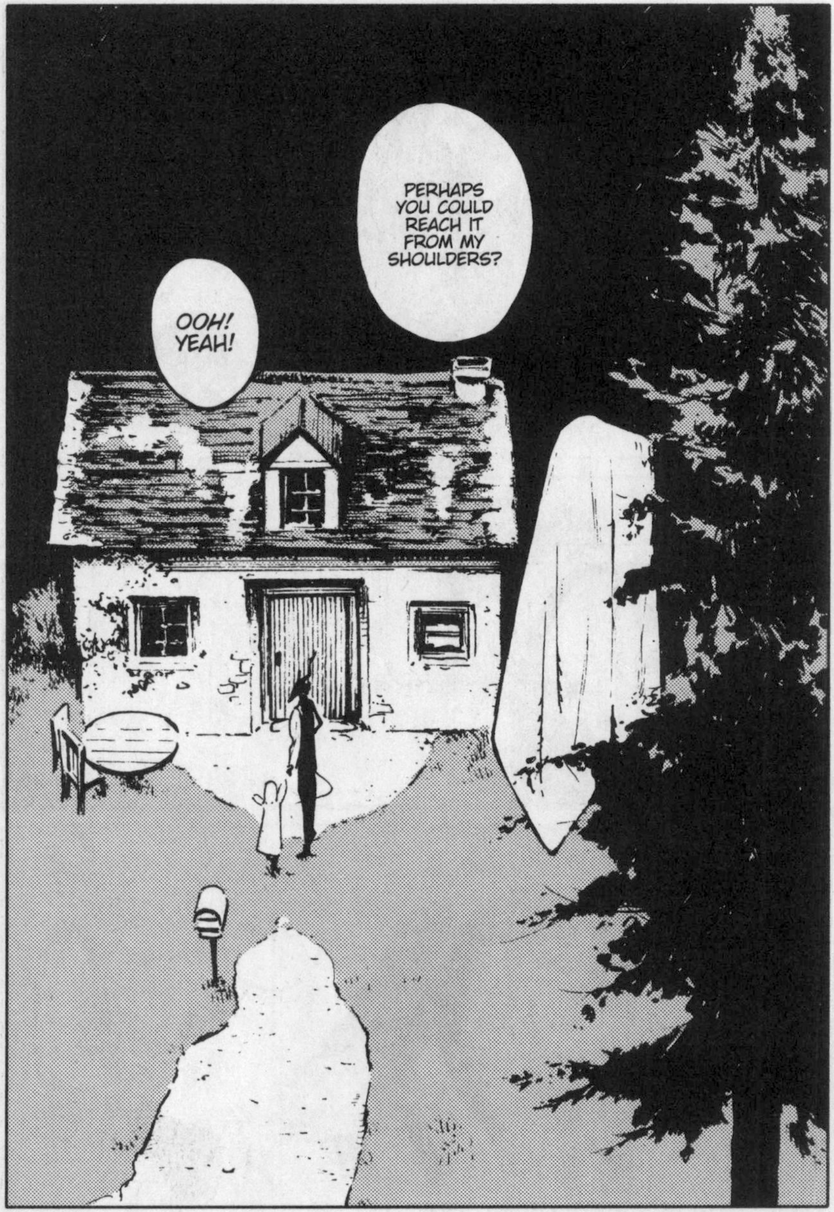
PERHAPS YOU COULD REACH IT FROM MY SHOULDERS?
OOH! YEAH!

Chapter 30

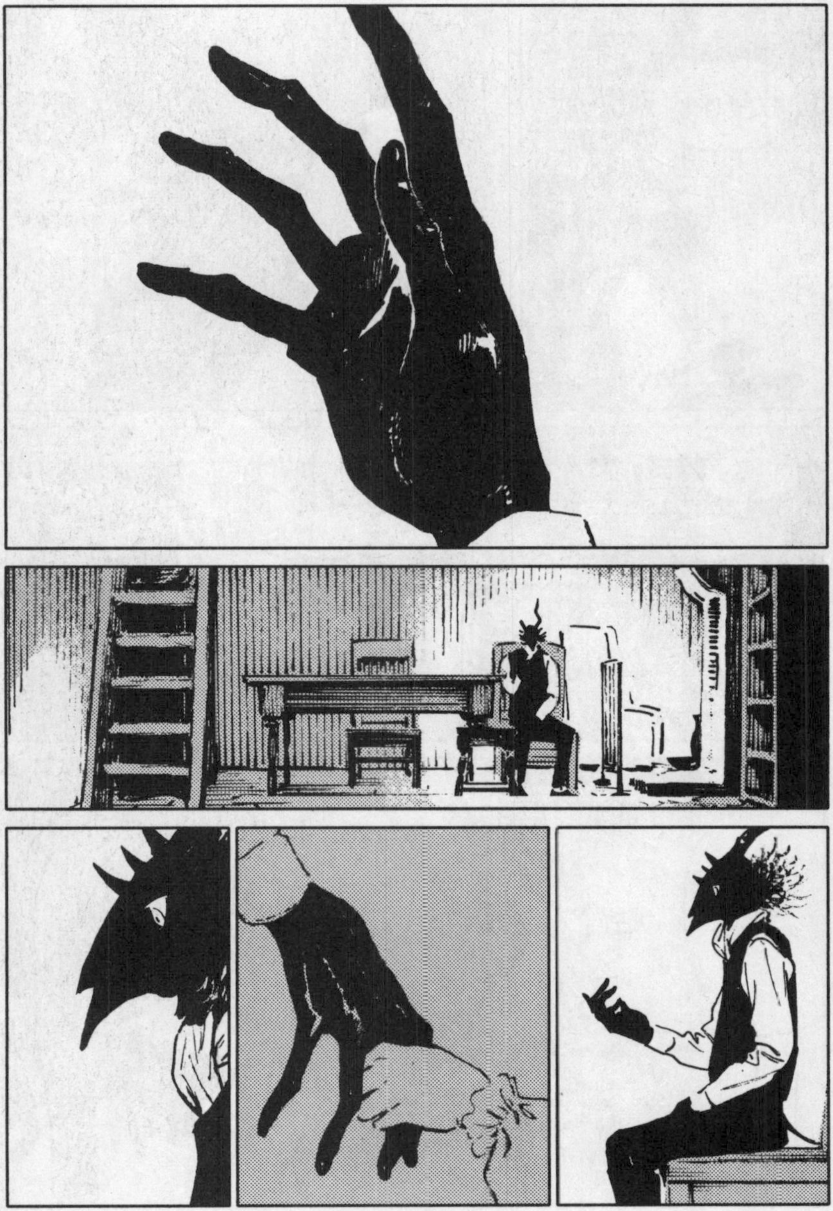

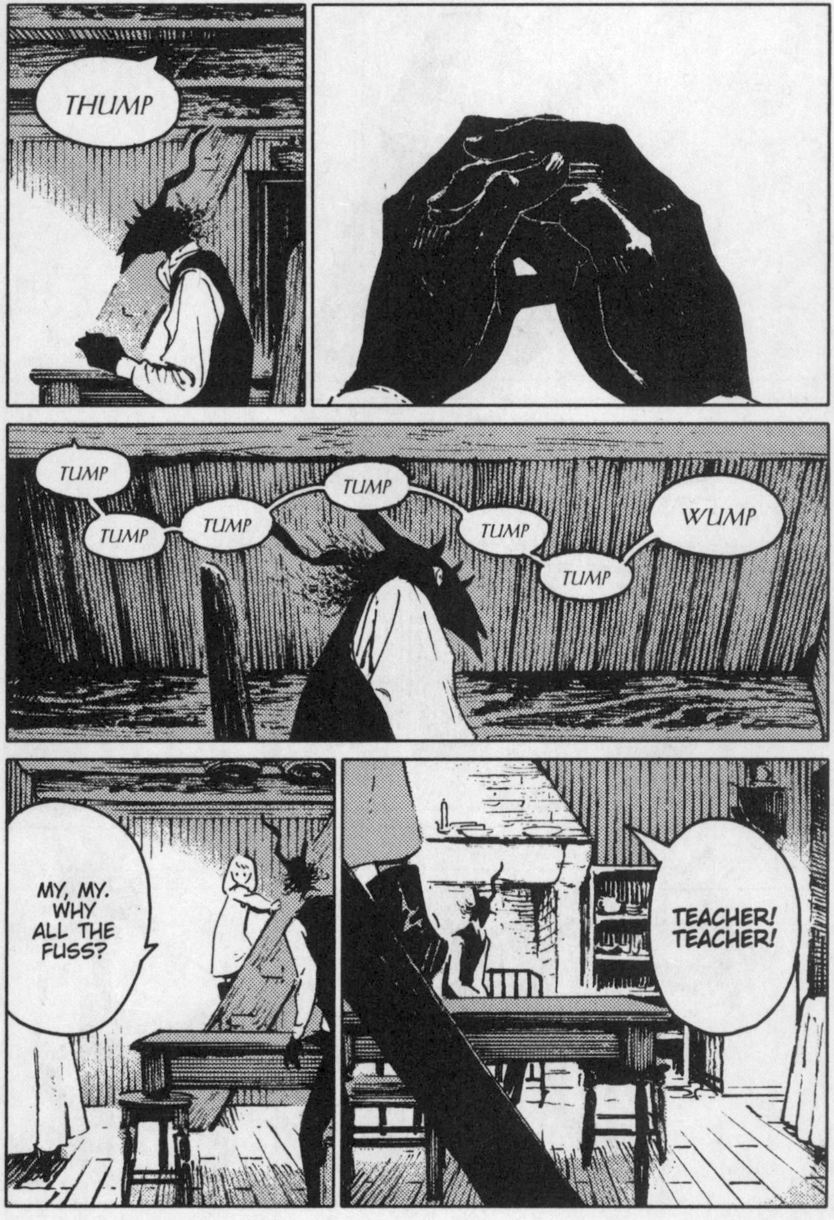
THUMP
TUMP
TUMP
TUMP
TUMP
TUMP
TUMP
WUMP
TEACHER! TEACHER!
MY, MY. WHY ALL THE FUSS?

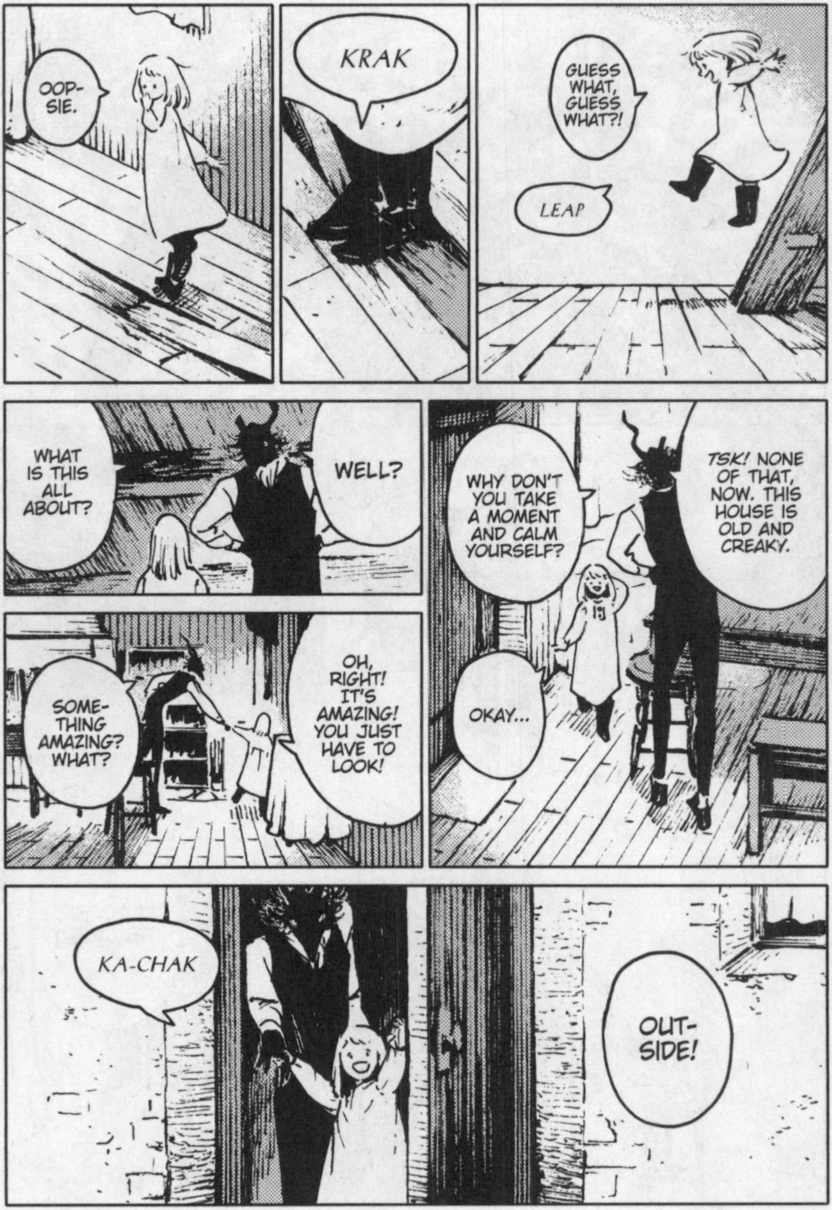
GUESS WHAT, GUESS WHAT?!
LEAP
KRAK
OOP-SIE.
TSK! NONE OF THAT, NOW. THIS HOUSE IS OLD AND CREAKY.
WHY DON'T YOU TAKE A MOMENT AND CALM YOURSELF?
OKAY...
WELL?
WHAT IS THIS ALL ABOUT?
OH, RIGHT! IT'S AMAZING! YOU JUST HAVE TO LOOK!
SOME-THING AMAZING? WHAT?
OUT-SIDE!
KA-CHAK

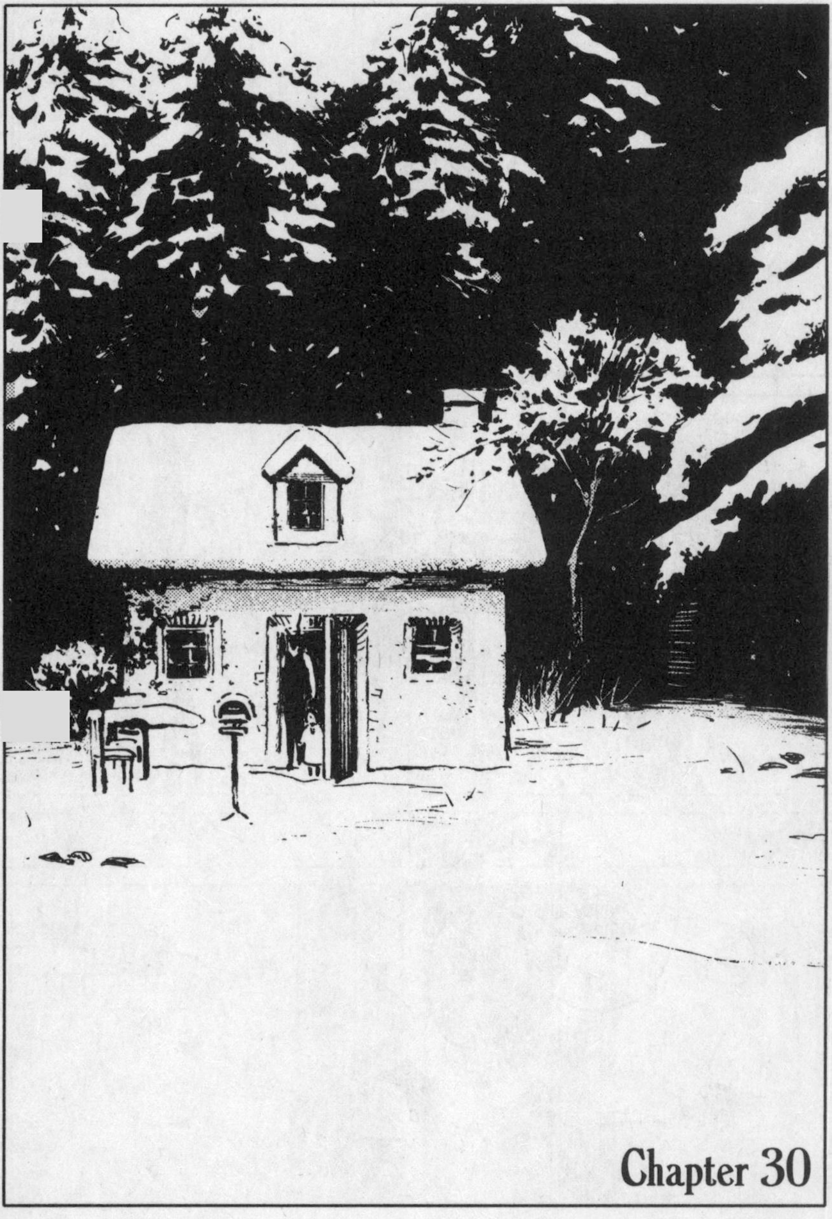

Chapter 30

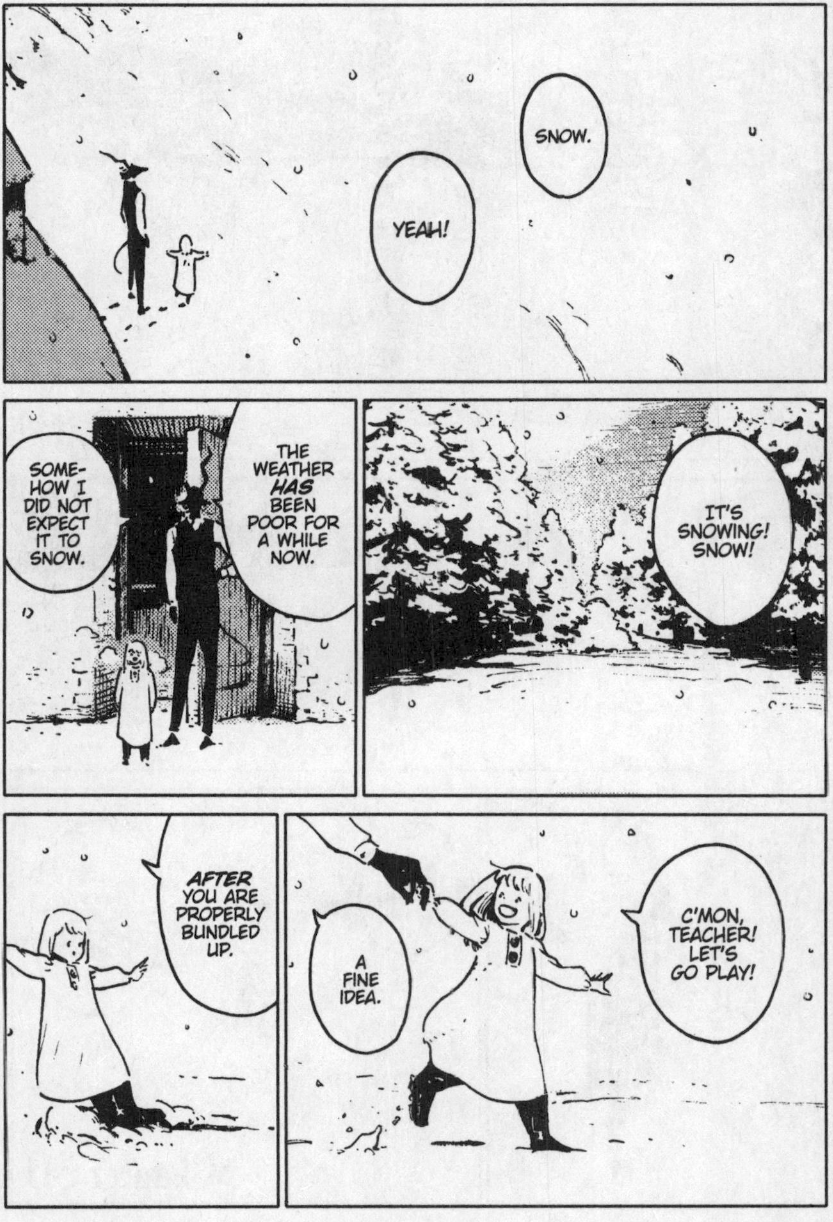
SNOW.
YEAH!
IT'S SNOWING! SNOW!
THE WEATHER *HAS* BEEN POOR FOR A WHILE NOW.
SOMEHOW I DID NOT EXPECT IT TO SNOW.
C'MON, TEACHER! LET'S GO PLAY!
A FINE IDEA.
AFTER YOU ARE PROPERLY BUNDLED UP.

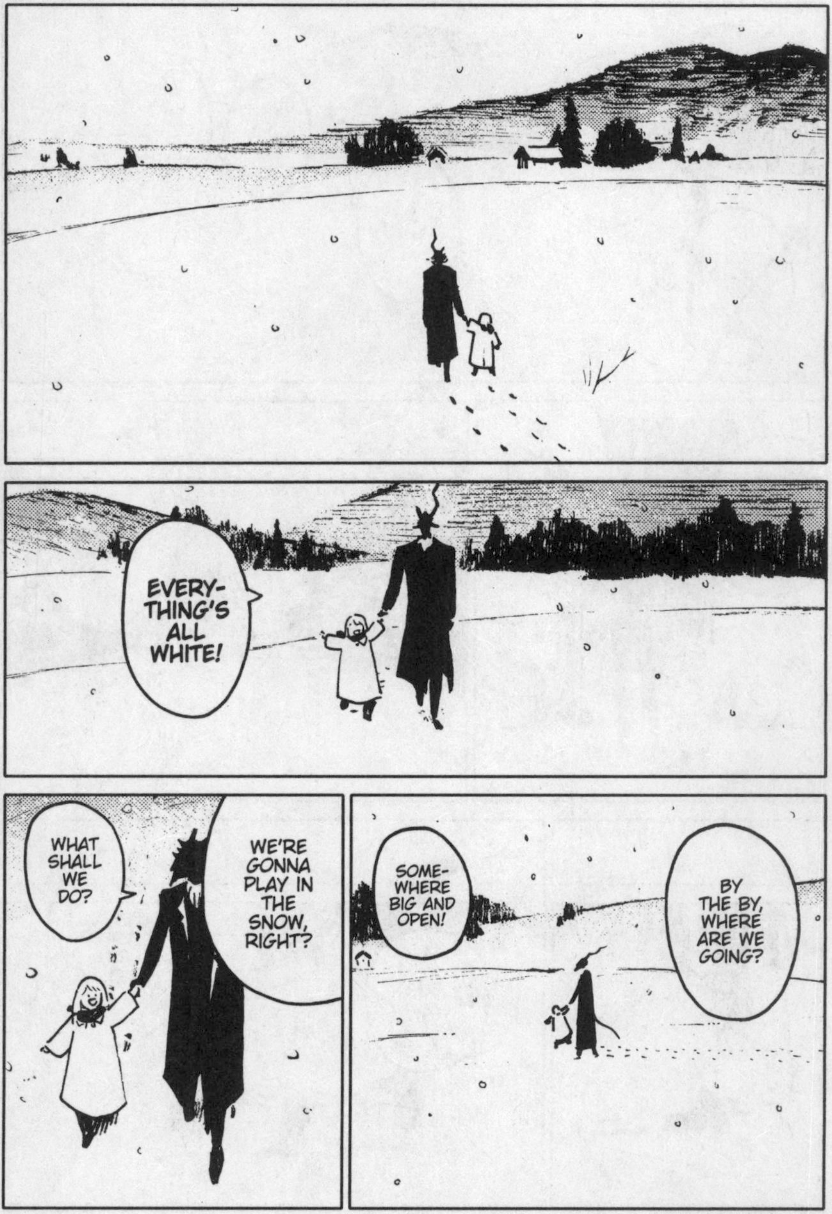
EVERY-THING'S ALL WHITE!
BY THE BY, WHERE ARE WE GOING?
SOME-WHERE BIG AND OPEN!
WE'RE GONNA PLAY IN THE SNOW, RIGHT?
WHAT SHALL WE DO?

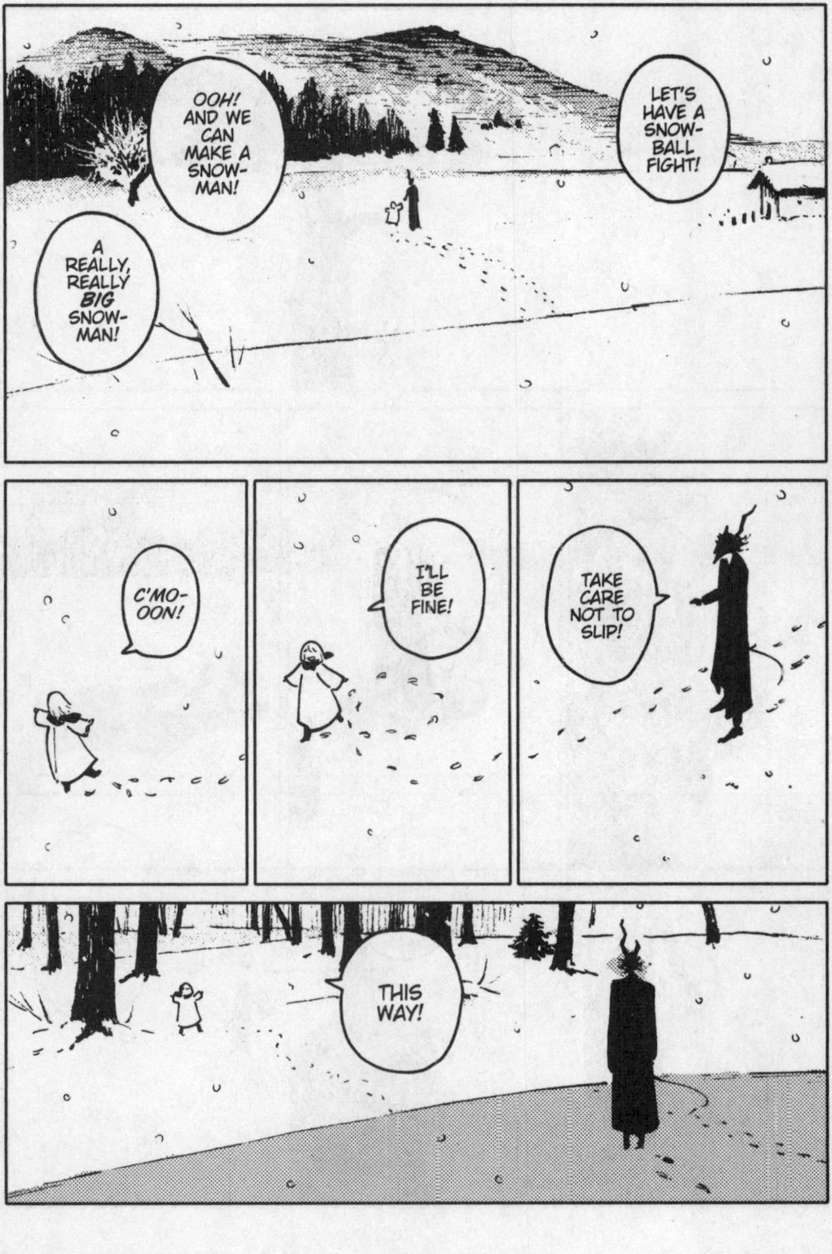
LET'S HAVE A SNOW-BALL FIGHT!
OOH! AND WE CAN MAKE A SNOW-MAN!
A REALLY, REALLY BIG SNOW-MAN!
TAKE CARE NOT TO SLIP!
I'LL BE FINE!
C'MO-OON!
THIS WAY!

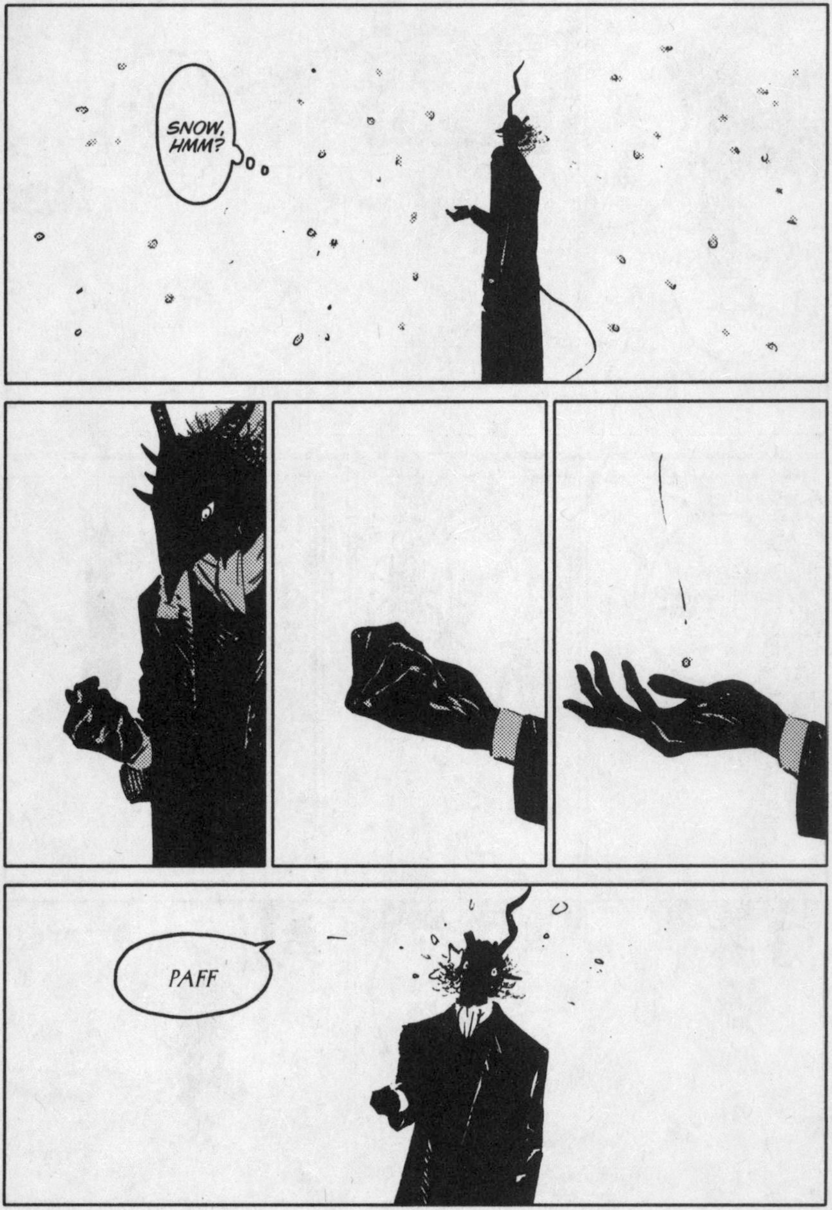
SNOW, HMM?
PAFF

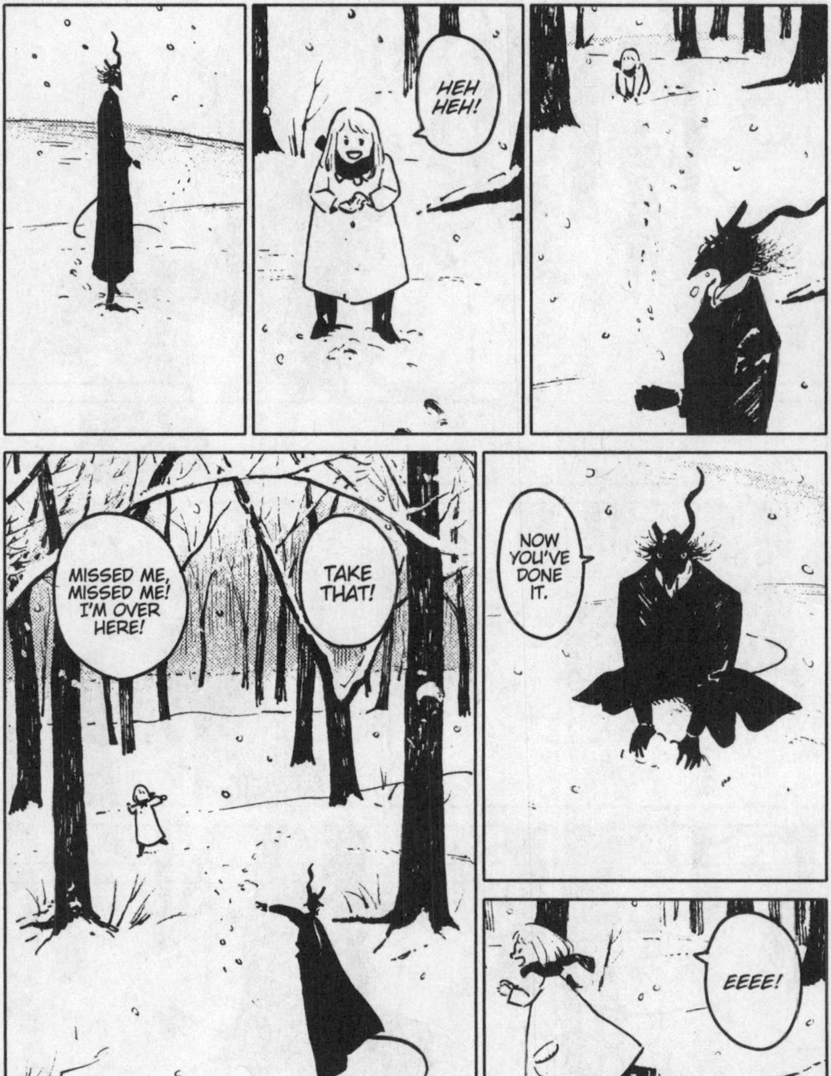
HEH HEH!
MISSED ME, MISSED ME! I'M OVER HERE!
TAKE THAT!
NOW YOU'VE DONE IT.
EEEE!

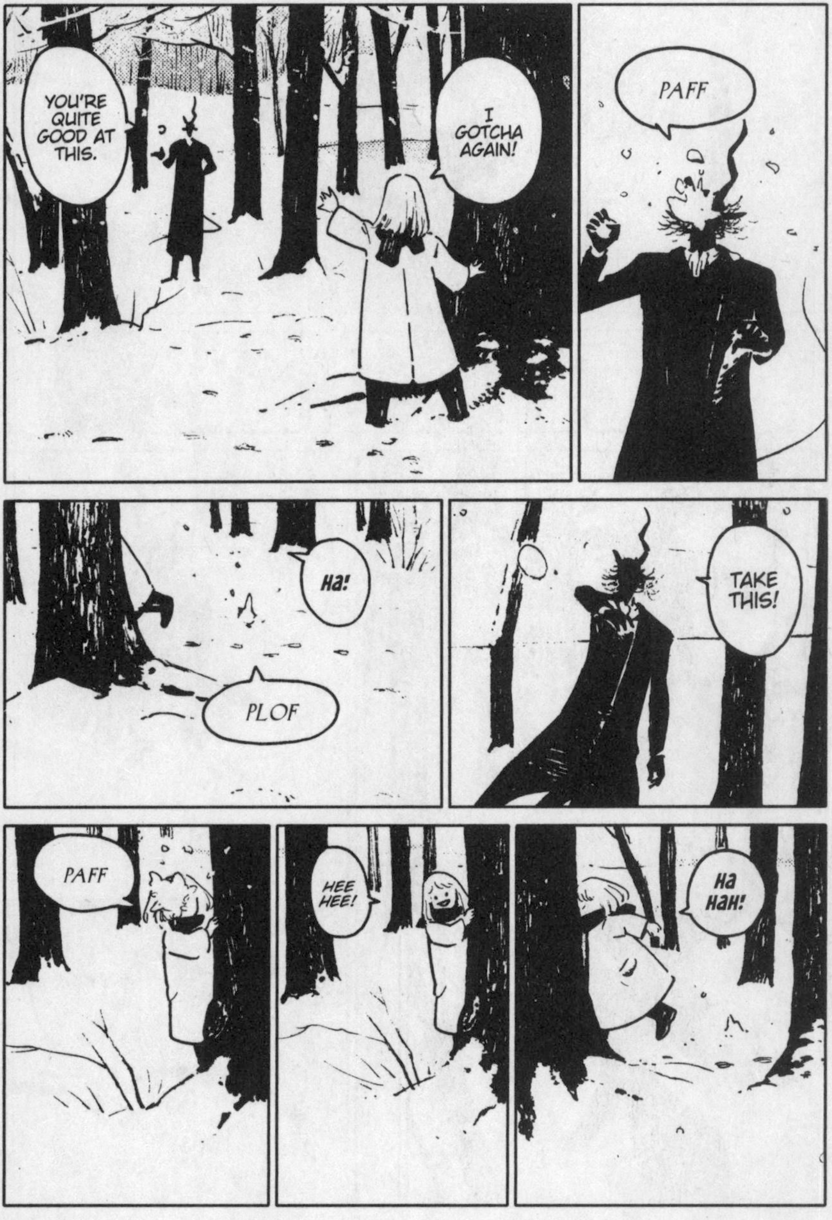
PAFF
I GOTCHA AGAIN!
YOU'RE QUITE GOOD AT THIS.
TAKE THIS!
HA!
PLOF
HA HAH!
HEE HEE!
PAFF

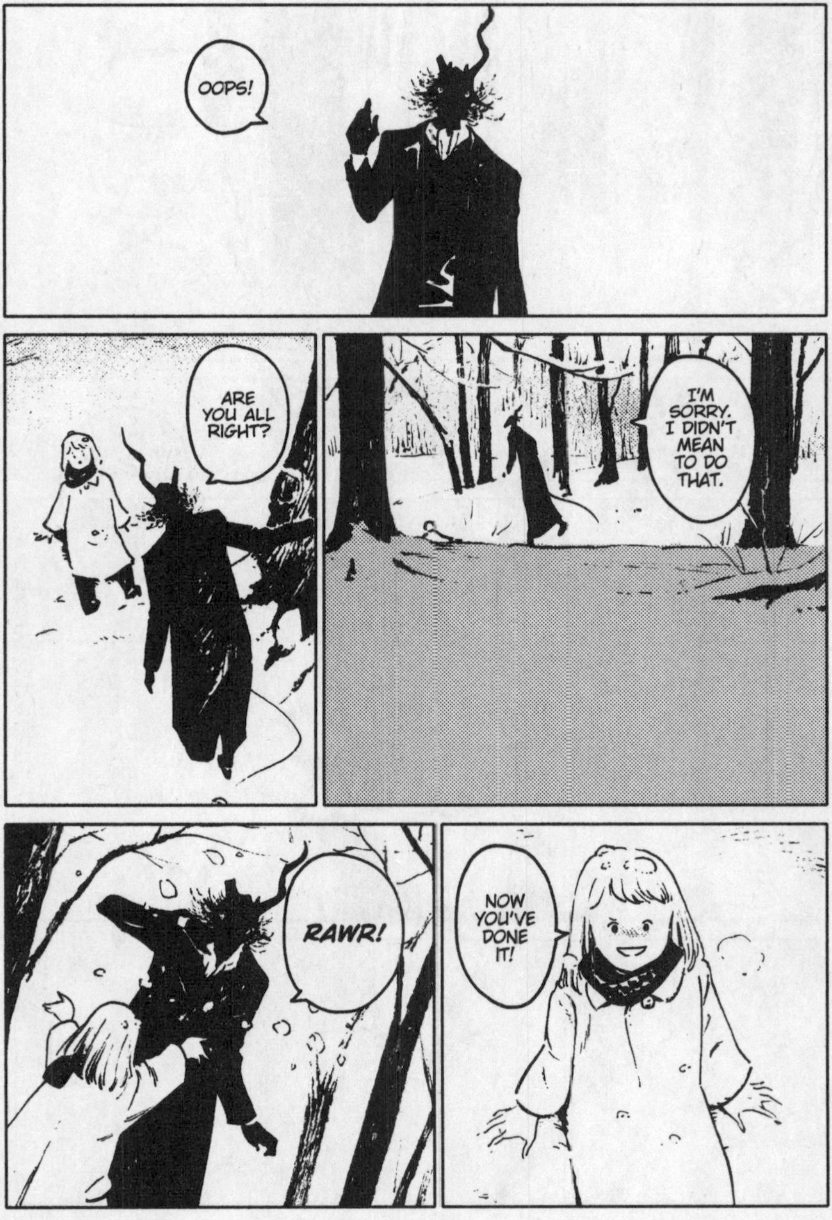
OOPS!
I'M SORRY. I DIDN'T MEAN TO DO THAT.
ARE YOU ALL RIGHT?
NOW YOU'VE DONE IT!
RAWR!

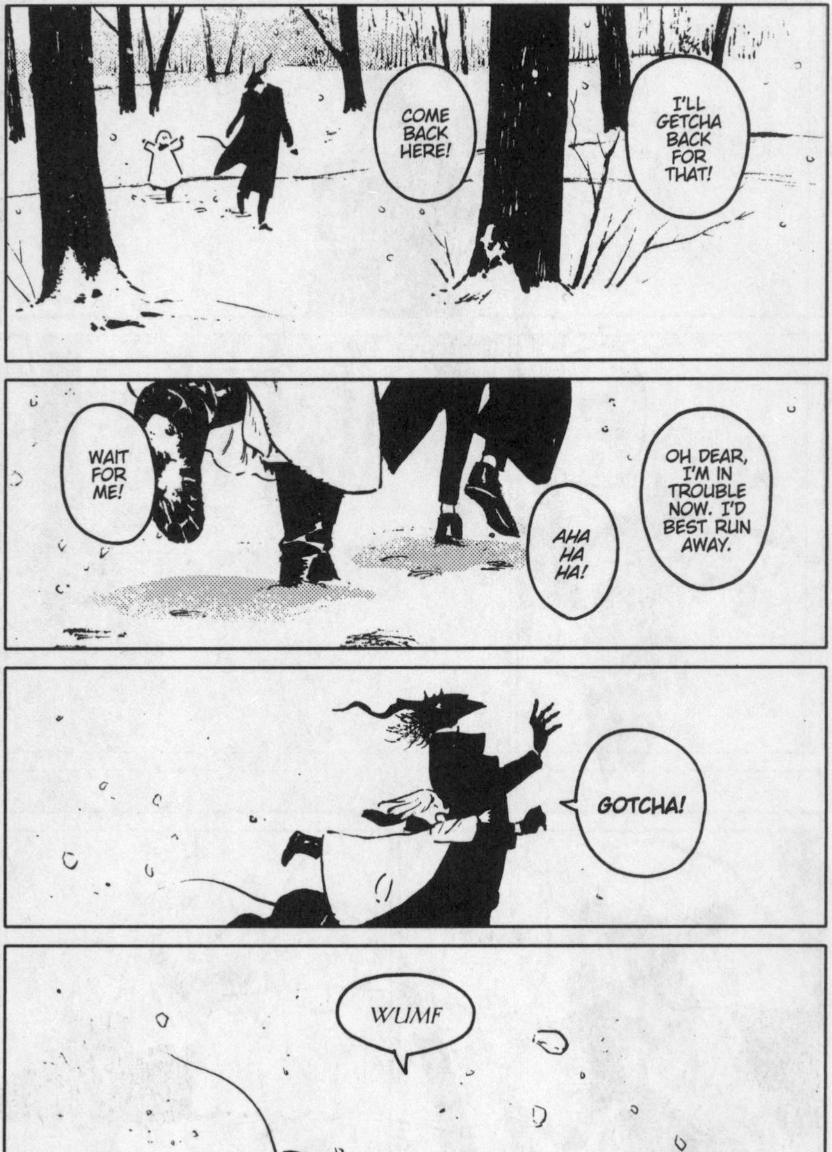
I'LL GETCHA BACK FOR THAT!
COME BACK HERE!
OH DEAR, I'M IN TROUBLE NOW. I'D BEST RUN AWAY.
AHA HA HA!
WAIT FOR ME!
GOTCHA!
WUMF

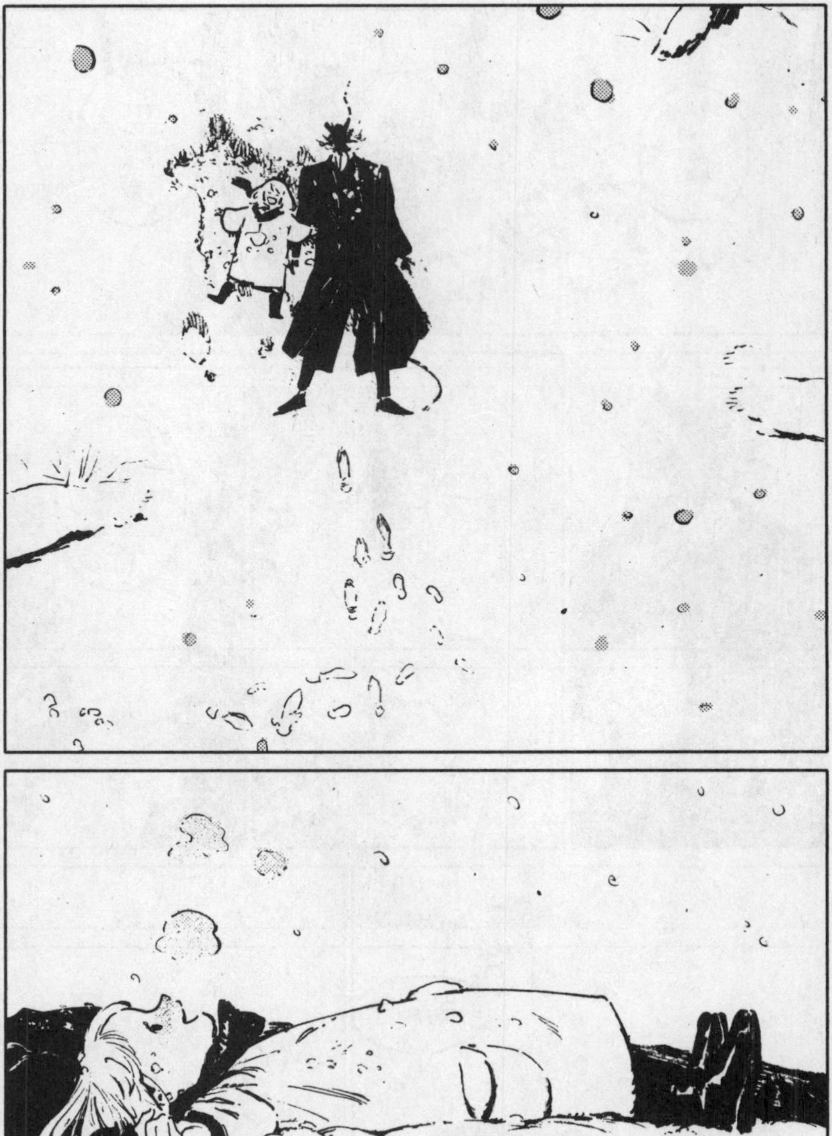

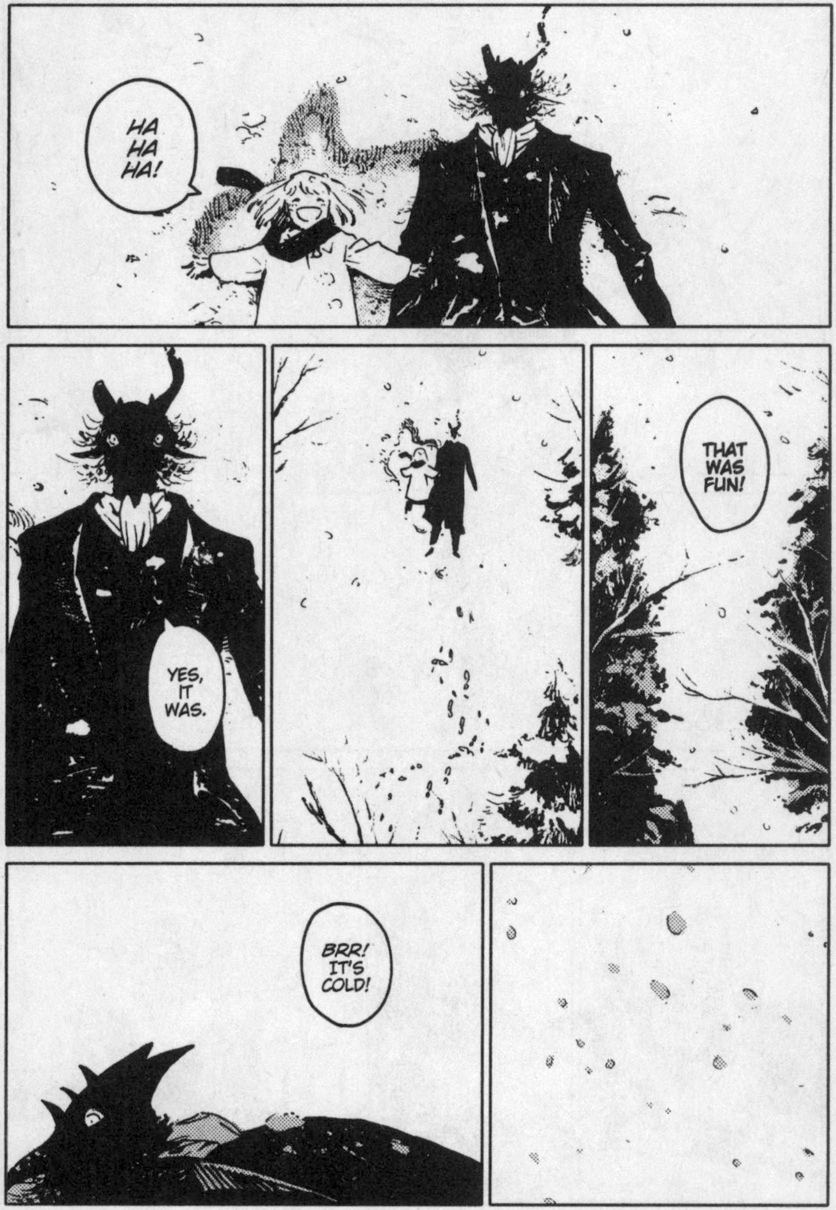
HA HA HA!
THAT WAS FUN!
YES, IT WAS.
BRR! IT'S COLD!

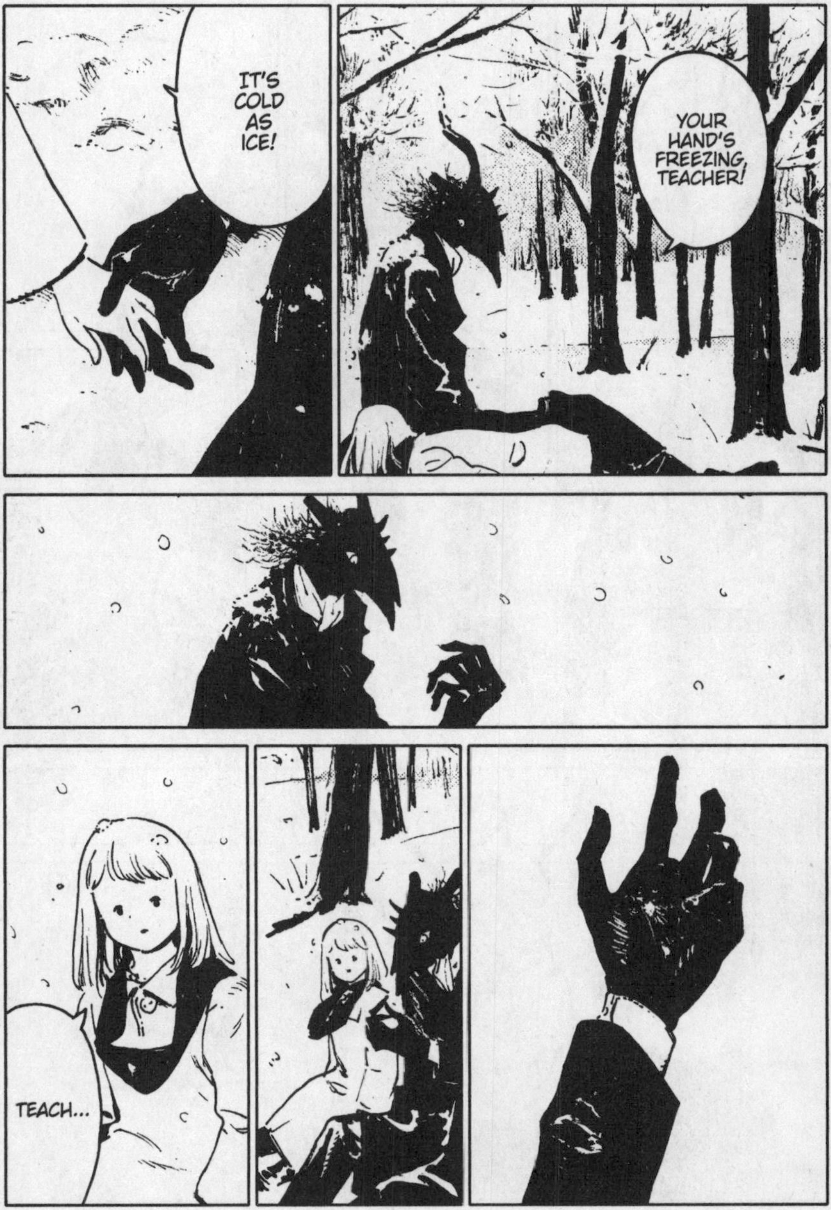
YOUR HAND'S FREEZING, TEACHER!
IT'S COLD AS ICE!
TEACH...

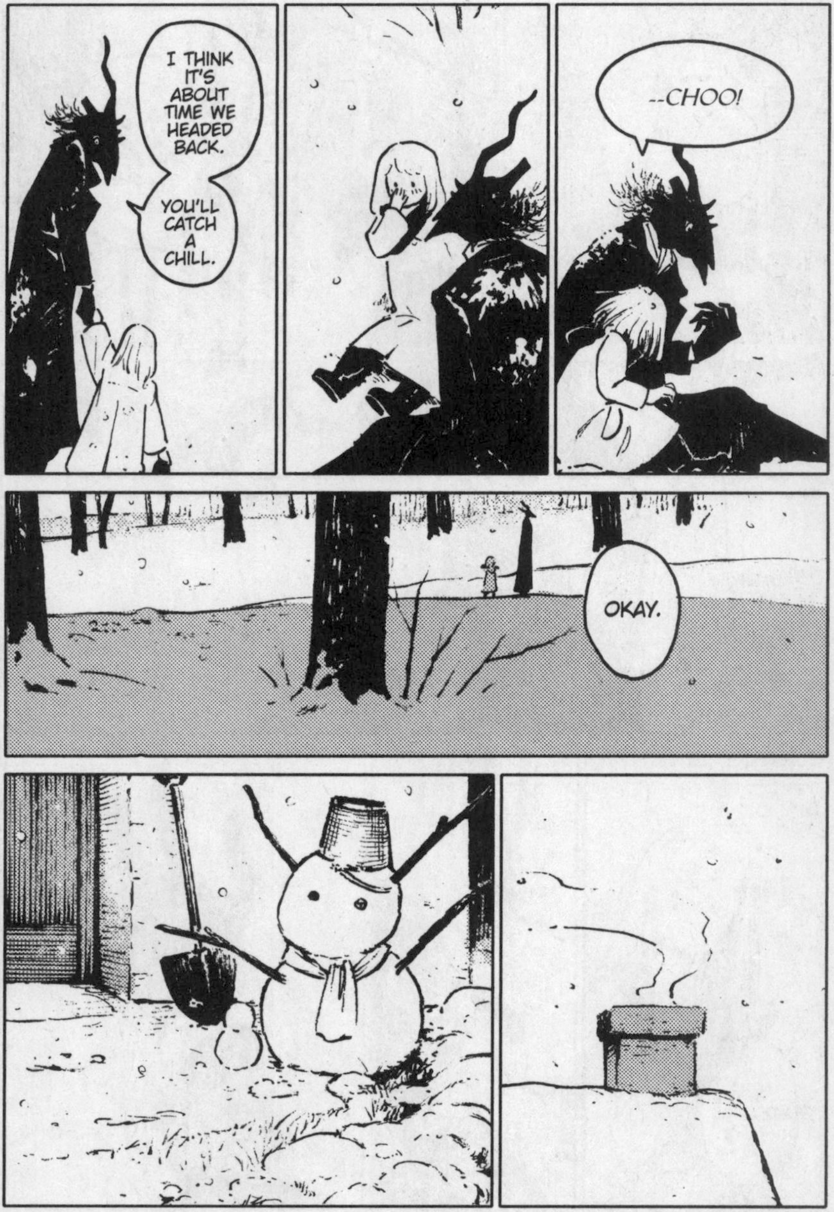
--CHOO!
I THINK IT'S ABOUT TIME WE HEADED BACK.
YOU'LL CATCH A CHILL.
OKAY.

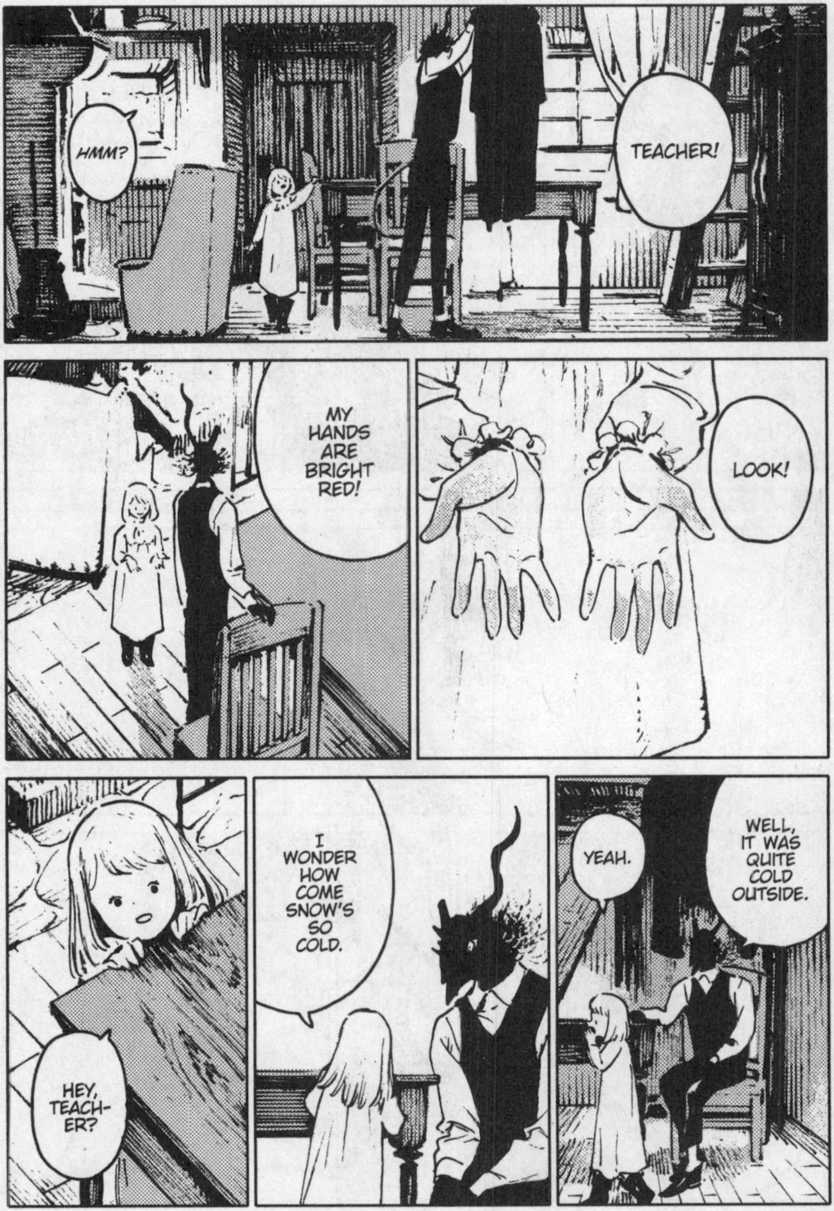
TEACHER!
HMM?
LOOK!
MY HANDS ARE BRIGHT RED!
WELL, IT WAS QUITE COLD OUTSIDE.
YEAH.
I WONDER HOW COME SNOW'S SO COLD.
HEY, TEACHER?

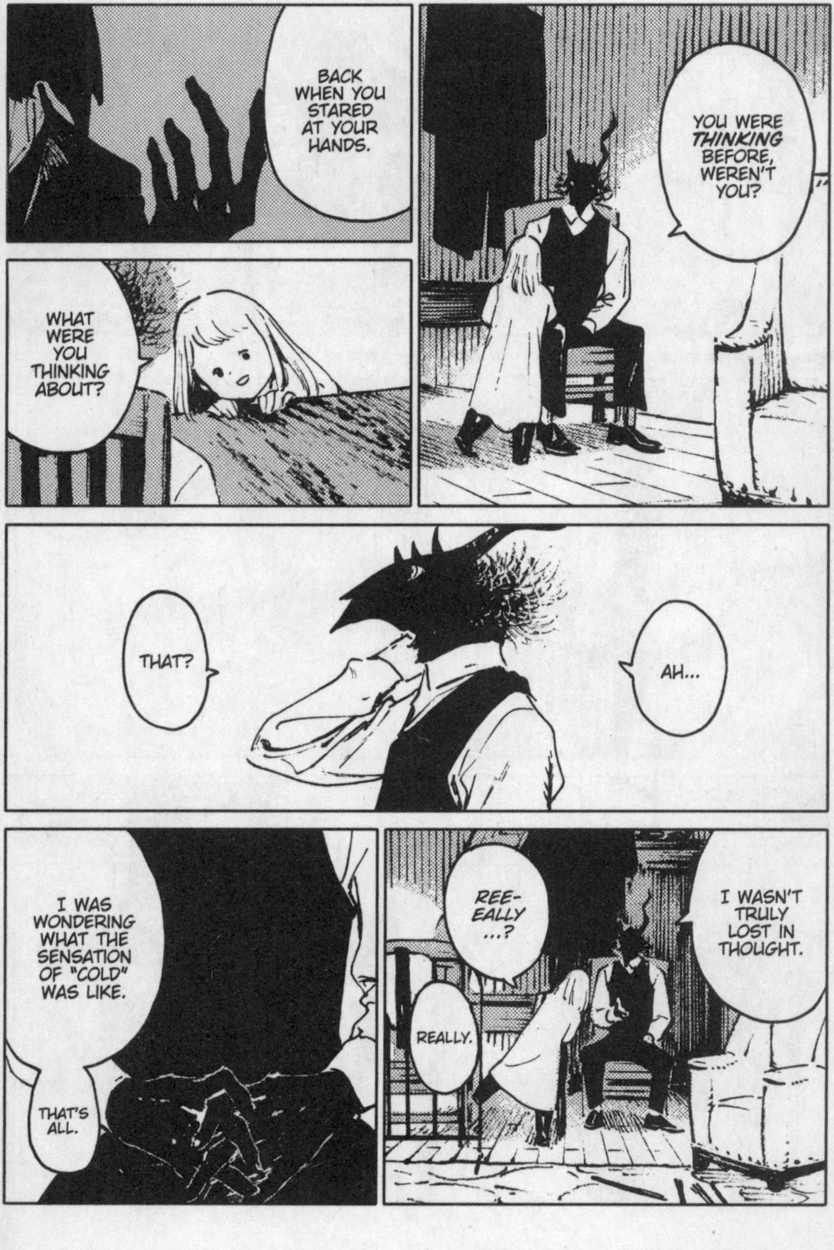
YOU WERE *THINKING* BEFORE, WEREN'T YOU?
BACK WHEN YOU STARED AT YOUR HANDS.
WHAT WERE YOU THINKING ABOUT?
AH...
THAT?
I WASN'T TRULY LOST IN THOUGHT.
REE-EALLY ...?
REALLY.
I WAS WONDERING WHAT THE SENSATION OF "COLD" WAS LIKE.
THAT'S ALL.

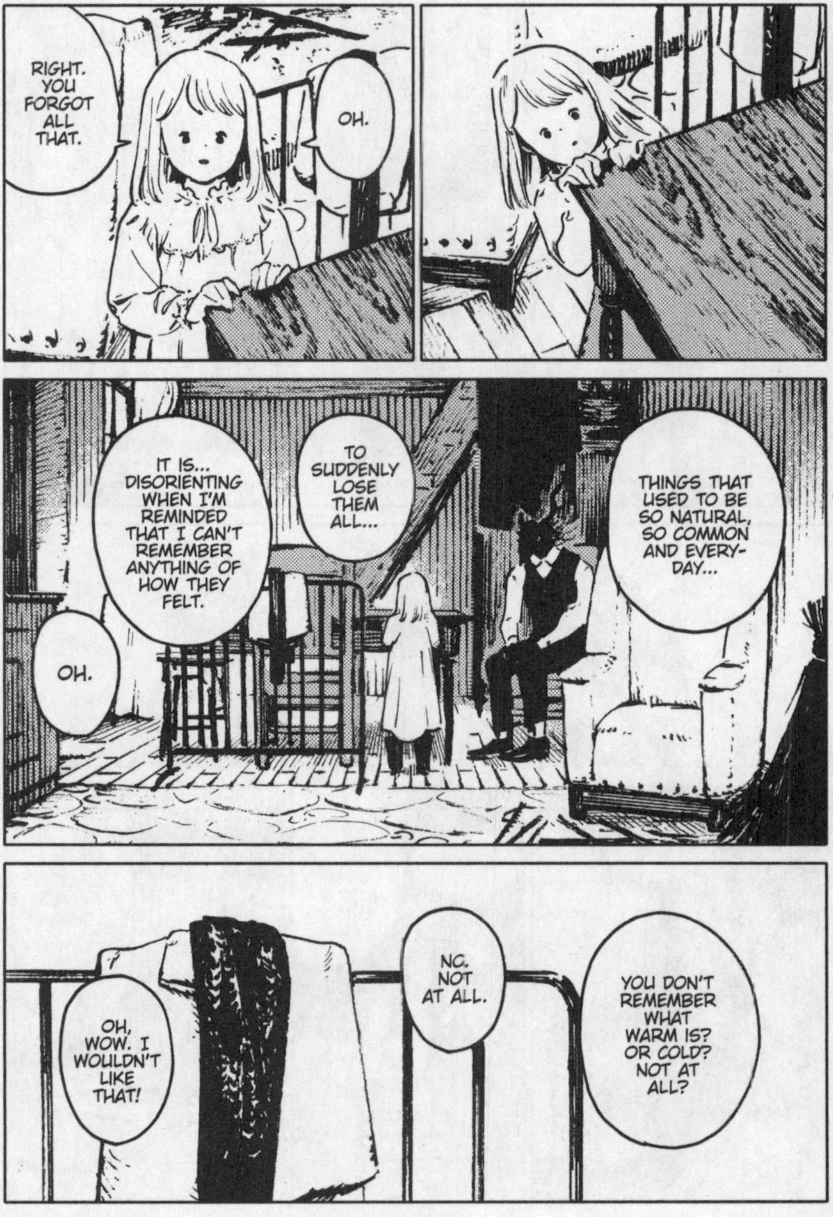
OH.
RIGHT. YOU FORGOT ALL THAT.
THINGS THAT USED TO BE SO NATURAL, SO COMMON AND EVERY-DAY...
TO SUDDENLY LOSE THEM ALL...
IT IS... DISORIENTING WHEN I'M REMINDED THAT I CAN'T REMEMBER ANYTHING OF HOW THEY FELT.
OH.
YOU DON'T REMEMBER WHAT WARM IS? OR COLD? NOT AT ALL?
NO. NOT AT ALL.
OH, WOW. I WOULDN'T LIKE THAT!

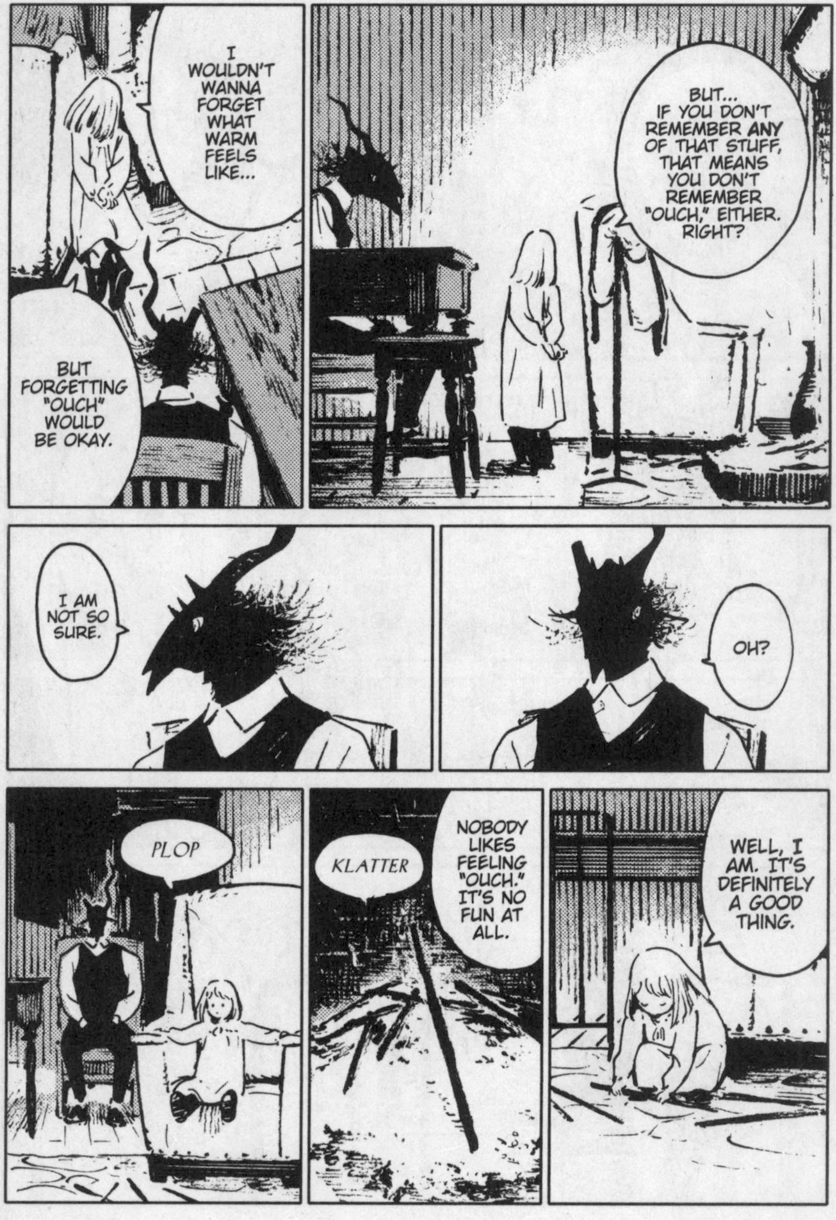
BUT... IF YOU DON'T REMEMBER ANY OF THAT STUFF, THAT MEANS YOU DON'T REMEMBER "OUCH," EITHER. RIGHT?
I WOULDN'T WANNA FORGET WHAT WARM FEELS LIKE...
BUT FORGETTING "OUCH" WOULD BE OKAY.
OH?
I AM NOT SO SURE.
WELL, I AM. IT'S DEFINITELY A GOOD THING.
NOBODY LIKES FEELING "OUCH." IT'S NO FUN AT ALL.
KLATTER
PLOP

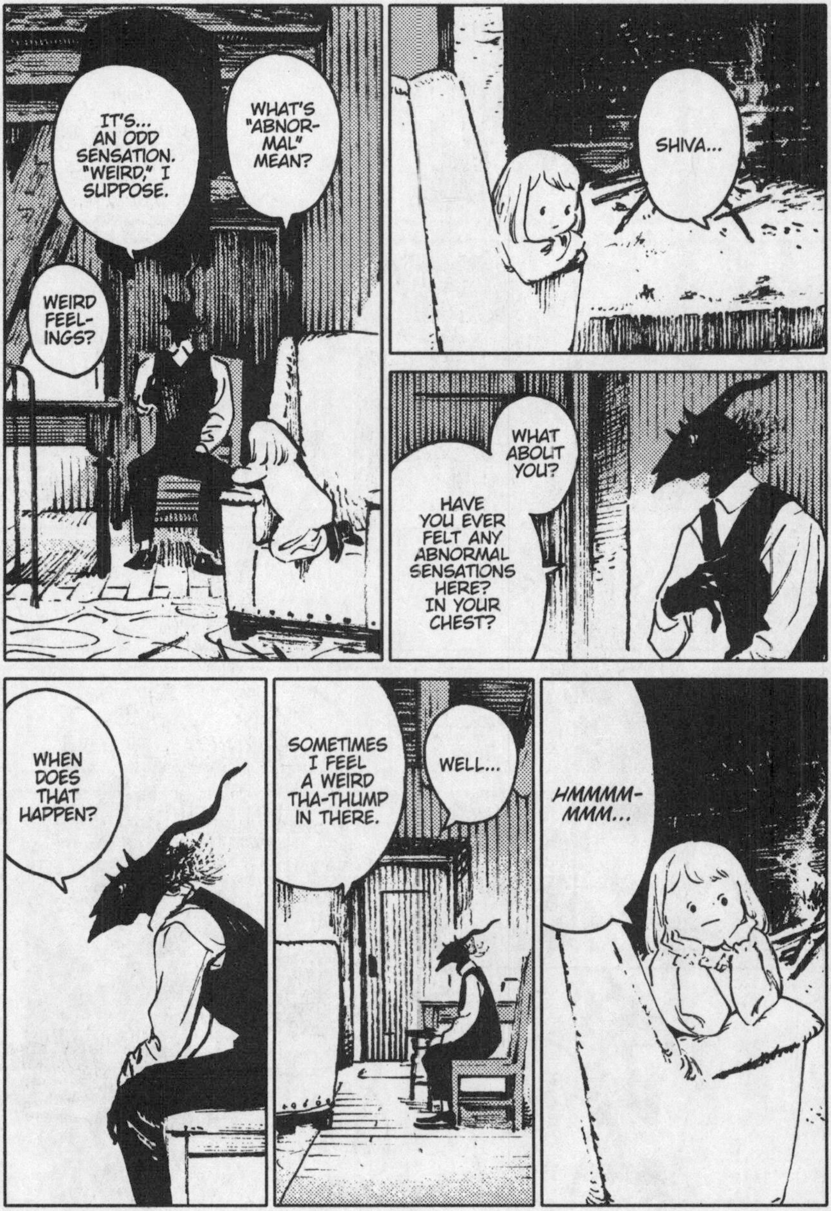
SHIVA...
WHAT ABOUT YOU?
HAVE YOU EVER FELT ANY ABNORMAL SENSATIONS HERE? IN YOUR CHEST?
WHAT'S "ABNORMAL" MEAN?
IT'S... AN ODD SENSATION. "WEIRD," I SUPPOSE.
WEIRD FEELINGS?
HMMMMMMM...
WELL...
SOMETIMES I FEEL A WEIRD THA-THUMP IN THERE.
WHEN DOES THAT HAPPEN?

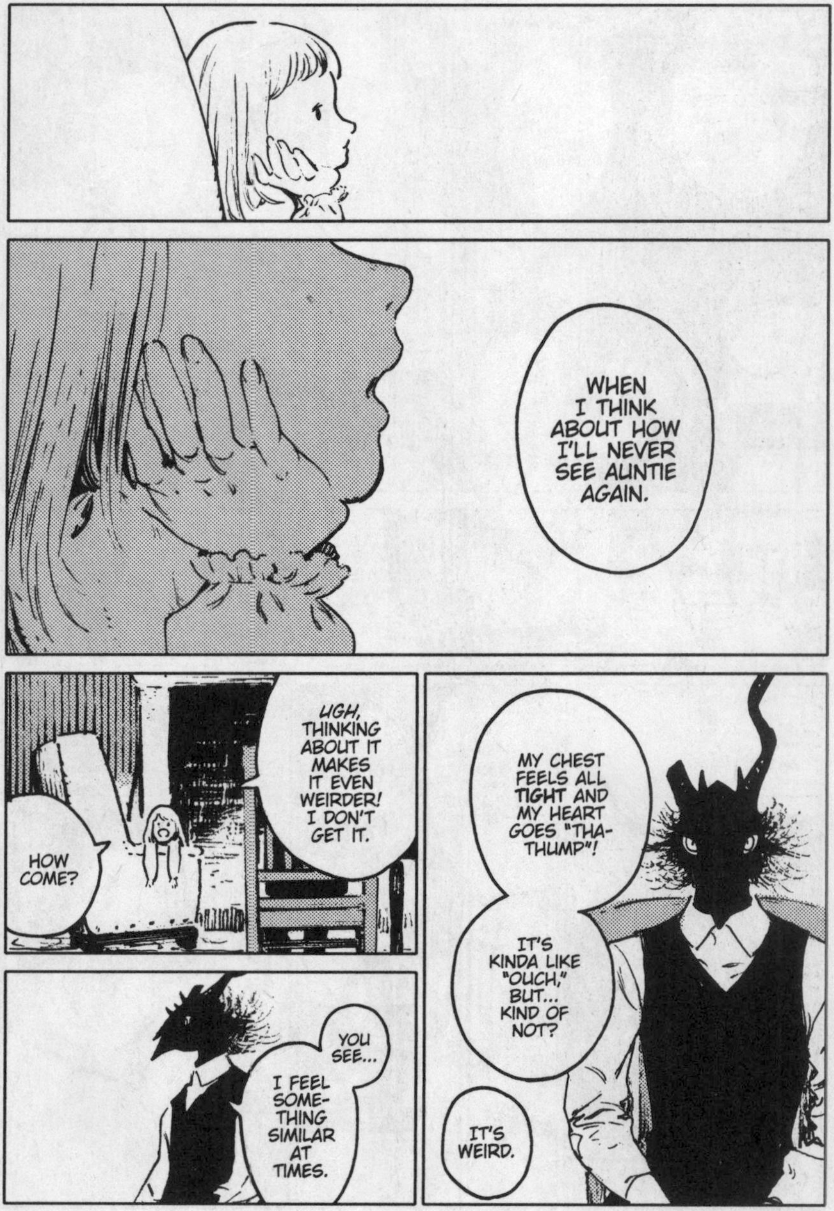
WHEN I THINK ABOUT HOW I'LL NEVER SEE AUNTIE AGAIN.
MY CHEST FEELS ALL TIGHT AND MY HEART GOES "THA-THUMP"!
IT'S KINDA LIKE "OUCH," BUT... KIND OF NOT?
IT'S WEIRD.
UGH, THINKING ABOUT IT MAKES IT EVEN WEIRDER! I DON'T GET IT.
HOW COME?
YOU SEE...
I FEEL SOME-THING SIMILAR AT TIMES.

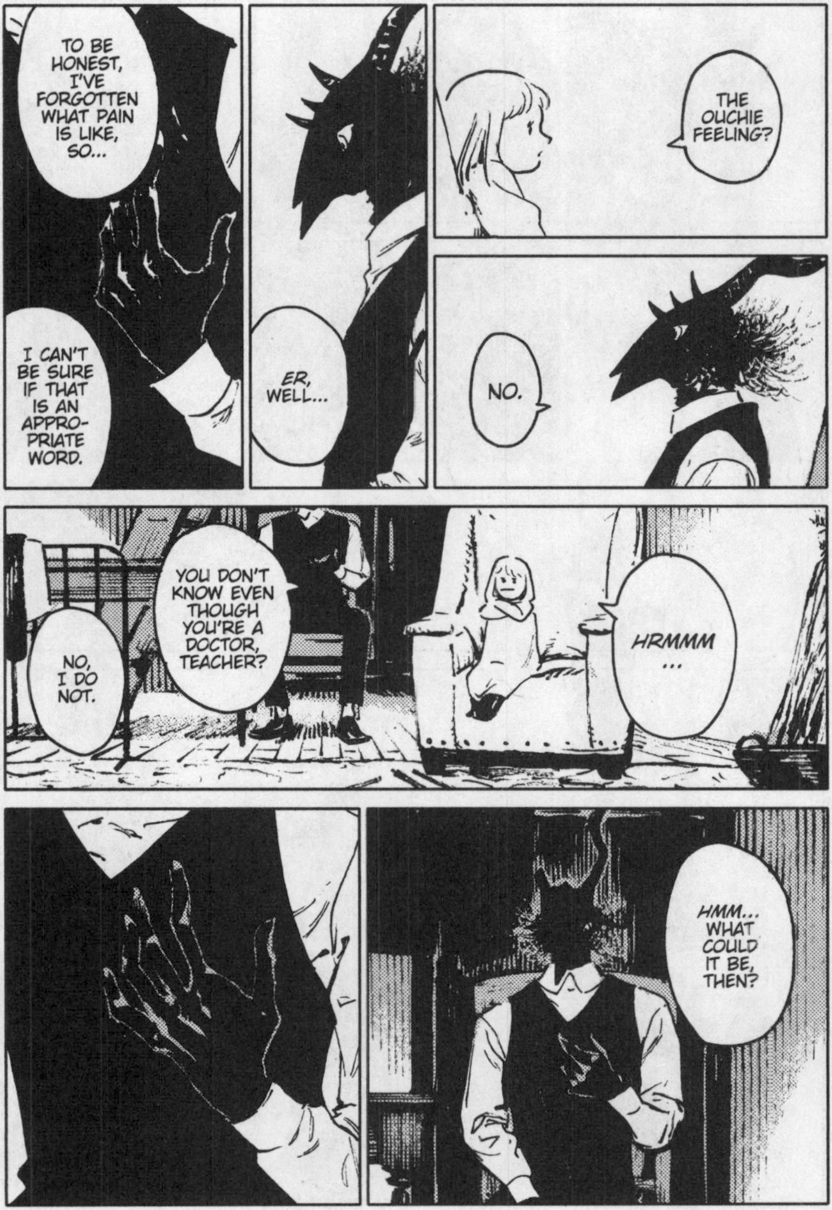
THE OUCHIE FEELING?
NO.
ER, WELL...
TO BE HONEST, I'VE FORGOTTEN WHAT PAIN IS LIKE, SO...
I CAN'T BE SURE IF THAT IS AN APPROPRIATE WORD.
HRMMM ...
YOU DON'T KNOW EVEN THOUGH YOU'RE A DOCTOR, TEACHER?
NO, I DO NOT.
HMM... WHAT COULD IT BE, THEN?

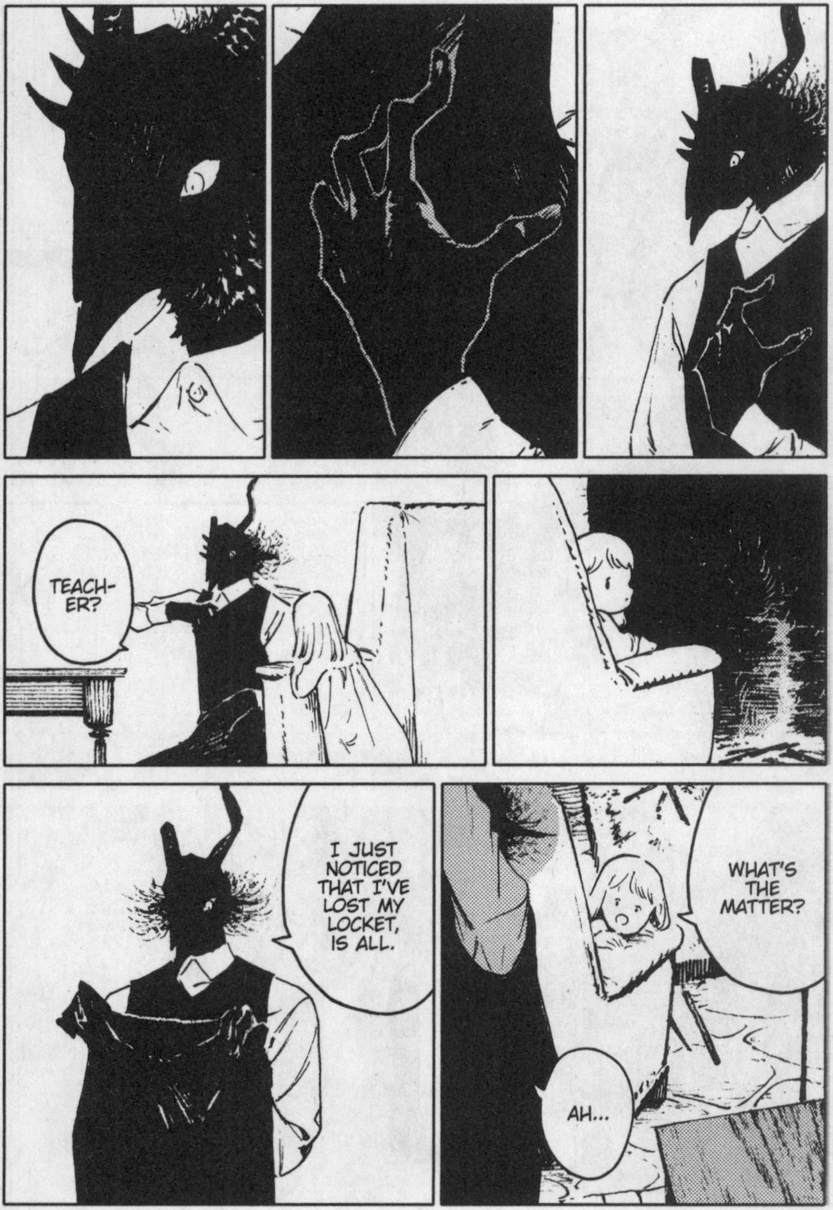
TEACH-ER?
WHAT'S THE MATTER?
AH...
I JUST NOTICED THAT I'VE LOST MY LOCKET, IS ALL.

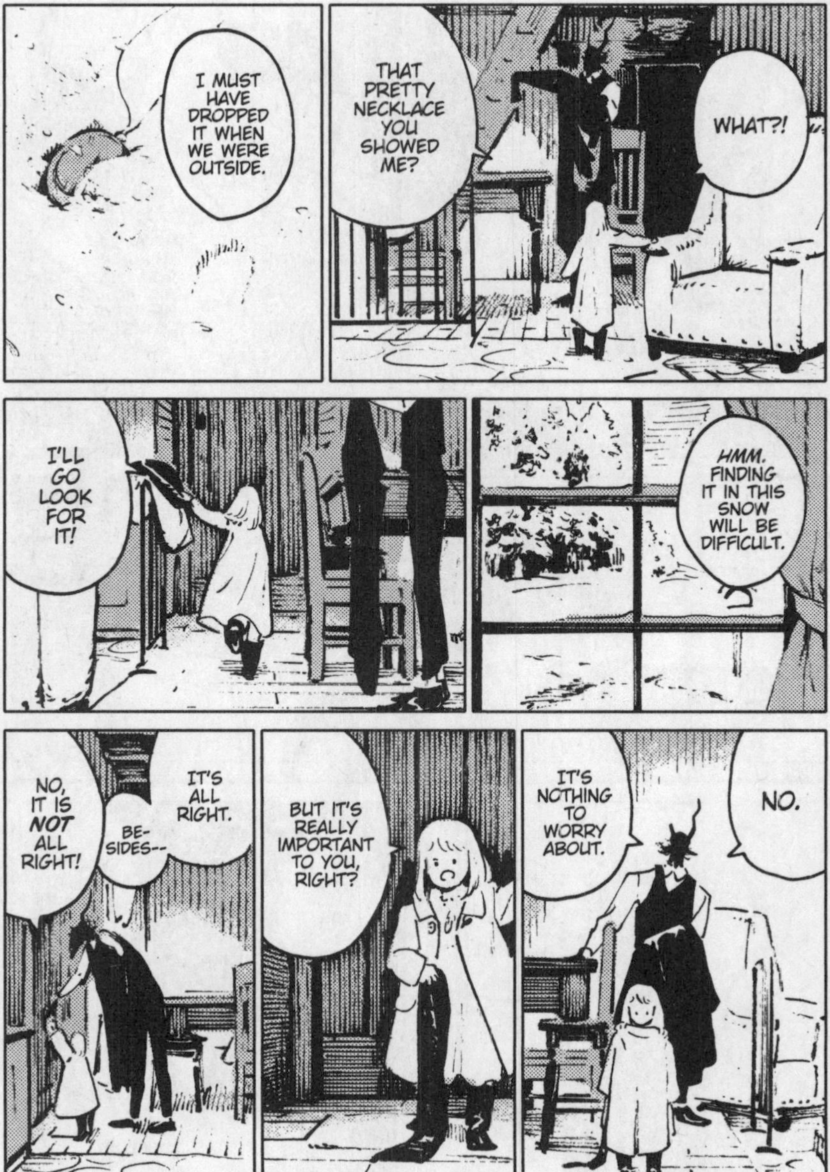
WHAT?!
THAT PRETTY NECKLACE YOU SHOWED ME?
I MUST HAVE DROPPED IT WHEN WE WERE OUTSIDE.
HMM. FINDING IT IN THIS SNOW WILL BE DIFFICULT.
I'LL GO LOOK FOR IT!
NO.
IT'S NOTHING TO WORRY ABOUT.
BUT IT'S REALLY IMPORTANT TO YOU, RIGHT?
IT'S ALL RIGHT.
BE-SIDES--
NO, IT IS ***NOT*** ALL RIGHT!

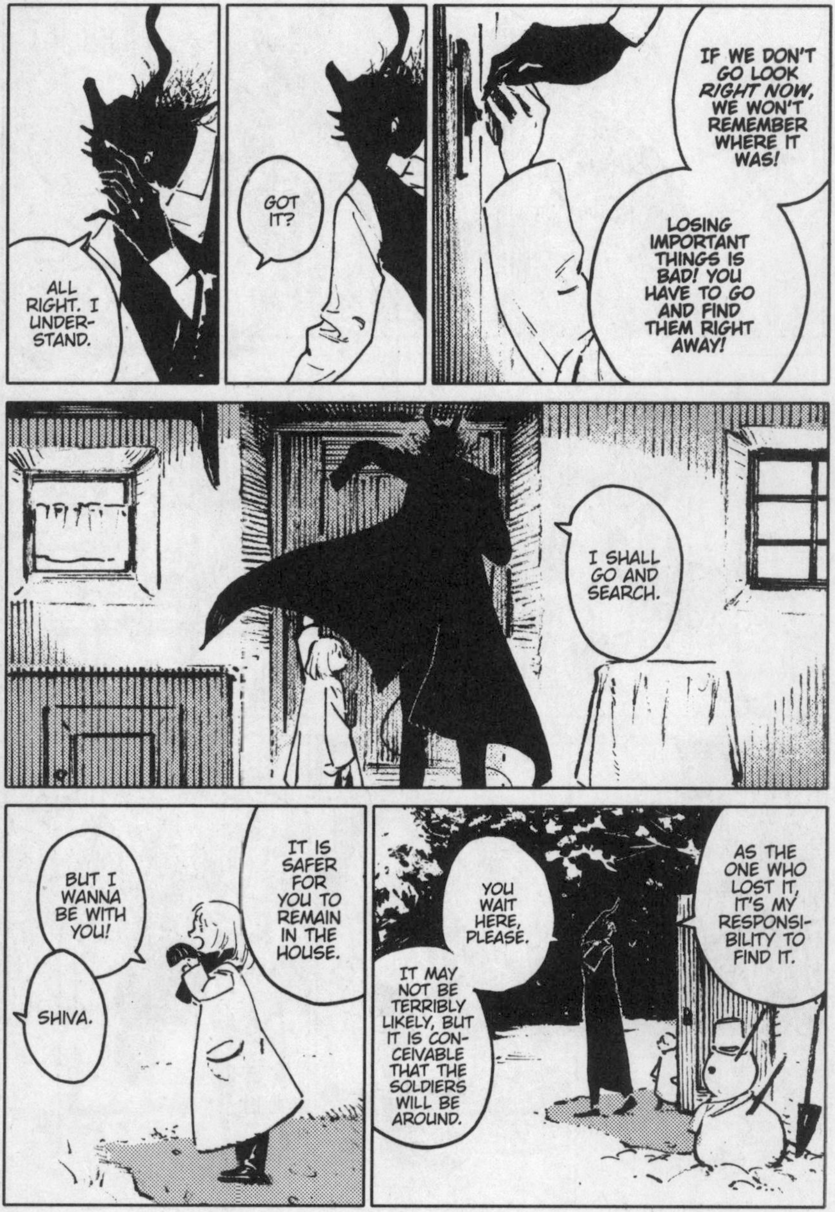
IF WE DON'T GO LOOK *RIGHT NOW*, WE WON'T REMEMBER WHERE IT WAS!
LOSING IMPORTANT THINGS IS BAD! YOU HAVE TO GO AND FIND THEM RIGHT AWAY!
GOT IT?
ALL RIGHT. I UNDER-STAND.
I SHALL GO AND SEARCH.
AS THE ONE WHO LOST IT, IT'S MY RESPONSI-BILITY TO FIND IT.
YOU WAIT HERE, PLEASE.
IT MAY NOT BE TERRIBLY LIKELY, BUT IT IS CON-CEIVABLE THAT THE SOLDIERS WILL BE AROUND.
IT IS SAFER FOR YOU TO REMAIN IN THE HOUSE.
BUT I WANNA BE WITH YOU!
SHIVA.

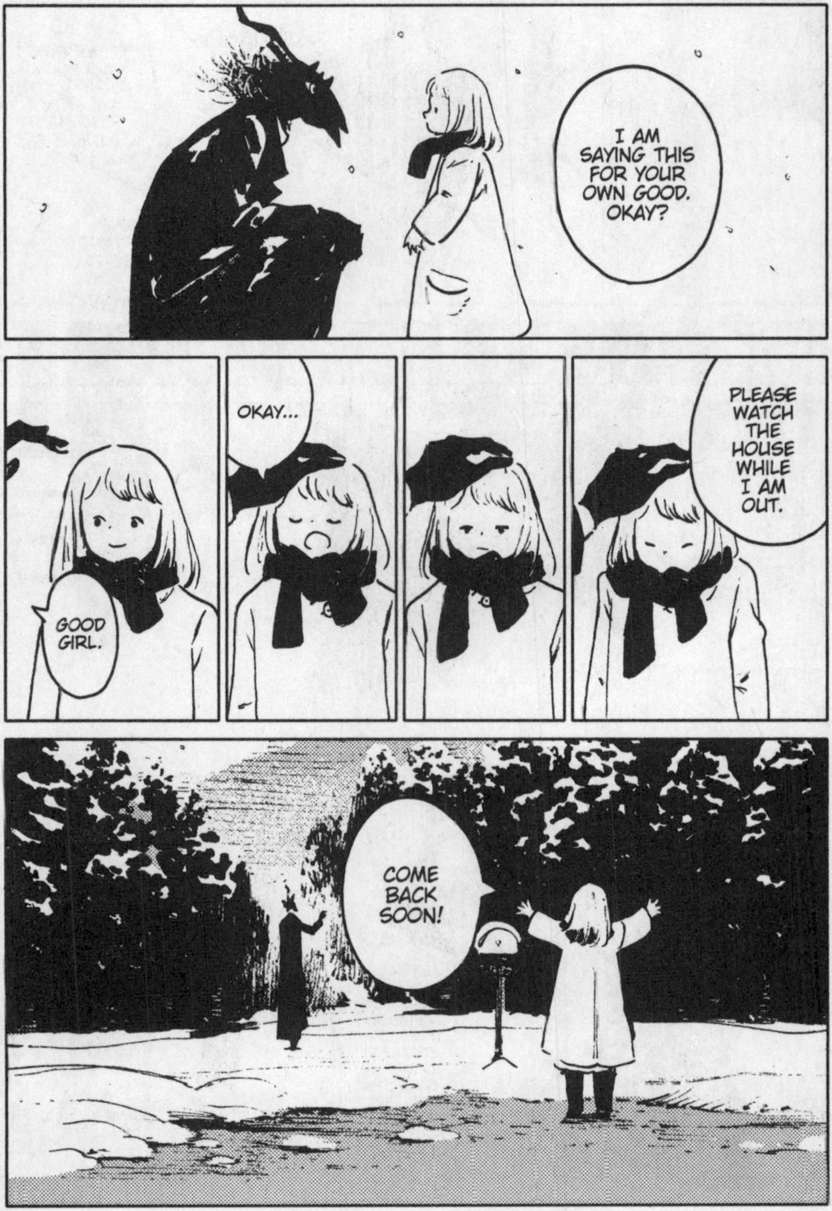
I AM SAYING THIS FOR YOUR OWN GOOD. OKAY?
PLEASE WATCH THE HOUSE WHILE I AM OUT.
OKAY...
GOOD GIRL.
COME BACK SOON!

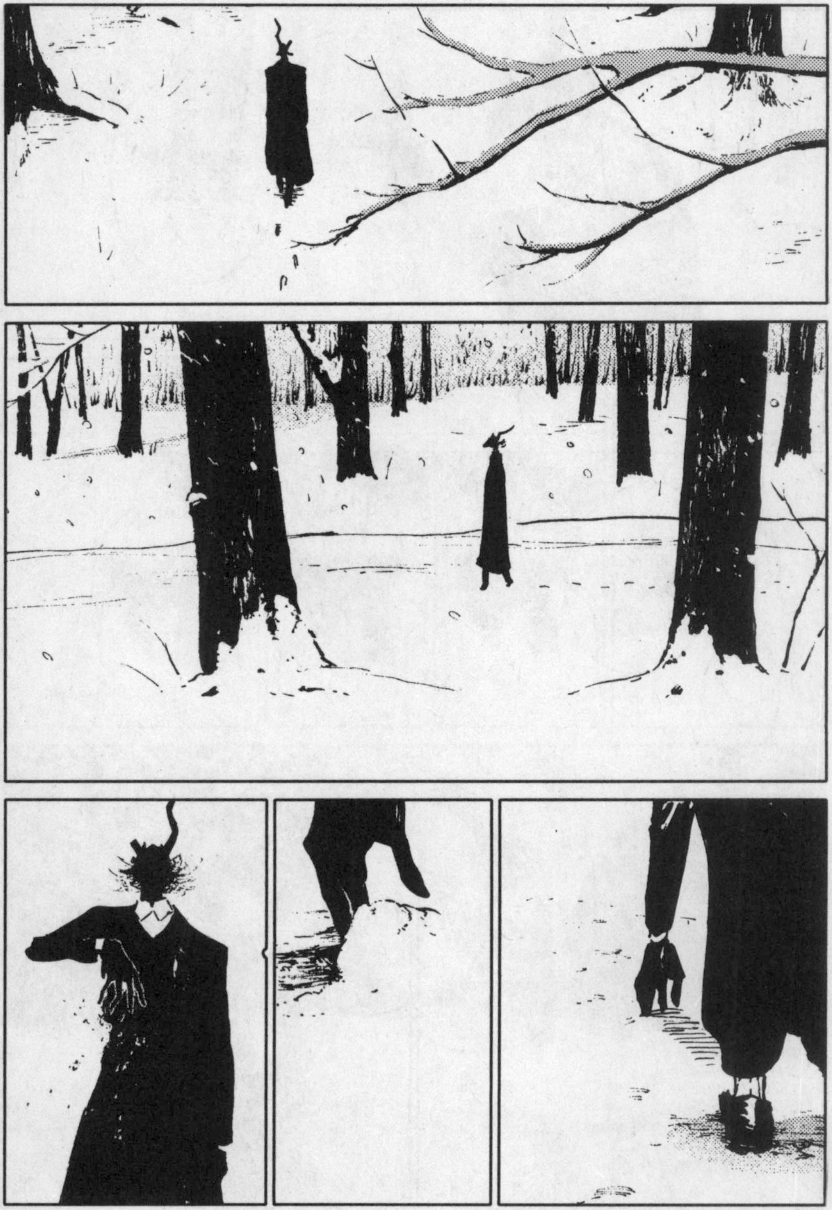

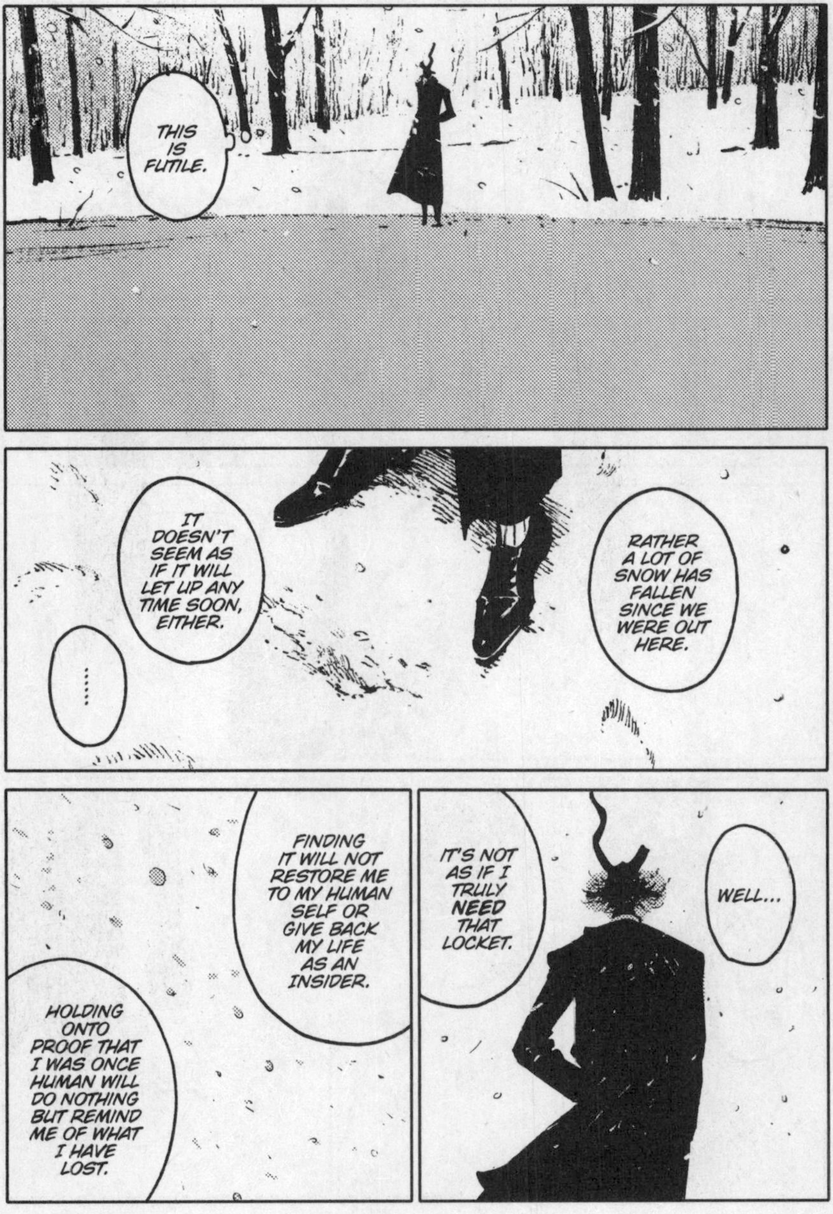
THIS IS FUTILE.
RATHER A LOT OF SNOW HAS FALLEN SINCE WE WERE OUT HERE.
IT DOESN'T SEEM AS IF IT WILL LET UP ANY TIME SOON, EITHER.
......
WELL...
IT'S NOT AS IF I TRULY NEED THAT LOCKET.
FINDING IT WILL NOT RESTORE ME TO MY HUMAN SELF OR GIVE BACK MY LIFE AS AN INSIDER.
HOLDING ONTO PROOF THAT I WAS ONCE HUMAN WILL DO NOTHING BUT REMIND ME OF WHAT I HAVE LOST.

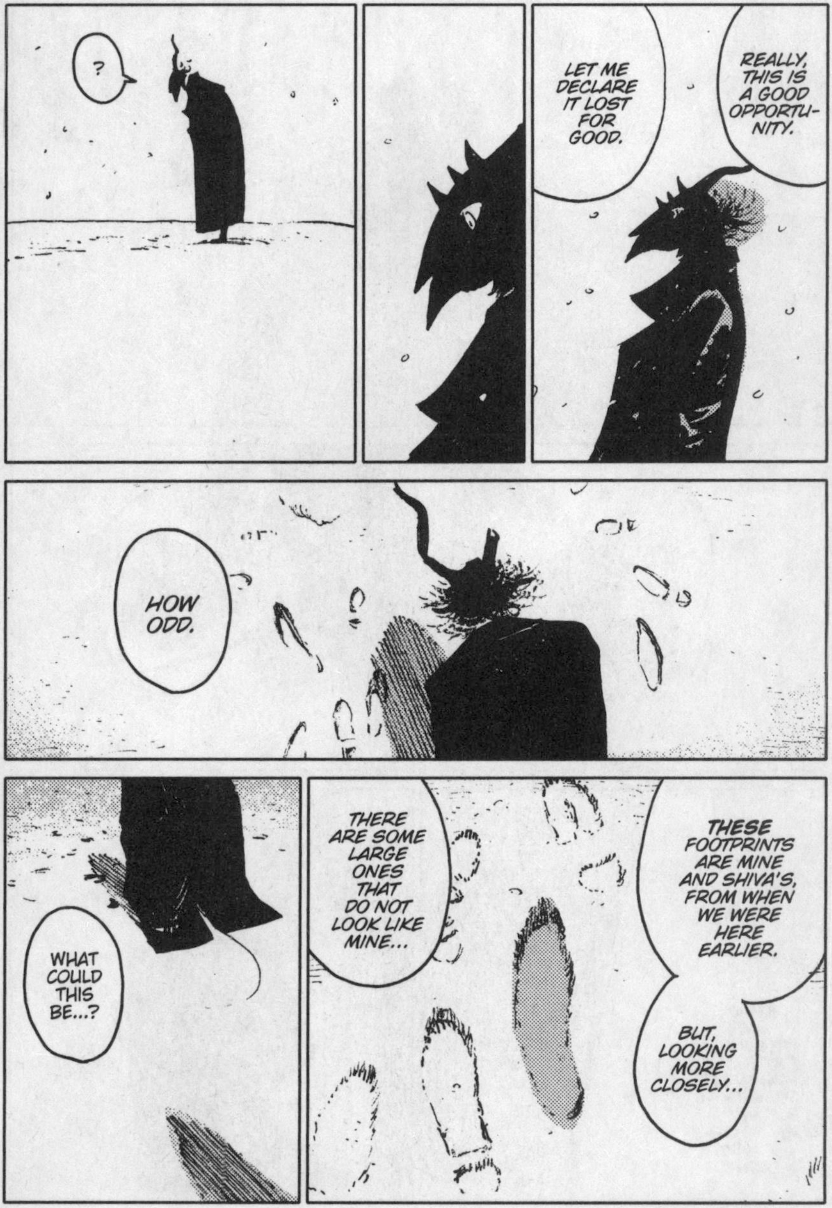
REALLY, THIS IS A GOOD OPPORTUNITY.
LET ME DECLARE IT LOST FOR GOOD.
?
HOW ODD.
THESE FOOTPRINTS ARE MINE AND SHIVA'S, FROM WHEN WE WERE HERE EARLIER.
BUT, LOOKING MORE CLOSELY...
THERE ARE SOME LARGE ONES THAT DO NOT LOOK LIKE MINE...
WHAT COULD THIS BE...?

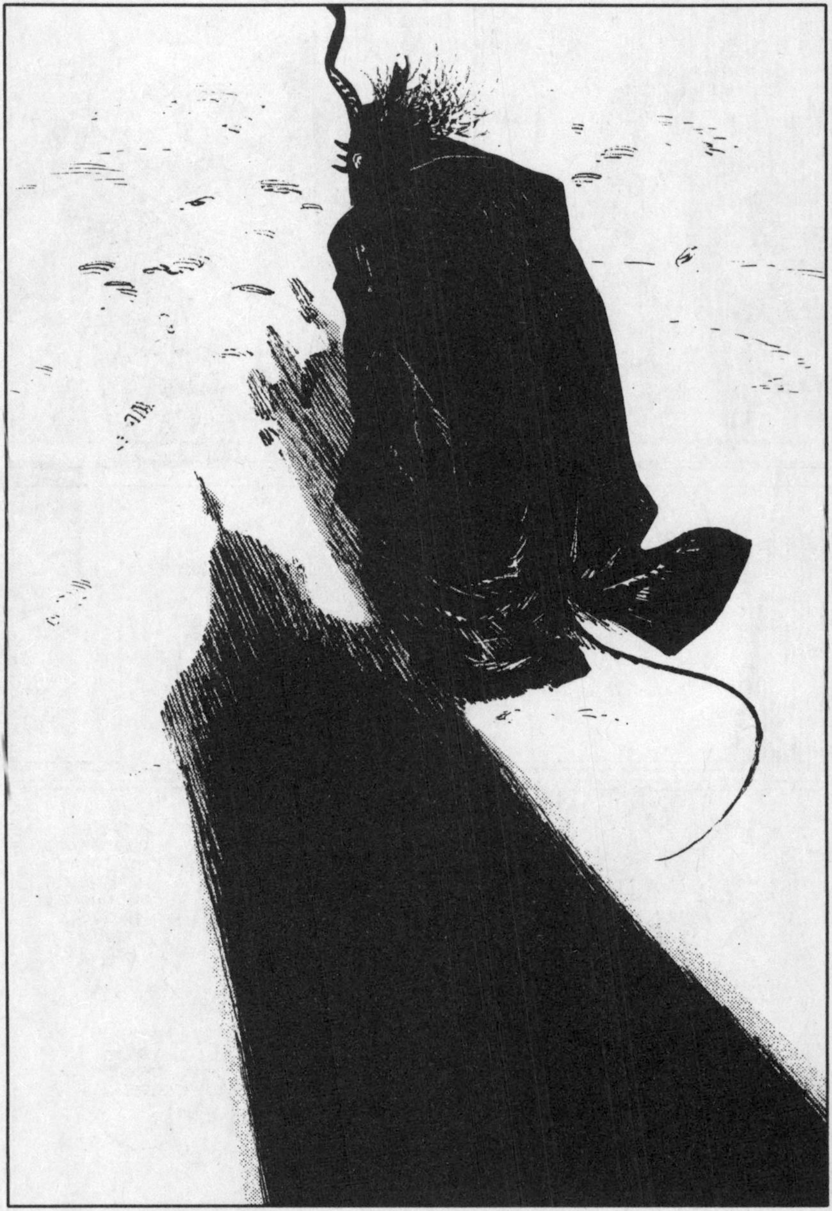

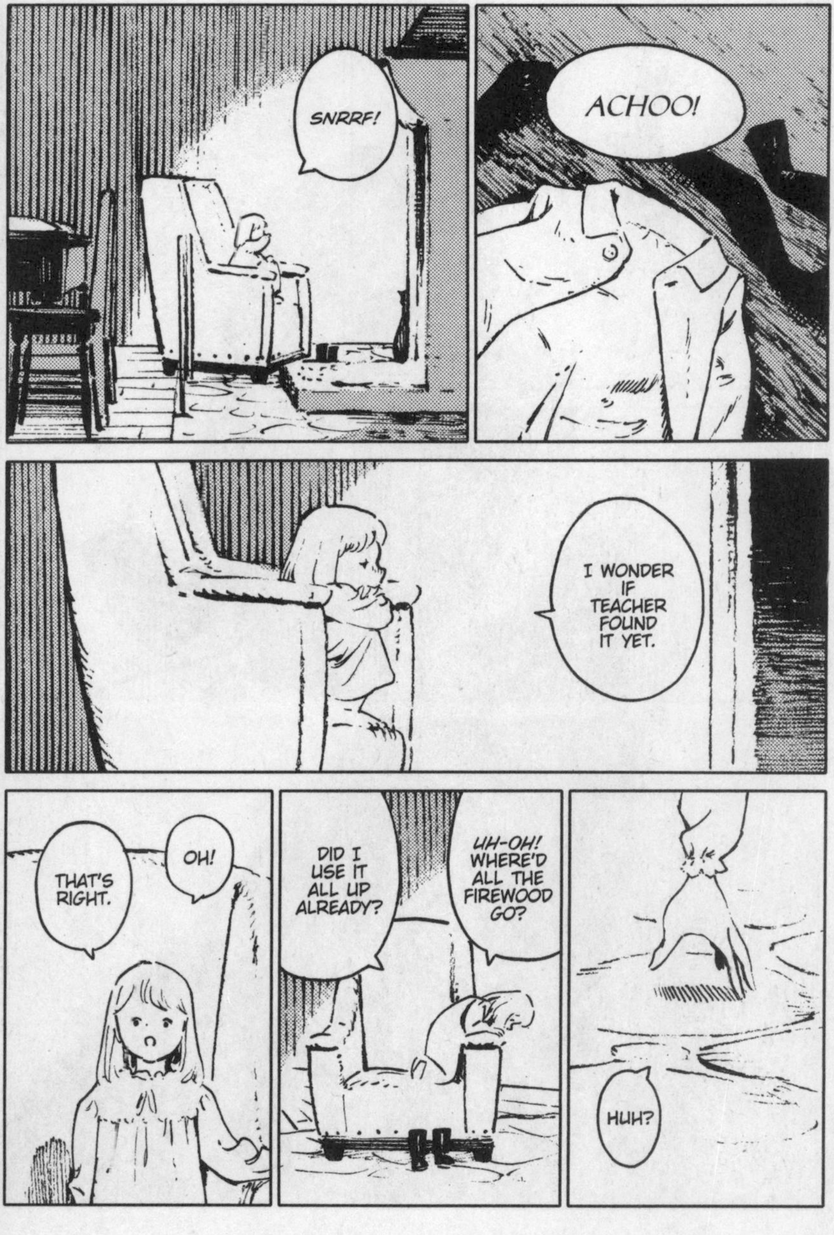
ACHOO!
SNRRF!
I WONDER IF TEACHER FOUND IT YET.
HUH?
UH-OH! WHERE'D ALL THE FIREWOOD GO?
DID I USE IT ALL UP ALREADY?
OH!
THAT'S RIGHT.

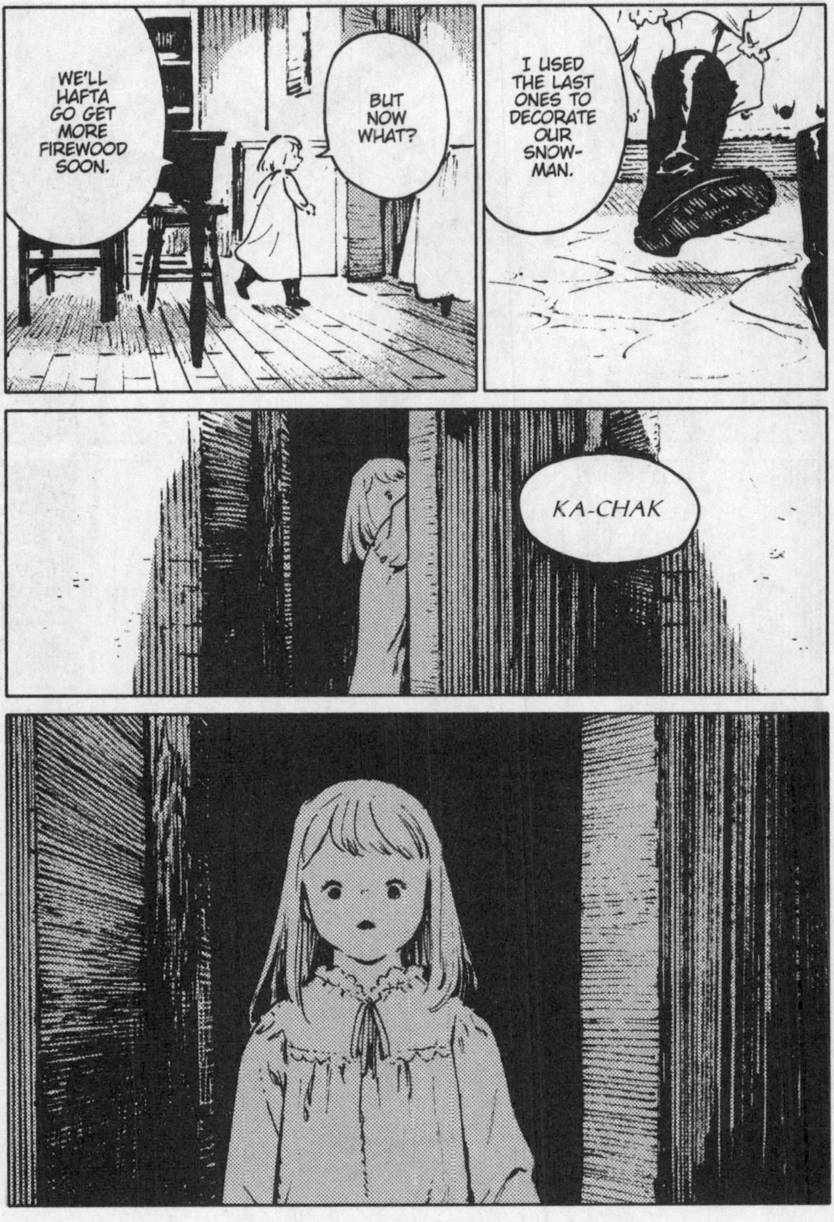
I USED THE LAST ONES TO DECORATE OUR SNOW-MAN.
BUT NOW WHAT?
WE'LL HAFTA GO GET MORE FIREWOOD SOON.
KA-CHAK

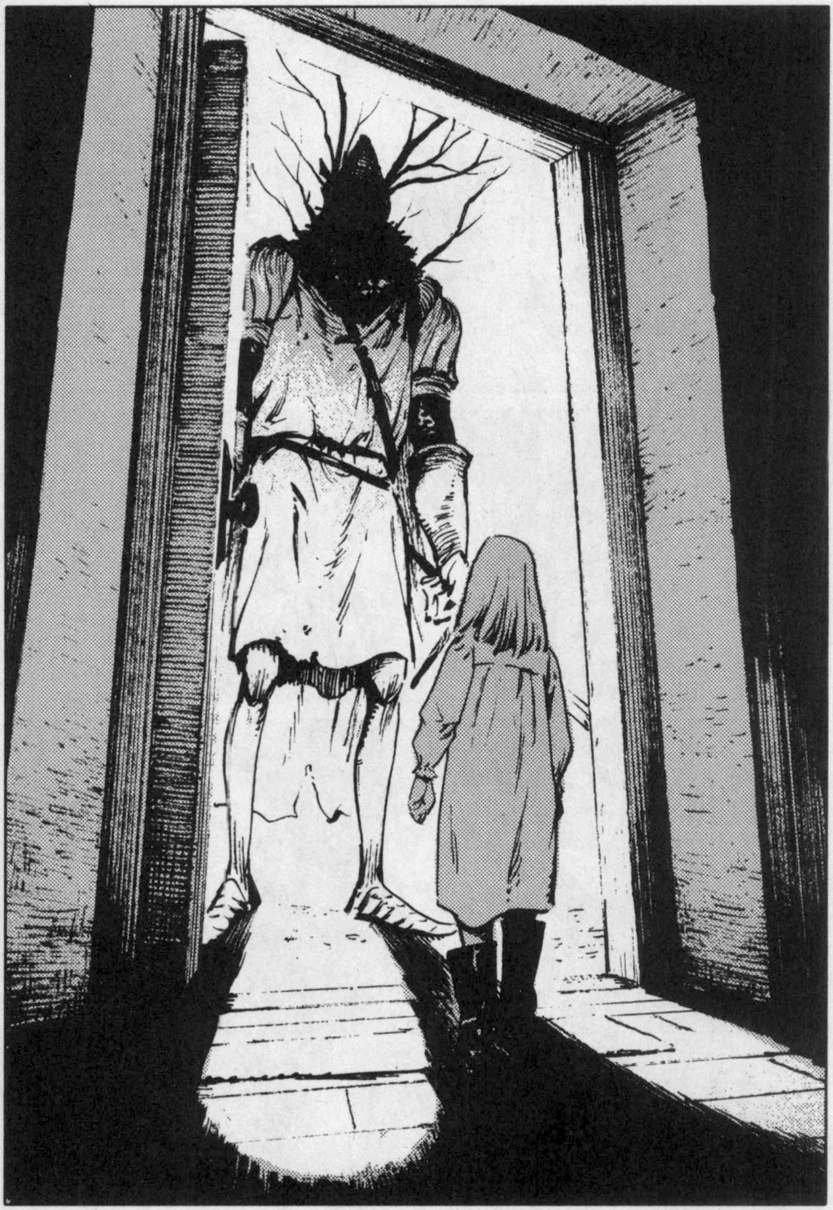

The Girl from the Other Side: Siúil a Rún Vol. 6 – END

Deuil à mer.

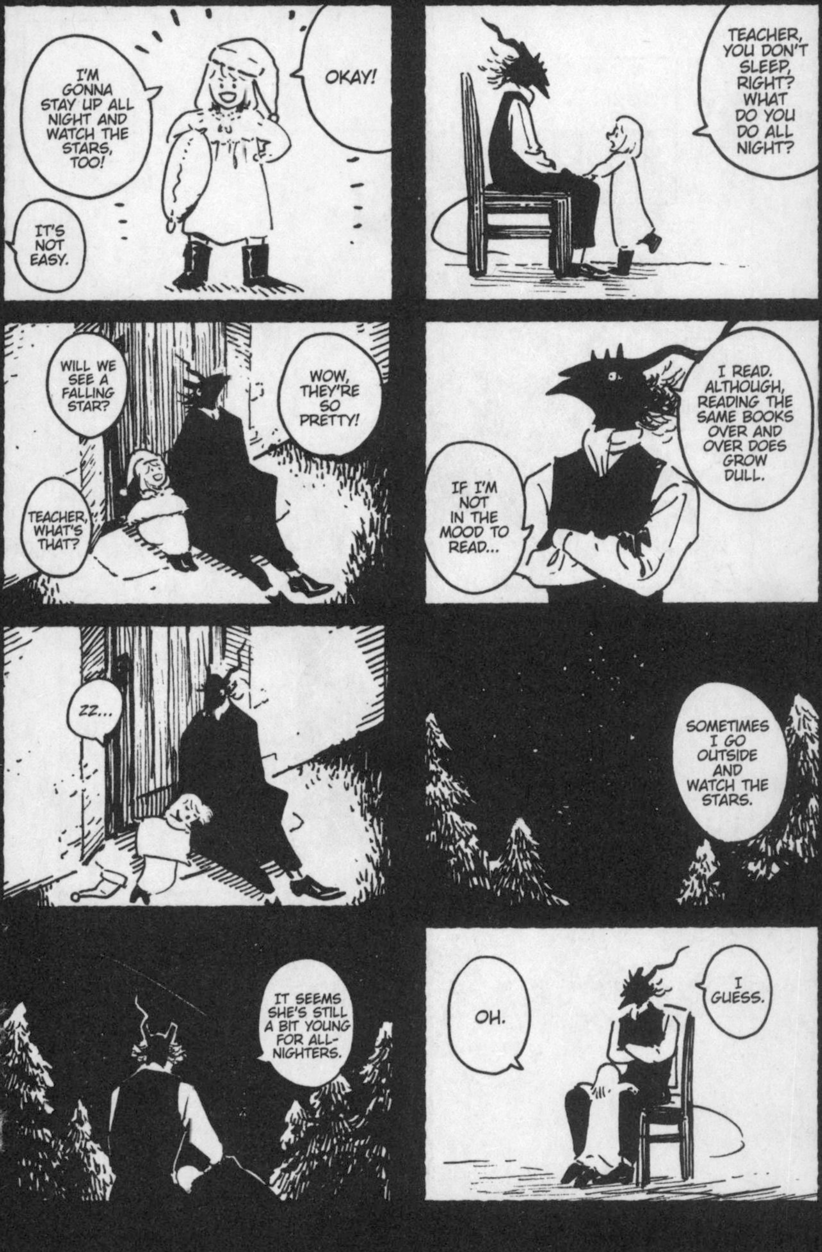
TEACHER, YOU DON'T SLEEP, RIGHT? WHAT DO YOU DO ALL NIGHT?
I READ. ALTHOUGH, READING THE SAME BOOKS OVER AND OVER DOES GROW DULL.
IF I'M NOT IN THE MOOD TO READ...
SOMETIMES I GO OUTSIDE AND WATCH THE STARS.
I GUESS.
OH.
OKAY!
I'M GONNA STAY UP ALL NIGHT AND WATCH THE STARS, TOO!
IT'S NOT EASY.
WOW, THEY'RE SO PRETTY!
WILL WE SEE A FALLING STAR?
TEACHER, WHAT'S THAT?
ZZ...
IT SEEMS SHE'S STILL A BIT YOUNG FOR ALL-NIGHTERS.

SEVEN SEAS ENTERTAINMENT PRESENTS

The Girl from the Other Side
Siúil, a Rún

story and art by NAGABE   vol. 6

TRANSLATION
Adrienne Beck

ADAPTATION
Ysabet MacFarlane

LETTERING AND RETOUCH
Lys Blakeslee

LOGO DESIGN
Karis Page

COVER DESIGN
Nicky Lim

PROOFREADER
Jocelyne Allen
Shanti Whitesides

ASSISTANT EDITOR
J.P. Sullivan

PRODUCTION ASSISTANT
CK Russell

PRODUCTION MANAGER
Lissa Pattillo

EDITOR-IN-CHIEF
Adam Arnold

PUBLISHER
Jason DeAngelis

THE GIRL FROM THE OTHER SIDE: SIUIL, A RUN VOL. 6
Enagabe 2018

Originally published in Japan in 2018 by MAG Garden Corporation, Tokyo.
English translation rights arranged through TOHAN CORPORATION, Tokyo.

No portion of this book may be reproduced or transmitted in any form without written permission from the copyright holders. This is a work of fiction. Names, characters, places, and incidents are the products of the author's imagination or are used fictitiously. Any resemblance to actual events, locales, or persons, living or dead, is entirely coincidental.

Seven Seas books may be purchased in bulk for educational, business, or promotional use. For information on bulk purchases, please contact Macmillan Corporate & Premium Sales Department at 1-800-221-7945 (ext 5442) or write specialmarkets@macmillan.com.

Seven Seas and the Seven Seas logo are trademarks of Seven Seas Entertainment, LLC. All rights reserved.

ISBN: 978-1-642750-06-5

Printed in Canada

First Printing: March 2019

10 9 8 7 6 5 4 3 2 1

FOLLOW US ONLINE: **www.sevenseasentertainment.com**

READING DIRECTIONS

This book reads from *right to left*, Japanese style. If this is your first time reading manga, you start reading from the top right panel on each page and take it from there. If you get lost, just follow the numbered diagram here. It may seem backwards at first, but you'll get the hang of it! Have fun!

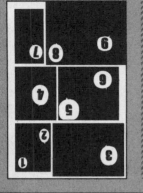

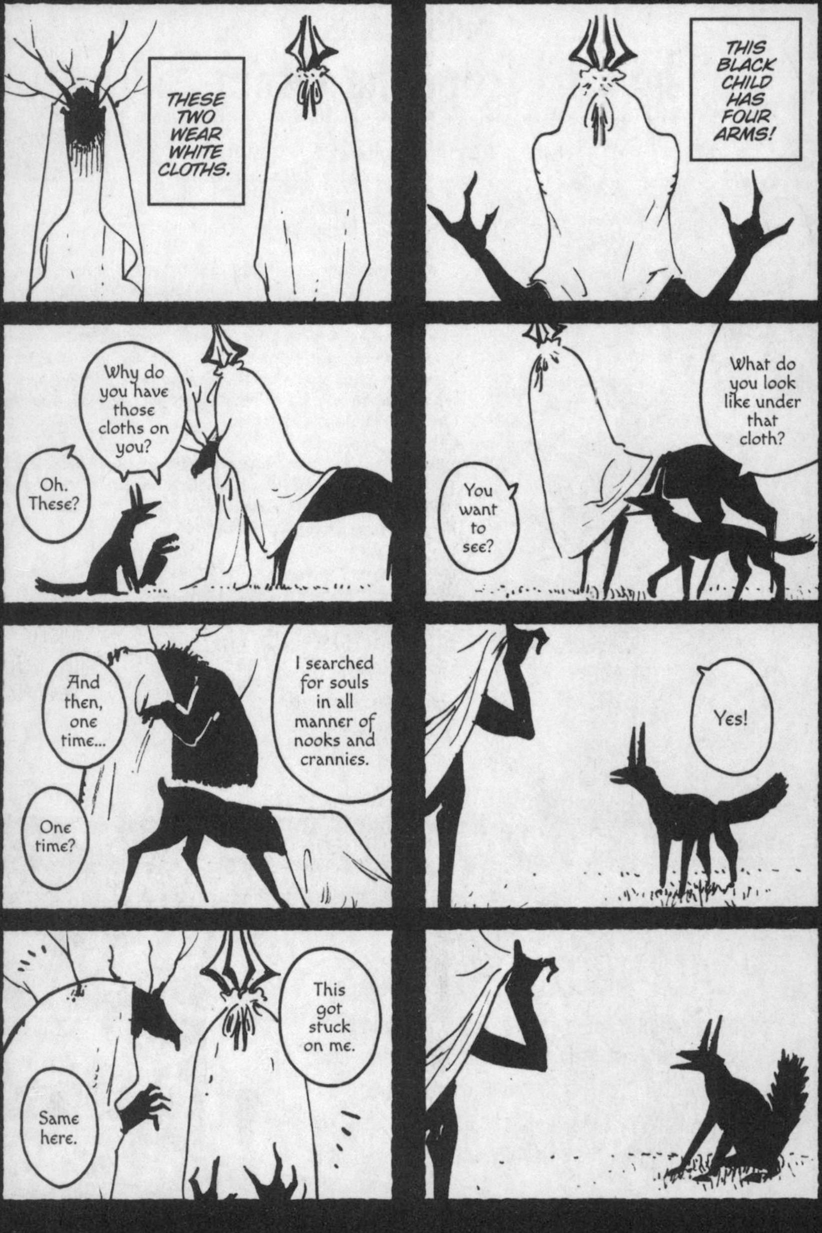
THIS BLACK CHILD HAS FOUR ARMS!
THESE TWO WEAR WHITE CLOTHS.
What do you look like under that cloth?
You want to see?
Why do you have those cloths on you?
Oh. These?
Yes!
I searched for souls in all manner of nooks and crannies.
And then, one time...
One time?
This got stuck on me.
Same here.